London School of Economics
Monographs on Social Anthropology

Managing Editor: Michael Sallnow

The Monographs on Social Anthropology were established in 1940 and aim to publish results of modern
anthropological research of primary interest to specialists.

The continuation of the series was made possible by a
grant in aid from the Wenner-Gren Foundation for
Anthropological Research, and more recently by a
further grant from the Governors of the London School
of Economics and Political Science. Income from sales is
returned to a revolving fund to assist further publications.

The Monographs are under the direction of an Editorial
Board associated with the Department of Anthropology
of the London School of Economics and Political
Science.

Pervasive in communication,
grounded in the very use of language,
symbolization is part of the living stuff
of social relationships.

Raymond Firth: *Symbols*

London School of Economics
Monographs on Social Anthropology
No 60

The Social Practice of Symbolization

An Anthropological Analysis

IVO STRECKER

THE ATHLONE PRESS
LONDON and ATLANTIC HIGHLANDS, NJ

First published 1988 by The Athlone Press Ltd
44 Bedford Row, London WC1R 4LY
and 171 First Avenue, Atlantic Highlands, NJ 07716

British Library Cataloguing in Publication Data
Strecker, Ivo, *1940–*
    The social practice of symbolization : an
    anthropological analysis. ———(London School
    of Economics monographs on social
    Anthropology. ISSN 0077–1074; no. 60).
    1. Symbolism – Anthropological perspectives
    I. Title II. Series
    306 .4
    ISBN 0–485–19557–7

Library of Congress Cataloging in Publication data
Strecker, Ivo A., 1940–
    The social practice of symbolization : an anthropological
    analysis.
        p. cm. — (Monographs on social anthropology / London School
    of economics ; no. 60)
        Bibliography: p.
        Includes index.
        ISBN 0–485–19557–7 : $65.00 (U.S)
        1. Hamar (African people)—Social life and customs. 2. Symbolic
    interactionism. 3. Social interaction—Ethiopia. I. Title.
    II. Series: Monographs on social anthropology ; no. 60.
    DT380.4.H36S77 1988
    306'.089935—dc19

Typeset by J&L Composition Ltd, Filey, North Yorkshire
Printed in Great Britain by Billings Ltd, Worcester

Contents

Foreword

Ivo Strecker's *The Social Practice of Symbolization* is based on extensive field work among the Hamar of Ethiopia. It is about the world of words and deeds, the pragmatics of communication. It tells how speakers and hearers willfully cooperate – and fail to cooperate – in the construction and interpretation of contexts of communication, how they bend and manipulate conventions in order to make the world respond to their will. It is, in a way, a story of the dark underside of communication – of the interpretive potential of cooperation withheld, hedged, or made deliberately ambigious through irony, vagueness, white lies, and outright prevarication, reminding us, in other words, of that messier and more interesting world of talk where speakers and hearers do not resolutely seek clarity, consensus, and agreement in harmonious communion, but exploit ambiguities, hint at meanings, create misunderstandings, and conspire against one another, seek some advantage in a slip of the tongue, or hear hidden insults in a pause or tone, or hide their intentions and meanings as they reveal them, or reveal them in the act of hiding them. This is the tale of the everyday world where meanings are in the spaces between words and in the contexts words evoke rather than in the facts they may purport to describe.

Ivo Strecker is interested in how the Hamar, and people generally, produce symbolism, and how they know the value of things, of differences of power, and of social distance, and how they use and manipulate this information when they communicate with one another. He is interested in 'symbolization' rather than the system of symbols, and consequently rejects the idea of the symbolic code as a pre-formed *ratio* inside the system of symbols but outside the speaker/hearer and independent of her will. He rejects this image because it implies that people know not of what they speak. It discounts their speaking, making it only a project of the anthropologist's exegesis, as in much of Turner's work. Strecker also rejects the notion that symbolization can be reduced to individual psychology, as in Sperber's version of speaking as a cognitive capacity, an inner rationality within the speaker/hearer's mind that is only poorly expressed in the outer garb of her words. It is the image of a defect in active or passive memory, of 'I know what I want to say but can't find the words to say it.' Strecker argues that this caricature of the speaker's intentionality neglects entirely the social context of communication.

He mediates these extremes by starting from an intersubjective notion of symbolization that stresses, in the manner of Grice and other speech act theorists and pragmatists, the idea of instrumentality, of speaking as a means-end rationality conditioned less by the cognitive capacities either of individuals or the symbolic code than by an emergent work of interpretation created by speaker/hearers in the course of talk itself. Using the schemata of Brown and Levinson, he shows how the Hamar deploy communicative strategies in order to preserve and enhance their self-images (called 'face' by Brown and Levinson). In this model speaker/hearers have a common understanding of this idea and of the means of its realization in discourse. They engage speaking strategies designed either for mutual maintenance of face or in order to enhance the face of one by threatening the face of the other. This is a model of both cooperation and competition. Speaker/hearers not only cooperate, as in Grice's version of speech acts, they compete. It is part of a metaphor of an economy of scarcity, not, as in Grice, of a scarcity of truth, but of power, of what truth seeks by other means. Face is desirable and scarce, and in order to get more of it workers (speaker/hearers) either collaborate or compete. This presupposition of scarcity enables and makes reasonable the ideas of contest, power, warfare, strategy, conquest, and domination, and justifies itself through its invocation of reasonable action in an unreasonable world. It is in the end ironic because it requires the simultaneous possibility of two mutually exclusive modes of discourse and interpretation – one involving Grice's model of cooperation, clarity, economy, and truth, and another involving competition, ambiguity, opacity, excess, and deceit.

Strecker thus captures the duplicity of talk and shows how the Hamar are able, in Bourdieu's terms, to euphemize the truth about social relations by what superficially appears to be a kind of self-deception, but is instead a practice of artful displacement. This leads Strecker to a reconsideration of the whole notion of displacement, which in turn enables him to formulate ideas about how different societies might favour one or another combination of cooperation and competition as normative modes of discourse in different contexts. Might the discourse of power, for example, manifest itself in a normative discourse of cooperation, and thus make cooperation only a disguised or displaced competition? Similarly in the case of ritual discourse. Does ritual discourse itself encode a distinction between sacred and profane or is it, as Strecker claims, a displaced discourse about power in which people achieve a kind of symbolization in no way different from that of profane symbolization? As these last examples indicate, Strecker adds to the somewhat overrational models of speech acts and pragmatism an element of the irrational, of a rational irrational in its creation of rationalized irrationalities.

This is a fascinating book, not only as an innovative and provocative extension of speech act theory, but also as an account of Hamar ways of talking and of interpreting talk. Along with the three volumes of *The Hamar of Southern Ethiopia* which Ivo Strecker has published already together with Jean Lydall, it makes an outstanding ethnography of speaking.

Stephen Tyler
Rice University
Houston
Texas

Acknowledgements

My thanks go first and foremost to the *genius loci* of the London School of Economics and Political Science and the Institut für Völkerkunde in Göttingen. When studying, researching and teaching, I gained a great deal from both places, and I welcome this opportunity to express my gratitude to all of those who created an atmosphere in which I liked to live and work.

Of the people whom I wish to thank individually it is Jean Lydall whom I want to mention first. Without the many discussions we had and without her professional advice the present study would never have materialized. I also owe a lot to our friend, host and teacher, the Hamar spokesman Aike Berinas (Baldambe). He helped me to understand Hamar culture and the social practice of symbolization to which the present study is devoted. I thank him in Hamar: *Misso Baldambe, gulpha assa ko kai'é. Inta annaka barjo älidine.*

Professor Erhard Schlesier accepted me as a *Habilitation* candidate, and I would like to thank him here for his trust and support. Some friends have read the manuscript and have made helpful comments. I thank them all, and in particular I want to mention Penelope Brown, Stephen Levinson, James Woodburn, Michael Sallnow and Stephen Tyler who made a number of detailed suggestions on how I could improve the text.

The fieldwork and the writing of this essay were made possible by grants from the Deutsche Forschungsgemeinschaft and Professor Carl-Friedrich von Weizsäcker. To both I want to express my gratitude. My thanks go also to the Cambridge University Press who allowed me to quote extensively from Penelope Brown and Stephen Levinson's work 'Universals in language usage: politeness phenomena' and to reproduce several of their charts. Finally I want to say that I am very grateful for being allowed to publish my *Habilitationsschrift* in the monograph series of the Department of Social Anthropology, London School of Economics and Political Science.

Introduction

The present essay was written as a partial requirement for a *Habilitation* at the University of Göttingen. It is based on fieldwork among the Hamar of southern Ethiopia which I carried out together with my wife, Jean Lydall. When we began to write up the results of our research, we decided that Jean, who was working for a PhD at the London School of Economics, would deal with kinship and economics while I would focus on ritual and politics.

As the topic for my *Habilitation* thesis I chose a Hamar rite of transition which had intrigued me immensely. My study was to be mainly ethnographic, but in a longer introduction I also wanted to sort out some problems which I had noticed in Turner's and Sperber's theories of symbolism. I found Dan Sperber's book *Rethinking Symbolism* especially thought-provoking as he had done fieldwork in the south of Ethiopia shortly before us. The problems which he encountered when trying to understand the symbolic behaviour of the Dorze were similar to those I met among the Hamar. Yet the way in which I have tried to solve the problems is very different from Sperber's. Generally speaking, Sperber and I differ in that he focuses on how people *process* symbolic statements while I have tried to find out how they *produce* them. After I had completed my thesis on symbolization, I sent the manuscript to Dan Sperber asking him for comment. In a letter to me dated April 6 1984, from which he has kindly permitted me to quote, he wrote: 'I am not convinced by your criticisms, although they do touch on an essential matter. I tend to believe that symbolic production adapts itself to symbolic reception, so that the essential properties of symbolism have to be studied at the reception end.' Both the production and the processing of symbolic statements are of course inseparable from one another and therefore must be treated within one single theoretical framework. In his more recent work on rhetoric and pragmatic linguistics Sperber has made steps in this direction. Especially in their book *Relevance* he and Deirdre Wilson (Sperber and Wilson 1986) have tried to take equal care of the communicator and the audience. Yet the thrust of the argument has still remained psychological and lacks the sociological dimension which I find so important for a proper understanding of symbolic communication. A certain difference has therefore remained and it emerges most clearly from our different understanding and use of the work of Paul Grice. In *Relevance* Sperber and Wilson expressly point to their psychological orientation and how it affects their understanding of Grice:

> Our aim is to identify underlying mechanisms, rooted in human psychology, which explain how humans communicate with one another. A psychologically well-founded definition and typology of communication, if possible at all, should follow from a theoretical account of these underlying mechanisms. We see Grice's analysis as a possible basis for such a theoretical account. From this perspective, the main defect of Grice's analysis is not that it defines communication too vaguely, but that it explains communication too poorly. (Sperber and Wilson 1986: 32)

From a purely psychological perspective it is indeed hard to appreciate Grice's theory fully, and it comes as no surprise that Sperber and Wilson find that the theory 'explains communication too poorly'. However, from a sociological perspective, I would argue, Grice's work and especially his theory of conversational implicature (Grice 1975) is not too poor but rather it contains a richness which still has to be tapped. As will become apparent in the present study, the Gricean notion of the co-operative principle should not be discarded (as by Sperber and Wilson) but examined more closely. For the co-operative principle is but one face of a Janus head which, if one turns it around, reveals another face, the principle of exploitation. It took me a while to discover that Grice has offered us nothing less than a *general theory of communicative exploitation*. But once I had understood this, and once I had grasped the sociological implications of what Grice has called 'flouting' (Grice 1975: 49), I could go ahead and make use of the riches in his theory.

As I tried to answer the problems arising from Turner's and Sperber's theories of symbolism, and as I tried to work out a general theory of the social practice of symbolization, my *Habilitation* thesis turned into a study predominantly concerned with theoretical questions. However, a number of observations which I have made among the Hamar still play a part in the present essay. First, I have often used data from the Hamar ethnography of speaking to think through the various interactional strategies which constitute the social practice of symbolization. Secondly, in the last section I deal briefly with a Hamar rite of transition. But this is only in order to show in principle how the theory of symbolization which I have worked out may be used to explain symbolism in ritual. A full ethnography of the rite will be provided in a separate publication.

Symbolism can be seen from many angles and, as the spectrum of studies in symbolic theory is very wide, it will be helpful, I think, to present a short overview of the field of problems in which my study is placed. Figure 1 serves as a first orientation. Let me go quickly through the diagram to indicate the content of the different problem-orientations in the field of symbolic theory.

Representation

The most general problems confronting symbolic theory are those of representation, the 'representation of one content in another and through another' as Cassirer has called it (1923: 41). This very general inquiry belongs, first and foremost, to the domain of philosophy, especially to the philosophy of language and the philosophical problems of meaning. All western cultures have their own history of philosophical writings in this field and the literature is immense.

Univocal representation or signification

Studies in univocal signification are the paramount domain of semiotics, the general theory of signs. Some of the most important authors in this field are Barthes (1964), Eco (1972; 1973), Lévi-Strauss (1958), Merleau-Ponty (1960), Morris (1938), Peirce (1931–35), Saussure (1968) and Seboek (1964). Furthermore, all philosophical treaties on logic and scientific method make contributions here (for example Cohen and Nagel 1934, Kamlah and Lorenzen 1967, Nagel 1961, Popper 1935), as do all linguistic studies on disambiguation. A basic knowledge of the findings in the field of univocal representation is a pre-requisite for the study of

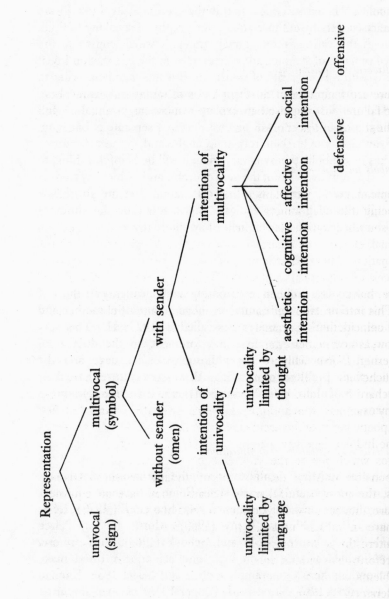

Figure 1 The field of problems in symbolic theory

the problems within the branch that extends from multivocal symbolization, as multivocality presupposes the existence of uni-vocality (see chapter 2 below).

Multivocal symbolization

There are a number of different kinds of multivocal expressions. The failure to distinguish between them accounts, I think, for most of the shortcomings of present-day symbolic theory in anthropology.

Symbols without senders

People may treat natural phenomena which have no personal author as being able to tell something. A constellation or movement of stars, the sounds of birds, black spots in the intestines of a slaughtered animal, etc., may be regarded as omens, oracles and other forms of divination. There is, strictly speaking, no sender here, no initial process of intentional codification. The communication dyad is, as it were, halved and reduced to the single act of decoding.

This interpretation of natural phenomena and of chance events and coincidents is extremely interesting and it acts, as we will see below, as a constant stimulus for the cognitive 'symbolic mechanism' (Sperber 1975). Chinese geomancy would be a case in point (Feuchtwang 1974) or forms of divination found in Africa (Evans-Pritchard 1937, Park 1963, Turner 1961), and then, of course, those many examples from antiquity, of which Aristotle has said that they are poetic because the accidental event may make sense and reveal some hidden necessity, like the example of the statue of Mitys in Argos which fell to the ground killing the man who had been responsible for Mitys' death. Events of this kind furnish, so Aristotle says, the most beautiful myths because they have an equivocal nature, they are outwardly accidental and at the same time they seem to have an intrinsic necessity (Aristotle, *Poetics*).

Interesting as the interpretation of symbols without authors – and therefore also without intention – may be, I think that all the problems which arise here can only be answered once one has understood the complete process of intentional multivocal coding and decoding. This is the problem area which branches off at this point in my diagram.

Multivocal statements intended to be univocal

Unintended multivocality pervades much of the communication in everyday life. Such multivocality is entrenched in the lexical and grammatical ambiguities which every natural language has, in contrast to the artificial languages of mathematicians, logicians, etc. On the lexical level, homonyms and homophones are a constant source of misunderstanding, and much effort is made to disambiguate the sources of possible ambiguity. Or, more correctly, a competent speaker takes special care that he does not construct sentences which contain badly placed homonyms or homophones. He will avoid sentences where, for example, the homophony of 'hair' and 'hare' or 'toupees' and 'two pees' lead to confusion, or where the homonymic alternatives of, for example, the German *Schloß* ('lock' and 'castle') are not taken into account.

Similarly, the competent speaker will try to avoid ambiguities which arise from correct but insensitive use of grammar. He will not say,

(1) 'All the guests won't eat a syllabub',

but will express himself more clearly and say either,

(2) 'Not all the guests will eat the syllabub', or
(3) 'None of the guests will eat the syllabub' (Smith and Wilson 1979: 63).

In so far as multivocality may be the unintended result of certain pitfalls inherent in the use of a language, it does not constitute the problem of my study and belongs to the problem-area of linguistics and the special theories concerning disambiguation.

A second source of unintended ambiguity lies not in the pitfalls of language but in the limitations of thinking itself. Often people simply do not think clearly and yet they utter seemingly multivocal statements with which they try to convince others that they hold a deep insight into this or that matter. Diderot had this in mind when on the first pages of his celebrated 'Jacques le fataliste' he attacked those lazy minds who always take recourse to allegory when they don't know what they really want to say. But whether it is intended to be univocal or multivocal, a statement which has not been thought through sufficiently is likely to turn out to be nonsense; it will be simply rubbish.

Intentional multivocality

Why and on what basis do we call some statements rubbish while calling others multivocal or even symbolic? What is the logic by which multivocal symbolization is achieved? Furthermore, what are the intentions which motivate the use of symbols in certain situations?

These are the questions which I will tackle in the subsequent study. In the first part I will try to assemble a general model of the cognitive basis of symbolization. This model should in principle be applicable to all possible human intentions. I have distinguished in this study four intentions: the aesthetic, the cognitive, the affective, and the social. These intentions are not mutually exclusive; in fact, they combine and support one another. Yet for heuristic purposes I – like so many before me – have found it useful to separate the four aspects of intention. I here briefly outline these.

Aesthetic intention

Multivocality has always been an element both of poetic practice and aesthetic theory. At the heart of art lies the process of mimesis by which the artist tries to delight us, move us, even cleanse us as the Greek term 'catharsis' implies.

'Tragedy through pity and fear effects a purgation of emotions' Aristotle has said (*Poetics*: 4) and, as the history of art shows, multivocality has been throughout one of the most powerful tools by which artists have effected a catharsis of their audience.

The literature is, accordingly, vast on the subject and great artists like Shakespeare, or Novalis (to name only two) have been analyzed again and again in order to find out 'how they have done it', how they have achieved the multivocal symbolization which moves us so deeply (see, for example, Mahood 1957 and Partridge 1968 on Shakespeare's wordplay, or Diez 1933, Haywood 1959 and Nivelle 1950 on the symbolism in 'Heinrich von Ofterdingen', Novalis 1802).

Furthermore, there have been whole schools and traditions in the arts which did not only use multivocality as a tool but made it their expressed aim not merely to leave the realm of univocality at certain moments but to part from it altogether.

Some of the German Romantics belong to this group (see Sørensen 1963) and the French symbolists of the second half of the nineteenth century: Mallarmé, Verlaine, Rimbaud and Baudelaire, for example. Anthropologists can learn much from these artists, whose works reveal to us what one might call the mechanics of symbolization. And if they do not learn from them directly, then they may learn from the writings of the art critics and the philosophers of art: from Empson's analysis *Seven Types of Ambiguity* (1930); from Frye's notion of 'outward' and 'inward' meaning (1957); from Gombrich (1960) and from Richards (1925) on the nature of metaphor, etc. I myself have learnt both from the critics and from the artists, and especially I have gained insight into the mechanics of symbolization through the work of one particular artist, the Belgian painter René Magritte (see section 2.2 below).

Cognitive intention

One of the most striking features of multivocality is its ability to activate our memories and stimulate our imaginative thinking, and because of this it has played an important role in the memory techniques and in the mental experiments of all ages. Analogy, simile, metaphor, metonymy, synecdoche, etc., these are multivocal figures of communication which constantly serve as tools for teaching. And yet, although we know that they work, we are far from knowing why they do so and their working has in many ways remained a puzzle.

For example, the problem of metaphor has generated an ever-increasing stream of studies by philosophers, linguists, psychologists and anthropologists alike (see Black 1962; 1979; Burke 1945; Turbayne (ed.) 1970; Geertz (ed.) 1974; Levin 1977; Loewenberg 1973; 1975; Mooij 1976; Ortony (ed.) 1979; Turner 1974; Wertheimer 1959; Polanyi 1966; Ricoeur 1978; J.D. Sapir 1977; Shibles 1971).

In my study I will deal with metaphor on several occasions. Also, symbolism as a cognitive mechanism will furnish the point from where I start my argument. Still the cognitive intentions as such will not be the centre of my attention. The general questions of how metaphors and, in a wider sense, all symbols may truly tell us, 'how things are' (see Black 1979: 41) I will leave unanswered.

Affective intention

One of the sources of multivocality is extremely difficult to fathom and has been largely excluded from my inquiry. I am thinking of the emotional states where psychological motives may lead to complicated forms of multivocal message construction.

The process has been well documented and analysed by Freud (1963), who has shown how dreams, myths, rituals, etc., may act as a disguise for people's deepest wishes. Some wishes are so problematic, both from the perspective of individual and social psychology, that people simply dare not admit them openly and are driven into multivocality. Ricoeur has spoken here of the 'semantics of wishes' which underlies the 'semantics of multivocality' (1970).

Similarly important have been Jung's contributions in this field (1948) but, like Freud's, they are rather different from the questions I am asking in this study.

Social intention

Of the large field of problems relating to symbolic theory I have staked out for study the *social* intentions which motivate the use of multivocality. The question is, why do people in certain social situations prefer to communicate through multivocal symbols rather than univocal signs? Why do they prefer symbolization rather than straightforward signification? To answer this question I will first turn to Brown and Levinson's theory of politeness. This theory I then extend, arguing that any theory of politeness is also a candidate theory of rudeness: how to honour provides the recipe for how to dishonour. Generally, politeness and social domination, help and exploitation, honour and dishonour, and truth and deceit have been at the centre of my attention and I have tried to work out a theory of symbolizaton which deals with these contraries in one single theoretical framework.

1 Ritual and symbolism

1.1 From the symbolic product to the principles of symbolic production

More than 125 years ago, Bachofen, who is one of the founding fathers of contemporary anthropology, began his contribution to the theory of symbolism by interpreting a picture which had recently (1838) been discovered in a columbarium of the Roman Villa Pamfilia (Bachofen 1859). The picture shows a group of five youths, four of whom are engaged in a discussion about three eggs, each painted white and black, which lie on a table in front of them. Now, there are two ways of looking at the picture. First, one can be attracted by the centre of attention within the picture itself: one can focus on the eggs. Secondly, one can view the picture as a whole: one can focus on the activity of the group. The two views sum up, I think, the history of symbolic theory rather well. Since Bachofen, anthropologists, historians, philosophers, philologists and others have been either discussing the eggs (as a product of symbolization) or discussing the discussions about the eggs (as meta-theories about the understanding of the products of symbolization). Thus, by choosing this particular picture as the object of his study, Bachofen enshrined in this early essay an essential wisdom about symbolism as a matter of scientific discourse. It provokes curiosity and thinking and an everlasting argument. All and everything which exists in this world may get dragged into the discussion, and all those involved may learn a lot of what there can be known about life; but in the end the symbols remain what they are; for example, three enigmatic eggs.

The literature on the interpretation of symbolism is accordingly rich, even vast. So why, if I know of the endlessness of symbolism, do I too enter the discussion? Well, I enter it in order to speak, as it were, for the fifth youth in the group who has until now been quiet and has even turned his back on the group. Instead of looking at the eggs, he has been looking at the world which surrounds the eggs and the boys who are talking about the eggs. To me, his eyes seem set on the world which provides the background knowledge and the source of motivation for symbolization. Similarly, in this book I will not ask what specific symbols mean, but why and how they are produced. I will turn away from the symbolic product and deal instead with the principles of symbolic production.

Bachofen himself and the majority of anthropologists have, as I have said, concentrated predominantly on the product of symbolic thinking, on the ϛυμβολον/symbol itself. In the present study I have shifted my viewpoint away from the ϛυμβολον and have focused on the active process which generates it. In other words, my interest lies in the act of ϛυμβάλλω.

The ancient Greek verb ϛυμβάλλω, from which the term symbol is derived, contains a highly dynamic element, as when 'rivers fall into one another', when items are 'thrown together' or are 'jumbled up together', or even when men are 'pitted' in war against each other and 'come to blows' and 'join in fighting'. Or, less dramatically, ϛυμβάλλω means 'roads join each other', 'straight lines meet in one point', people make contracts, etc. Then again there is the aspect of contribution and enrichment, such as to 'store up', 'accumulate', 'contribute an opinion, help or judgement'. And finally, there are all the various shades of comparing; that is, to 'reckon', 'compute', 'conclude', 'infer', 'conjecture', 'interpret', 'understand', 'agree', 'make a treaty', 'fix' and 'settle' (Liddle and Scott 1968). It is the active element within the ϛυμβολον which has roused my interest and which I want to explore. But I will not do so as a philologist, nor will I be concerned with the Greeks. Rather, I will approach the issue as an anthropologist, and the people from whom I draw my knowledge will be the Hamar of southern Ethiopia.

1.2 Symbols, ritual and the analysis of social systems

I originally became interested in questions related to symbolism when I attempted to understand the basic problems of anthropological observation and description. In a study entitled *Methodische Probleme der ethno-soziologischen Beobachtung und Beschreibung* (Strecker 1969) I tried to identify the factors which cause the distortions which we find so often in anthropological representations. One factor, I found, has to do with problems related to the

interpretation of symbolism in ritual. As this problem of anthropological representation furnishes the general background of the
present study, let me explain in some detail.

Anthropological fieldwork is no one-way process where A.
observes B. Rather, fieldwork always necessitates co-operation and
communication between the observer and the observed. Ideally, a
fieldworker would find all the people of the society he is studying
willing to co-operate with him. This is, however, not the case, as
various social factors oppose such unlimited co-operation. In every
society the movements of a fieldworker are restricted in particular
ways and the opportunities for observation and inquiry are
accordingly quite limited. The observer's situation may vary
considerably, just as languages differ in that one may be difficult,
another easy to learn (Maybury-Lewis 1967: XX); but the restrictions are always there, and any theory of fieldwork which does not
take these restrictions into account deludes itself. Anthropological
fieldwork, then, is faced with a selectivity which is not generated by
the observer's interests and preoccupations alone, nor by the present
state of the discipline's technology (tape recorders, for example), but
also by the practice of fieldwork, by the social factors which influence
the opportunities for empirical work.

The practical limitations of fieldwork are in turn married to the
following dilemma of anthropological theory. The theoretical
interest of anthropology has as its focus the 'totality', the total system
that exists within cultures and societies. Malinowski's focus was on
'culture ... an integral composed of partly autonomous, partly co-
ordinated institutions' (1944: 40). Nadel spoke of 'culture ... the
integrated totality of standardized behaviour patterns' (1951: 29).
Radcliffe-Brown's concern was with 'social structure ... a complex
network of social relations' (1952: 19). Evans-Pritchard studied
'social institutions as interdependent parts of social systems' (1951:
8), and Gluckman spoke of 'customs ... having an interrelated
dependance on one another ... operating within systems of social
relations' (1965: X).

Now, given the fact that the practice of fieldwork makes heavy
selectivity inescapable, an anthropologist can never hope to reach his
aim of describing a totality without flagrantly distorting it. And yet
the anthropologist has no choice but to pursue the unattainable goal
of totality. The reason for this is that unlike his colleagues in the

other social sciences he usually works in an alien culture. Here he cannot proceed like his colleagues who work in the basically familiar society at home. He cannot focus on any single variable in a generally known social formation, because there is no such generally known social formation which would justify him in isolating a single variable and looking at it more closely. An anthropologist in the field must never isolate any phenomenon assuming that its social and cultural context may be taken for granted. Rather, he has to describe and analyse each phenomenon which he observes within the context to which it belongs. This context may be called 'pattern' (Benedict 1934), '*ethos*' and '*eidos*' (Bateson 1958), 'structure' (Radcliffe-Brown 1952; Lévi-Strauss 1963), 'system' (Evans-Pritchard 1951; Gluckman 1965) or some other term, according to the particular theoretical orientation of the anthropologist. Whatever the name, all aim at a totality, a *Gestalt* which gives the individual and isolated phenomenon its place in a wider context. As Malinowski's classic presentation of the *kula* has shown (Malinowski 1922), and as many anthropologists have demonstrated in their monographs ever since (for example, Firth 1936, Fortes 1945 and 1949, Evans-Pritchard 1940, Meggitt 1965, Maybury-Lewis 1967, Nadel 1942 and Turner 1957), anthropological description succeeds as a description of social life only when it takes into account the intrinsic relationship between the parts and the whole of a society or culture. Thus the holism of empirical anthropology has a theoretical and not a practical reason.

If we realize that holistic orientation is a theoretical necessity, and if we realize at the same time that for practical reasons the goal cannot be attained, how do we solve the problem? In my 'critical theory of description' (1969: 38), I tried to provide at least a partial answer to the dilemma, and it was then that I first encountered the problems of symbolic action which constitutes the topic of the present study. At that early stage I did not explicitly deal with symbolism but with ritual.

Ritual, and in turn symbolism, both tie in with problems of anthropological description (or simply ethnography) as follows. Actions which we call 'ritual' tend to provide a pitfall for the ethnographer, because in the practice of fieldwork ritual is often relatively easy to observe. It is strongly patterned (Firth 1951: 222); it is expressive and dramatic (Beattie 1966: 60); it is standardized

(Nadel 1954: 99); it is repetitive and publicly sanctioned (Firth 1951: 222), etc. For these reasons ritual is particularly visible.

This visibility makes it, not surprisingly, an ideal object for anthropological documentation, and many anthropologists have accordingly organized their description of 'other cultures', to use the title of Beattie's book (1964), around data that predominantly stem from the realm of ritual. Yet this is precisely where the problem lies: because of its practical visibility to the anthropological observer, ritual is prone to lead him towards a bias in perception. What is more, this bias, which initially stems only from practical reasons, soon becomes a bias with theoretical implications.

In my study of the practical and analytical aspects of the study of ritual (1969: 42) I have argued that there is nothing wrong with using ritual for the study of a social system or any other totality provided that one is aware of the analytical limitations of concentrating on ritual.

Durkheim (1912) and Radcliffe-Brown (1922) long ago showed that ritual action provides a key to an understanding of the processes of integration within a social system. As Radcliffe-Brown put it, rituals create and perpetuate the 'collective sentiments and the representations connected with them, upon which ... the very existence of the society depends' (1922: 404). If one wants to understand the social cohesion prevailing within any society one has indeed to study its rituals. Another analytical value of ritual lies in the fact that it often serves to establish role and status demarcation within a social structure. Van Gennep in his classical study of rites of passage has aptly summarized this point: 'A society is similar to a house divided into rooms and corridors. The more the society resembles ours in its form of civilization, the thinner are its internal partitions and the wider and more open are its doors of communi- cation. In a semi-civilized society, on the other hand, sections are carefully isolated, and passage from one to another must be made through formalities and ceremonies' (1977: 26).

One can see how ritual can thus be used as an analytical indicator which allows an insight into the inner differentiation or anatomy of a social system. But at the same time there are serious analytical limitations. Ritual belongs, after all, to what has come to be called since Marx the superstructure (*Überbau*) of society. Ritual is ideology in action. Any anthropological description which does not take this into account and uncritically bases its generalizations on observations from the realms of ritual is bound to present not the true but the ideological form of society. Although there are exceptions like, for example, millenarian rituals, this ideological view will tend to be static and harmonic, and the less developed the theory of ritual is with which the anthropologist operates, the more static and harmonic it will be. If he holds a simple theory of reflection which assumes an almost one-to-one correspondence between ritual and the other spheres of social order, then the social structure which the anthropologist describes will appear to be static, harmonic and in a state of equilibrium. A classic example of such a one-sided analytical use of ritual is Fortes's work on the Tallensi (1945; 1949); for a detailed critique of Fortes's approach, see Worsley (1956) and Strecker (1969).

1.3 An improved analytical use of ritual: Gluckman and Turner

By 1970, when I set off to carry out fieldwork, Gluckman and Turner seemed to offer the most refined theories of ritual. Both followed Radcliffe-Brown in stressing the normative aspect of ritual, but they also asked questions concerning the nature of the norms that are stressed. In particular, they asked whether in their rituals people stress those social norms and values which, in the practice of everyday life, are problematical rather than those to which they unproblematically adhere.

In answer to this question, Gluckman elaborated on two aspects of ritual. First, in his celebrated treatment of rituals of rebellion (1963), he was able to show that certain African rituals occur at those points in society where the confrontation of interests between different actors is most prominent. The rituals act here as a kind of catharsis, and this catharsis reinforces the social cohesion of the group. Thus ritual may both indicate the equilibrium of a society and show the points where the equilibrium is endangered and potentially off-balance. Or, to put it differently, ritual may serve equally as an indicator of the harmony and of the latent conflicts within the society. The second aspect is also related to conflict. When examining 'rituals of social relations' (1962), Gluckman developed the theory that ritual arises wherever there is the need for social demarcation. The theory may be seen as an application of Van Gennep's early theory of ritual demarcation to role theory.

In societies where multiplex face-to-face relations prevail, the question of who at a certain moment in time is acting in which of his many roles may often need an immediate answer if social conflict or, at least, insecurity is to be avoided. Therefore, the identity of an actor is often defined by way of ritual, the ritual acting as a means of orientation which prevents the different roles of a person from being mixed up. As Gluckman has put it, the effect of ritual is 'to mark off and segregate roles in social groups where they may be confounded' (1962: 28). This segregation of roles not only prevents unnecessary social conflict but also counteracts what Gluckman has called the spreading effects of breach of role:

> Because men and women in tribal society play so many of their varied purposive roles with the same set of fellows . . . every activity is charged with complex moral evaluations, and default strikes not at isolated roles but at the integral relations which contain many roles. I think that it is this compound of moral evaluation, and the spreading effects of breach of role, which accounts for the way rituals are attached to so many changes of activity in tribal society. (1962: 28)

Like Gluckman, Turner explored the relationship between ritual and social conflict. His theory constitutes a logical development of Radcliffe-Brown's theory of ritual integration. In his study of the Andaman Islanders, Radcliffe-Brown had asserted that a society in order to persist has to exercise and express certain (unspecified) collective sentiments by means of ritual. 'The only possible way,' he said, 'by which such collective sentiments can be maintained is by giving them regular and adequate expression' (1922: 404). But not everything gets ritualized in society, not every collective sentiment is based on ceremony. Only in certain kinds of situations of life do rituals abound, in others they are absent. What characterizes the situations in which rituals occur, and why do they occur? Turner's studies have made an important contribution to these issues. I am not, at the moment, thinking of his analysis of individual affliction and healing by means of ritual (1968), but of his study of schism and continuity among the Ndembu of Central Africa (1957). The interesting point of this study is the way in which Turner has integrated ritual into the study of conflict within a social structure.

When analyzing the social life of the Ndembu, Turner found that certain social conflicts tended to recur in a particular patterned way: 'On a number of occasions during my fieldwork I became aware of marked disturbance in the social iife of the particular group I happened to be studying at the time... After a while I began to detect a pattern in these eruptions of conflicts: I noticed phases in their development which seemed to follow one another in a more or less regular sequence' (1957: 91). Turner called these eruptions 'social dramas', and he described the processual form of these dramas as consisting of four phases (1957: 91–2):

(1) The public breach or non-fulfilment of some crucial norm occurs between two interacting persons or groups.

(2) The violation of the norm leads to a phase of mounting crisis within the social group to which the persons belong.

(3) Adjustive and redressive mechanisms are brought in to limit the spread of breach.

(4) The reintegration of the group or the recognition of irreparable breach between the contesting parties takes place.

Now, for an understanding of ritual, the relation between phase 2 and phase 3 is of crucial interest. During the period of mounting social crisis (phase 2), structural cleavages and contradictions between social norms, values and interests become visible. The crisis leads, as it were, to a moment of truth, it 'exposes the pattern of current factional struggle', as Turner puts it, 'and beneath it there becomes visible the less plastic, more durable, but nevertheless gradually changing basic social structure' (1957: 91).

The conflict of interests which the crisis reveals is, however, not socially acceptable. Therefore, in phase 3 mechanisms of redress and adjustment are brought into action, and it is here, according to Turner, that ritual comes in as a prime agent of social reconciliation. It acts as a means of overcoming the insufficiencies of the social structure, and it directs the value orientation of the contestant parties away from the particular conflicts on to a higher level of sociability where once again every one is interested in living in harmony with everyone else. To quote Turner on this once again:

[Ndembu] life is full of manifold and unceasing struggles, of schism and fission. I believe ... that the society exhibiting this turmoil and unrest could not maintain any sort of coherence for long were it not for its plastic and adaptable system of ritual ... the ritual contrives to stimulate in its members sentiments of tribal unity, of a general belonging together, which transcend the irrepairable divisions and conflicts in the secular social structure. (1957: 302)

This is certainly an improved approach to ritual. What is especially valuable is the fact that, unlike Durkheim's and Radcliffe-Brown's theories, which made the fieldworker close his eyes, Turner's and also Gluckman's approach alerts the fieldworker. As ritual is no longer seen as mirroring social harmony, an understanding of it becomes more urgent. Behind every ritual there may lie some hidden, even explosive, danger and manifold latent social conflicts.

So it was that when in 1970 I went to do fieldwork among the Hamar of southern Ethiopia I treasured Gluckman's and Turner's theories as some of the most important analytical tools with which I intended to tackle the social system of the Hamar.

1.4 Towards a theory of ritual symbolism: Turner

While Turner's (and Gluckman's) theory of ritual constitutes the general background to the present study, it is particularly his theory of symbolism which prompted me to write this book. In what follows, I will try to overcome some of the shortcomings in Turner's theory. Only when the defects of this theory of symbolism are amended can his very powerful theory of ritual be used for the analysis of social systems. Let me explain by first outlining some of the main elements of Turner's theory of symbolism and then formulating my critique.

Turner treats symbolism, as he does ritual, always with an eye on method and on fieldwork. In fact, considerations of method are his starting-point. At the beginning of his chapter on 'Symbols in Ndembu ritual' (1967: 19–47) he says: 'The structure and properties of ritual symbols may be inferred from three classes of data: (1) external form and observable characteristics; (2) interpretations offered by specialists and by laymen; (3) significant contexts largely worked out by the anthropologist' (1967: 20). A second chapter entitled 'Ritual symbolism, morality and social structure among the Ndembu' (1967: 48–58) contains the same three methodological steps. This time they are related to meaning, a term which Turner puts in inverted commas: 'When we talk about the "meaning" of a symbol, we must be careful to distinguish between at least three levels or fields of meaning. These I propose to call: (1) the level of indigenous interpretation (or, briefly, the exegetical meaning); (2) the operational meaning; and (3) the positional meaning' (1967: 50). The classes of the first essay correspond to the levels of the second essay in the following way:

I	II
observable characteristics	operational meaning
indigenous interpretation	exegetical meaning
significant context	positional meaning

The content of each of the three pairs may be summarized as follows:

1. *Observable characteristics – operational meaning* The observer watches someone do something. Turner, for example, watches how, at a girl's puberty ritual, 'a novice is wrapped in a blanket and laid at the foot of a *mudyi* sapling' (1967: 20). He also observes (at this or another time) that the *mudyi* tree 'is conspicuous for its white latex, which exudes in milky beads if the thin bark is scratched' (1967: 20). Furthermore, as he continues to observe Ndembu ritual life, Turner finds that Ndembu do not use the *mudyi* tree only once, but operate with it in more than half a dozen different kinds of ritual. He also observes how different people operate with the same symbol during the same ritual differently (1967: 56). All these observable characteristics of the particular use of an object, plant, living being, mimetic action, etc., constitute its operational meaning in the ritual. The operational meaning of a symbol is thus always defined situationally.

2. *Indigenous interpretation – exegetical meaning* The observer asks the actor or someone else about a symbolic action he has observed. Or, if he does not ask, he still tries to get statements about the event by listening to conversations, examining the statements which go with the ritual performance and studying related oral tradition, songs,

stories, riddles, etc. Thus Turner can tell us of the *mudyi* tree that
Ndembu women 'say with reference to its observable characteristics
that the milk tree stands for human breast milk and also for the
breasts that supply it' (1967: 20). Indigenous interpretation does not
stop here; rather it starts with the concrete and observable and then it
expands into more and more general and abstract formulations. For
example (1967: 53), Turner's informants moved as follows:

> *mudyi* tree equals breast milk
> *mudyi* tree equals a mother and her child
> *mudyi* tree equals matrilineage
> *mudyi* tree equals a novice's children
> *mudyi* tree equals womanhood
> *mudyi* tree equals women's wisdom.

The fact that exegesis runs from the particular to the general and
from the concrete to the abstract does not, however, mean that
people think of the symbol as internally divided. On the contrary,
Turner emphasizes that symbols are felt and experienced as single
entities. The Ndembu 'can break down the concept "milk tree"
cognitively into many attributes, but in ritual practice they view it as a
single entity' (1967: 54). This entity merges the most concrete and
the most abstract referents or 'significata' of a symbol.

Furthermore, the entity contains meanings which belong to very
different semantic domains. Both domains constitute two poles of a
continuum. At one pole of the meaning continuum cluster significata
which are basically physiological in character and affect human
emotion; at the other pole cluster referents which relate to the social
structure and affect human morality. Turner calls the emotional pole
'orectic' and the social or moral pole 'normative' (1967:54). Both
fuse in the single entity of the symbol and this is what gives the
symbol its power. The 'intimate union of the moral and the material'
turns the obligatory into the desirable and charges the symbol 'with
power from unknown sources, and to be capable of acting on persons
and groups coming in contact with them in such a way as to change
them for the better or in a desired direction' (1967: 54).

Here we are, of course, no longer in the realm of indigenous
interpretation, but have moved to an anthropologist's interpretation
of indigenous interpretation. That is, we have already entered the
third pair of Turner's three methodological steps.

3. *Significant context – positional meaning* According to Turner, the working-out of the significant context or the positional meaning of a symbol is largely the job of the observer. The task is essentially a synthetic one; it consists of analyzing the symbol as part of a whole: 'The positional meaning of a symbol derives from its relationship to other symbols in a totality, a *Gestalt*, whose elements acquire their significance from the system as a whole' (1967: 51). In Turner's view, no single actor who takes part in a ritual thinks of the positional meaning of any symbol he uses. By its very definition, the positional meaning escapes his awareness. Being a part of the ritual event, the actor is limited by what Turner (following Lupton) has called a 'structural perspective'.

The structural perspective of an actor is the result of his 'occupancy of a particular position, or even a set of situationally conflicting positions, both in the persisting structure of his society, and also in the role structure of the given ritual' (1967: 27). The role involvement is enhanced further by the personal interests, purposes and wants which the actor tries to satisfy, and by his belief in the ideals, values and norms which are symbolized in the ritual. All this leads to the fact that in ritual each participant views the event 'from his own particular corner of observation' (1967: 27). Therefore, the job of the anthropologist is to overcome this selectivity and assemble a whole, a *Gestalt*, which reveals more than the single views which the participants individually hold. To quote Turner and the example of the *mudyi* tree once again:

Thus in the '*Nkang'a*' ritual, each person or group in successive contexts of action, sees the milk tree only as representing her or their own specific interests and values at those times. However, the anthropologist who has previously made a structural analysis of Ndembu society, isolating its organizational principles, and distinguishing its groups and relationships, has no particular bias and can observe the real interconnections and conflicts between groups and persons, in so far as these receive ritual representation. What is meaningless for an actor playing a specific role may well be highly significant for an observer and analyst of the total system. (1967: 27)

These are very proud words and they stand at the apex of Turner's

theory of symbolism. It is he, the anthropologist, who reveals the
final and deepest truth and meaning of the symbols used by the
people whom he, the outsider, has come to study. They, the
participants, hold only a partial view and have only limited insight
into what they are doing, but the anthropologist arrives at a complete
and unbiased understanding of the meaning of the symbols.

1.5 Symbolic effects without a cause: a critique of Turner

I had to go and carry out fieldwork in order to find out that Turner's
theory is not only too proud, attributing too much competence to
the anthropologist and too little to the people, but also that it
lacks something which is indispensable for an understanding of
symbolism. Furthermore, the theory also contains an unnecessary
ballast, a misleading element which is quite inessential for an
understanding of symbolism.

According to Turner, the anthropologist arrives at an interpretation of symbols by means of the three steps described above: that is,
he observes, records exegeses and works out the significant context.
Now, as soon as I arrived in Hamar, the Hamar situation taught me the
interesting lesson that the ritual life of a people can function very well
without any exegesis, that is, without the second step in Turner's
explanatory model. There are no such specialists in symbolic
exegesis among the Hamar as seem to exist among the Ndembu.
True, the Hamar are eloquent and able to explain their social life
(see, for example, Lydall and Strecker 1979b), but when it comes to
the meaning of symbolic statements, they usually remain silent. This
silence is not meant to hide anything from the inquisitive anthropologist, but rather tells him that he is asking the wrong questions,
that he expects words where they are inappropriate. Or, more
correctly, that he expects words to be put to the wrong kind of use.

For example, at the climax of a Hamar rite of transition the initiate
leaps on to and then runs across the backs of a row of cattle. What
does this action 'mean'? During my early days in Hamar I often asked
people this question and always the answer was silence. After a
while, when I had learnt more about their social life and about the
world they live in, I began to understand the inappropriateness of
certain questions and stopped asking them.

If Turner had been right, then the participants in the Hamar rituals should each have voiced their structural perspective I would then have pieced the different views together and combined them with other knowledge about the social system and the rite as a whole. This would have helped me to arrive at the positional meaning of each symbol. However, as it is normally impossible in Hamar to elicit any exegesis from a participant in a ritual it is also impossible to piece together multiple exegeses. Any attempt at piecing together the 'positional meaning' (in Turner's sense of the term) of a symbol is thus hampered from the start, and Turner's model is, in fact, inapplicable. If people constantly use symbols, as the Hamar do, but do not say what the symbols mean, then we certainly need a theory which accounts for this fact. We need a theory for the explanation of symbolism in ritual which embraces both the 'said and the unsaid', to use the title of Tyler's magnificent book (Tyler 1978).

It is not sufficient to postulate, like Turner, that whenever people do not offer an exegesis to the anthropologist, 'certain conflicts would appear to be so basic that they totally block exegesis' (Turner 1967: 38). This negative factor, though surely playing a role in symbolization at times, is not the only cause of the lack of exegesis of ritual which is found so often. As I will show below, there are other positive factors which convincingly explain why the Hamar participants in a ritual offer no exegesis when asked about the meanings of their symbolic actions.

But the most crucial limitation of Turner's theory of symbolism lies in the fact that it is, after all, not strictly speaking a theory of symbolization but of signification. This may sound odd, because Turner has criticized Nadel and Wilson precisely on this point, saying that their difficulties in the interpretation of ritual 'derive from their failure to distinguish the concept of symbol from the mere sign' (Turner 1967: 26). Yet Turner's theory too is more a theory of signification than of symbolization. Polysemy or multivocality means for him only 'that a single symbol may stand for many things' (Turner 1967: 50). He explains symbols as 'economic representations' which are able 'to interconnect a wide variety of *significata*' (Turner 1967: 50).

Interesting as this view may be, it only goes half-way towards a theory of symbolization because Turner nowhere considers the actor as being someone who purposefully constructs statements which carry multiple meanings. He never considers the possibility that someone may want to say something in such a way that a message may pass indirectly and in a hidden way. Sperber (1975) has rightly identified this facet as Turner's 'cryptological view' of symbolism. His true intellectual forefathers are not Marx or Nietzsche (1887) but the 'revelationists' such as Creuzer (1819) and Jung. He quotes the latter as saying, 'a symbol is always the best possible expression of a relatively unknown fact, a fact, however, which is none the less recognized or postulated as existing' (Turner 1967: 26; Jung 1949). Turner evidently accepts this view of symbolism (although he rejects Jung's theory of the collective unconscious as the principal source of ritual symbolism and replaces it with the social structure) and thus, in a very fundamental way, people are always separated from the meaning of the symbols which they are using, and they are forever longing for the revelation which would terminate the separation. People are thus not the masters but the slaves of their symbols. In order to be free they need the psychoanalyst or the anthropologist.

Truly, things cannot really be like this and the separation between the people and their symbols must be only an illusion. The knowledge of the positional meaning of a symbol cannot be the privilege of the outside observer alone. On the contrary, without the positional meaning in mind people would not and could not embark on the creation and use of symbolic statements. Furthermore, no matter how learned and informed an outside observer may become during his fieldwork, his understanding of the positional meaning of symbols will always at best only approach the understanding of those who, so to speak, 'positioned' the symbols in the first place – positioned them within the context of their specific culture in such a way that they are able to carry meaning. Not a simple and univocal meaning, but the complex and multivocal meaning which we call symbolic.

What has gone wrong then is that Turner has treated multivocality only as the effect and not as the cause of symbolization. Yet if we want to explain symbolism in ritual we must also include in our analysis the causes of symbolism, the authors of symbolic statements who think symbolically and know and anticipate the multivocality of the statements which they create. We must think of people as actors who do not only think of their own interests but also of the interests of others, and who therefore choose at specific moments to communicate not by means of univocal signs but rather by means of multivocal symbols. We have to try to understand the processes which go into symbolic codification. Once we have understood the practice of symbolic coding or, as I have called it in this study, the practice of symbolization, then we will also be able to cope with symbolic statements more competently and use our findings for an analysis of the social system. This, then, is the point from which this book departs.

I would have started off my analysis of the cognitive basis of symbolization as a direct critique of Turner's approach to symbolism in the way I have indicated above had Dan Sperber not published his extremely thought-provoking book, entitled *Rethinking Symbolism* (1975).

When, together with Jean Lydall, I was beginning to study the Hamar, Sperber was just completing fieldwork among the Dorze who are neighbours of the Hamar in southern Ethiopia. Like the Hamar, the Dorze employ abundant forms of symbolism in their social life and, like the Hamar, the Dorze only rarely offer any indigenous interpretation of their symbols. And again, just as among the Hamar, a mythological background which would provide meaning to the symbols is almost totally missing. The following quotation in which Sperber describes the situation among the Dorze could, in fact, apply equally well to the Hamar:

> In a general way, the Dorze, who utilize a large number of symbols in connection with multiple, lively and complex rituals, do not explain them, and restrict their comments to the rule of use. Transition rituals are not accompanied by any initiation into a body of esoteric knowledge. The few bits of exegesis that I gathered were improvised by good-natured informants in response to questions that no Dorze would have dreamt of asking. (1975: 18)

As I have already shown above, this apparent discrepancy between an abundance of symbolic action on the one hand and a striking absence of indigenous symbolic interpretation on the other, cannot be explained by Turner's model. Sperber is quick to realize this when he writes that the Dorze situation shows 'that a complex symbolic system can work very well without being accompanied by any exegetic commentary' (1975: 18). But not only does Sperber offer a critique of Turner, he also offers the outline of an approach to symbolism which is altogether new. And in this way Sperber has moved, as it were, in front of Turner and therefore it is he with whom I will begin.

2 The cognitive basis of symbolization

2.1 Symbolism as a cognitive mechanism (Sperber)

In his important contribution to the general theory of symbolism Dan Sperber has developed the hypothesis that symbolism is a cognitive mechanism which has specific functions in the construction of knowledge and in the working of the memory (Sperber 1975). Furthermore, the specific structure of symbolism, he says, cannot be predicted and explained in reference to social communication as most theories, at least those proposed by anthropologists, have tried to do. If Sperber's contention is true it should radically affect our understanding of symbolic processes and I therefore begin this inquiry into symbolization with a close look at Sperber's theory. In this subsection I only sum up briefly what I consider to be Sperber's main line of argument, but in subsections 2.2–2.4 I go into detail and try to evaluate Sperber's achievements.

The critical point of departure in Sperber's thinking is his view that a semiological approach to an understanding of symbolism is bound to fail. Symbolic forms, he says, do not have the properties of signs and thus cannot operate within systems of interdependent meanings. The condition which would allow us to study symbolism in the way we study codes is simply not fulfilled. In symbolic systems, 'no list gives, no rule generates, a set of pairs (symbol, interpretation) such that each occurrence of a symbol finds in it its prefigured treatment' (1975: 16). Therefore symbolic interpretation cannot be a matter of decoding. Furthermore, the semiological view has not appreciated the nature of the pairs which it says are constituting the entities of symbolic codes. Contrary to what the semiologists have asserted, the exegesis of a symbol does not furnish its interpretation, not even a part of its interpretation, but rather must be seen as an extension of it. The relationship between symbol and exegesis is not one of prediction and substitution but of addition. The exegesis is added to the symbol itself, it does not provide a substitute for it, and just like the symbol itself it in turn needs its own exegesis. Thus one moves on from exegesis to exegesis logically *ad infinitum* without ever arriving at an independent interpretation of the symbol.

Sperber takes Turner's treatment of the *museng'u* symbol which occurs in Ndembu hunting ritual as a case in point: 'The Ndembu first explain that the *museng'u* is good for a certain hunting ritual because it means a "multiplicity of kills"; secondly, that it means this by the etymology of its name and the abundance of its fruits' (1975: 29). In this way a branch of a tree called *museng'u* is conceptually represented three times and each representation consists of a development of the preceding one:

(1) The *museng'u* brings success in hunting.
(2) The *museng'u* signifies multiplicity.
(3) The *museng'u* bears many fruits.

Statement 3 justifies statement 2 and statement 2 justifies statement 1. This regressive process leaves the exegesis for ever on a symbolic level. Add to this the fact that although pairing of symbol and exegesis may be achieved *ex post facto* it can never be predicted with certainty, and the semiological dilemma becomes evident. As Sperber sees it, semiological analysis fails because of a defect derived from a 'disproportion between symbols and the representations they are said to encode ... a restricted number of explicit symbols is associated with certain representations in such a ruleless manner that any object at all could as well have been symbolised. An arbitrary exegesis makes an unforseeable selection among all these possible symbolisations' (1975: 47).

This then is the situation of the semiologists of whom Sperber singles out Turner for detailed criticism. (I leave out here his parallel critique of Freudian semiology.) He says that he generally agrees with Turner's methodology and he acknowledges the good results which Turner's refined analysis of symbolism has furnished. Only on the place of meaning in the study of symbols does he differ. Thus he writes:

> I disagree with Turner only on a single point: the use he makes of the notion of meaning – in his eyes a descriptive category, in mine a misleading metaphor. If I have used his works, it is not to underscore this disagreement, but on the contrary because his analyses implicitly discard the idea of a symbolism organized like a

code, so that he cannot speak of meaning except by refraining from defining or even circumscribing the concept. It would be better, in fact, not to speak of meaning at all. (1975: 33)

After he has dealt with Turner and what he calls the 'cryptological' semiologists, Sperber turns to examine the work of Lévi-Strauss. In a chapter entitled 'Absent meaning' he comes to the surprising conclusion that Lévi-Strauss, the most avowed and most sophisticated of all semiologists, has proved, contrary to his intentions, that symbols cannot possibly have any meaning. He has 'demonstrated the opposite of what he asserts, and myths do not constitute a language' (1975: 83). In an extended argument which is too long to reiterate here, Sperber shows how the rules which Lévi-Strauss has found governing myths do not constitute a grammar, if this is understood as 'a device that generates the sentences of the language it describes by means of given axioms and by the operation of rules, independently of all external input' (1975: 82). On the contrary, these rules show that 'myths are generated by the transformation of other myths or of texts which carry a certain mythicism' (1975: 82). Myths are a device 'that allows an infinite and non-enumerable set of possible inputs' (1975: 82). It is Lévi-Strauss's great achievement that in his *Mythologiques I–IV* (1964–71) he has established this fact, that he has demonstrated how 'the device that would generate myths depends on an external stimulus' (1975: 82–3) and that no grammar could by itself generate a set of myths. Thus the semiological notion of meaning has no place in the study of symbolism. Once 'we strip the work of Lévi-Strauss of the semiological burden with which he has chosen to encumber it,' Sperber writes, 'we will then realise that he was the first to propose the fundamentals of an analysis of symbolism which was finally freed from the absurd idea that symbols mean' (1975: 84).

Furthermore, Sperber says Lévi-Strauss suggested the idea that symbolic elements 'organise the mental representation of systems of which they are parts' (1975: 70). This organizing nature of symbolic activity brings back to mind the comparison between symbolic thinking and the working of a *bricoleur* which Lévi-Strauss makes in the first chapter of *The Savage Mind* (1966). Sperber sums up this comparison by saying:

The *bricoleur* gathers objects, various odds and ends of which he may always make something but never just anything; for each element, once one wishes to utilise it, suggests some plans and rejects others, just as each symbolic element suggests some interpretations not of itself, but of the set in which it finds its place. (1975: 70–1)

In analogous fashion, symbolic thinking is understood by Sperber as being concerned with the processing of odds and ends, with the treatment of mental 'waste' and with inventing a relevance and a place in the memory for 'defective conceptual representations'. To understand these latter points I now leave Sperber's criticism of the semiological view and examine the alternative theory of symbolism which he has put forward.

Already early on in his polemic against the semiologists Sperber signals the distinctive character of his own view in a splendidly constructed metaphor:

In contrast to what happens in a semiological decoding, it is not a question of interpreting symbolic phenomena by means of a context, but – quite the contrary – of interpreting the context by means of symbolic phenomena. Those who try to interpret symbols in and of themselves look at the light source and say, 'I don't see anything'. But the light source is there, not to be looked at, but so that one may look at what it illuminates. (1975: 70)

This metaphor of the symbol as a light source certainly sums up Sperber's distinct shift in perspective. 'Don't look at the symbol thinking it means anything,' he says, 'but look inside yourself and see what memories it activates and evokes.' The shift is from external meaning to internal evocation.

Keeping the central metaphor of the symbol as a light source in mind, let us assemble the elements of Sperber's theory. These elements consist of three related processes that define symbolism as a cognitive mechanism. Sperber calls them:

(1) putting in quotes a defective conceptual representation;
(2) focalizing on the condition responsible for the defectiveness of a conceptual representation;
(3) letting an evocation occur in a field delimited by the focalization.

At first sight this terminology, which is derived partly from linguistics and partly from logic, appears strange to the eyes of an anthropologist, but, as will soon become clear, the terminology does justice to the processes it tries to describe.

'Putting in quotes a defective conceptual representation' (1975: 141) describes what happens when we react mentally to statements which we commonly classify as symbolic. All symbolic statements (and acts, for that matter) share the property that they are figurative. Being figurative they violate the canonical forms of explicitness of information in communication and therefore are not acceptable. Not acceptable, that is, until they are put into quotes.

An analytical statement which is about the semantic relationship of categories is acceptable:

Example 1: The lion is an animal

A synthetic proposition which is about the speaker's encyclopaedic knowledge of the world is acceptable:

Example 2: The lion is a dangerous animal.

However, a statement which is neither about the semantic relationship of categories nor a synthetic proposition about the world that may be affirmed or falsified is not acceptable:

Example 3: The lion is king of the animals.

This figurative statement constitutes what Sperber calls a 'defective conceptual representation' and its apparent defect is overcome by putting it into quotes. By doing so it becomes 'logically possible to hold a synthetic statement to be true without comparing it with other synthetic statements which are susceptible of validating or invalidating it' (1975: 99). Thus example 3 becomes an acceptable statement as:

Example 4: 'The lion is king of the animals.'

Only when it is put in quotes does the statement in example 3 receive a place in the knowledge of an individual.

Here we have the first step of the symbolic mechanism. It aims at rescuing defective conceptual representations and does not let them go to waste. Like the Lévi-Straussian *bricoleur* it picks them up and by putting them into quotes makes them admissible, despite their apparent lack of truth value; and then it stores them in the memory, to use them whenever there arises the need to construe a set of symbolic statements in which it may play its part. Let me quote Sperber at length as he yet again utilizes Lévi-Strauss's metaphor of the *bricoleur* in order to demonstrate the mechanism of putting a defective conceptual representation in quotes, which he says lies at the root of symbolization:

> To return to Lévi-Strauss's image, the symbolic mechanism is the *bricoleur* of the mind. It starts from the principle that waste products of the conceptual industry deserve to be saved because something can always be made of them. But the symbolic mechanism does not try to decode the information it processes. It is precisely because this information has partly escaped the conceptual code, the most powerful of the codes available to humans, that it is, in the final analysis, submitted to it. It is therefore not a question of discovering the meaning of symbolic representations but, on the contrary, of inventing a relevance and a place in memory for them despite the failure in this respect of the conceptual categories of meaning. (1975: 113)

Here then lies the function of the process of putting a representation into quotes. With the help of 'putting into quotes' the mind enriches itself with entries that otherwise would be indigestible. The resulting knowledge is neither semantic, that is about the analytical relationships among categories, nor encyclopaedic in a strict sense, but rather it consists of the memory of words and things enshrined in the quotations.

The second process which defines the symbolic mechanism follows immediately upon the 'putting into quotes'. Sperber calls this second process 'focalization'. As soon as the conceptual attention focuses on some distinct piece of information it begins to calculate its validation. It describes it by entirely analyzed statements and then mobilizes all previous knowledge that this information may enrich or modify. Thus it compares the implications of the new statements with the statements previously validated. 'A conceptual representation therefore comprises,' as Sperber puts it, 'two sets of statements: focal statements, which describe the new information, and auxiliary statements, which link the new information to the encyclopaedic memory' (1975: 112).

Now, when we deal with symbolic statements the same process occurs. The only difference lies in the fact that the focal statement is defective in the way described above and that in order to overcome the defect the original focal statement is supplemented by a second representation which 'is not constructed by the conceptual mechanism which turned out to be powerless, but by the symbolic mechanism that then takes over' (1975: 113). Focalization as part of the symbolic mechanism, then, is the focusing of attention on an initially defective conceptual representation. Indeed, the very defectiveness mobilizes the attention and thus causes the focalization which in turn leads to the putting in quotes of the representation. The relationship between a defective conceptual representation and the active and passive memory which becomes activated by it is visualized by Sperber as conical:

> Firstly, the focus of attention moves from the statements at the 'top of the cone' to the unfulfilled conceptual conditions... Secondly, this unfulfilled condition itself becomes the top of a cone the base of which, this time, is the passive memory. This base is a field whose limits vary and which contains all the information by means of which the unfulfilled condition may be re-evaluated and possibly fulfilled. (1975: 121)

The re-evaluation of information in the passive memory Sperber calls evocation and it constitutes the third element in his theory of the symbolic mechanism. The opposite of evocation is invocation, a term which, if I understand rightly, Sperber uses to mean a deduction that follows a logical inference rule. Whereas invocation is an orderly process which allows intersubjectivity, evocation is, or so it seems to me, anarchic and radically subjective. A statement which is acceptable without having to be put into quotes allows that all the encyclopaedic entries which it subsumes may be directly invoked, but a statement which has been put into quotes, that has become symbolic, does not allow such direct invocation. Rather it necessitates the focalization described above and a resulting search in the memory of the field which is in turn delimited by the focalization. To illustrate the difference between invocation and evocation Sperber uses the example of a student in a library:

He has before him a certain number of books: the active memory.
The vast majority of books, which are still on the shelves, are the
passive memory. When, in the course of his work, he comes across
a reference which interests him, he may, by using the card
catalogue, immediately find the book he needs. But it may also
happen that he wants further information on a subject he has not
entirely defined, and does not know which volume to consult. The
only option is to search through the shelves on which the relevant
works might be found. Often, he stops to thumb through books
that at the outset he had no need of. And, just as any library user
acquires at length a dual knowledge of the stacks, on the one hand
by consulting the card catalogue, and on the other by scanning the
shelves in a more and more confident manner, so, aside from the
direct invocation of encyclopaedic knowledge which is the job of
the conceptual mechanism, the symbolic mechanism creates its
own pathways in the memory, these evocations which anything
may set in motion and nothing seems able to stop. (1975: 122–3)

Thus evocation is essentially idiosyncratic. It consists of a search
in the memory the depth and extent of which can never be predicted.
And yet it is compatible with a collective sharing of beliefs, rituals,
etc. The plural individual evocations that constantly occur in the
cultural symbolism of a society lead to what Sperber calls 'a
commonality of interest but not of opinions' (1975: 137). The more
symbolic representations there are, the more evocational fields will
determine each other and the more individuals will share similar
evocations.

The sharing is situational, it does not last. If people want to ensure
it they have to 'set the endless evocation in motion again' (1975:
145). Hence the repetitive side of cultural symbolism, which, once
enacted, forces the members of a society to actively remember the
background of all that is most important to them and dearest to their
hearts. This then, according to Sperber's theory, is the final *raison
d'être* of symbolism and this is what gives it its structure. Sperber's
view of the symbolic mechanism could be summed up as re-search in
opposition to the research done by the conceptual mechanism. A 're-
search' which sees the old representations each time in a different
light; a re-search that makes use of any new information that might
have materialized in daily life and a re-search that continues even as

one generation after the other passes through time: 'The same rituals are enacted, but with new actors; the same myths are told, but in a changing universe, and to individuals whose social position, whose relationships with others, and whose experience have changed' (1975: 145).

2.2 A closer look at focalization and displacement (Magritte)

Having outlined Sperber's theory, let me now proceed to examine his contribution critically. To start with, in my view Sperber's contribution is much more valuable than some rather rash reviewers of the book seem to suggest (see, for example, Bloch 1976). It is valuable already for the very reason that it has achieved a major shift in theoretical perspective. On the spiral of anthropological inquiry Sperber has arrived back at the cognitive pole. For the time being, he is not looking at what happens 'out there' in the cultural and social field, but at what happens inside the human mind as it copes with symbolic phenomena. He has turned his eyes away from the '*opus operatum*' (Bourdieu 1977: 36) and tries to understand the process rather than the product of symbolization. By doing so he has been able to make an important achievement: he has given the concept of evocation a new and clearly defined status as a tool in the study of symbolism. True, the term has been used before by almost everyone who has written in this field, but always the use has been intuitive. Now that Sperber has explicated the processes involved in evocation, we are able to use the concept more precisely and hence more fruitfully when we try to understand what happens when people perform rites together, tell each other myths and generally engage in cultural symbolism.

However, although Sperber is concerned with general symbolism, his contribution does not amount to a general theory of symbolism. This becomes evident when one looks more closely at the two processes which, according to Sperber's theory, complete the symbolic mechanism. He has not sufficiently analyzed either the 'putting into quotes of a defective conceptual representation' or 'focalization'. In fact, he has only used them as constructs for his central aim; that is, to formulate a theory of evocation. Had he looked more closely at these processes, which obviously play a central role in symbolization, he would have come nearer to his avowed aim of establishing a general theory of symbolism. But to accomplish this he would have had to come full circle and admit that symbols cannot, after all, be understood without reference to meaning. And he would have also come to realize that symbolism not only involves cognition but social practice as well.

Sperber has throughout looked at symbolism only from the receiving side of things. He has asked, 'What happens when I try to digest a symbolic statement?' Such a perspective corresponds to the existential situation of an ethnographer. He observes more than he acts. He listens more than he speaks. He does not influence people and tries to remain unobtrusive. In short, his concern is first and foremost one of deciphering messages and pondering what they might be about. But surely this is not all there is to symbolism and I wonder why Sperber never turned the question around and asked, 'What happens when someone cooks and dishes up a symbolic statement?' He never followed up the problem of what might be involved in the creation of symbolic statement. His cognitive theory does not relate to this aspect of symbolism at all.

Any 'defective representation' may be, but only a few in fact are, used symbolically within a specific cultural set-up. To return to Lévi-Strauss's image of the *bricoleur*. Many of the waste products of the conceptual industry, as Sperber calls them, are, after all, rubbish and no *bricoleur* worth his name would bother to keep them. What he keeps are conceptual representations which are only superficially defective and contain below their defective surface a well-designed structure.

Let me begin to explain this by examining Sperber's notion of focalizaton. He defines it as a 'displacement of attention' (1975: 119). By this he means the way in which the mind focuses its attention immediately on any seemingly displaced element in a statement or action rather than on its unproblematic parts. Thus the word 'king' is seemingly displaced in the statement:

The lion is king of the animals.

Our attention focuses on 'king' rather than 'lion' or 'animal'. Or, to give an example of symbolic action, butter is seemingly displaced when it is carried in large lumps on the heads of the Dorze as they enact a certain ritual (Sperber 1975: 37).

Now, it is crucial to realize that not all displacements cause the same intensity and persistence of focalization. One displacement will be quickly judged and dismissed as non-sense, error, etc., while another will be taken more seriously. It may worry or interest the mind, which therefore keeps focusing on it and begins the prolonged search in the active and passive memory which Sperber has described as evocation.

To test such differential effects of displacement one only has to conduct some simple experiments in substitution. Take, for example, the familiar statement:

(1) 'The lion is king of the animals.'

Substitute as follows:

(2) 'The lion is the Paul Brown of the animals.'
(3) 'The lion is the Muhammed Ali of the animals.'
(4) 'The lion is the Maggie Thatcher of the animals.'

Structurally the sentences are similar. They contain the same apparent semantic anomaly of a species being equated with an individual and in addition the comparisons are in some way or other far-fetched. It is hard to cope with them and only by an act of deliberate focusing and a continued process of unobstructed evocation can one establish a relevance for them. Thus Maggie Thatcher may perhaps evoke bossiness and Muhammed Ali a certain kind of physical power. But what about Paul Brown? Who is he? Who would take pains to focus on him for any length of time? There may well be a Paul Brown. He may even be the 'king of animals' for that matter, but here and now I don't know him and, therefore, I immediately dismiss that statement as irrelevant for myself. No 'putting into quotes' has turned the statement

'The lion is the Paul Brown of the animals.'

into something I am motivated to keep in my memory. We can see, therefore, that in order for focalization to be effective and able to trigger off evocation (or a set of evocations), the displacement that is the condition of focalization must not be arbitrary.

To understand this point more clearly let us at last turn away from the receiving end of things and join the camp of those who create symbolic statements rather than only interpret them. I already had this interest while I was doing fieldwork in Hamar. One day I jotted down the following remarks in my diary:

> Today I read *Ulysses*. Yet I don't enjoy it: Joyce's richness seems empty to me, at least from my Hamar perspective. I read with delight and surprise his discovery of the properties of water and then it lets me down because it is not a discovery with an internal structure but a gush of mixed and repeated associations. I wonder which authors I will like to read when we have returned to Europe. I dream of texts about general themes such as fire, water, wind, sky, earth, male, female. Texts that structure these generalities, bring to light their different possibilities and the conditions of these possibilities. I have a great appetite for good surrealism, surrealism that explores the qualities of symbols of rich and poor, hard and soft, hot and cold, continuous and discontinuous – surrealism that implicitly deals with all the symbols contained in our Hamar material. Surrealists explore symbols by counter-posing them. They find the forms in which symbols exist and then they try to invent them themselves, following the code of those symbols that already exist. Think of the contrasts between Hamar symbols of peace, richness, abundance, harmony, temperance, etc.: the heart-shaped green, soft, thick creepers like '*gali*' and '*kalle*'. Then think of the symbols of aggression: the bright, hard and pointed spikes of such trees as '*zaut*' and '*sobala*'. Or the simple ritual action of rubbing the white and soft fat of a sheep on to someone's heart by means of a black and hard stone. (Lydall and Strecker 1979a: 66–7)

Anthropologists can indeed learn a lot from the surrealists. Generally speaking they both try to reach the same goal. They both ask the question, 'Who are we?' and embark on a journey to find the answer in terms of 'who we are not'. They differ in that the anthropologist (as ethnographer) journeys in space and his procedure is empirical, while the surrealist travels in the mind and proceeds by ways of the imagination. But both are similarly concerned with overcoming their immediate cultural and social conditions, to see them for what they ultimately are, 'arbitrary systems of control', as the anthropologists might say, or, in the more polemical voice of a surrealist, a 'second-rate reality that has been fashioned by centuries of worshipping money, races, fatherlands, gods, and, I might add, art' (Magritte in Torczyner 1979: 118). In their quest for otherness, the surrealists have systematically explored the hidden background of the superficial world in which we find ourselves and by doing so they have provided us with an insight into the elementary processes involved in the creation of symbolic statements. In fact, they make transparent the input of that which anthropologists in the field are usually condemned to encounter as output only. To prove this point let me concentrate for the moment on one of the surrealists who, in my view, has carried the insights of the surrealist school to the most convincing conclusion: the Belgian, René Magritte.

I visualize at the moment a painting by Magritte which he has called *The Castle of the Pyrenees*. On it I see a massive rock with a castle on top hovering in mid air above the ea. There has certainly been a displacement here, but I am not inclined to dismiss it as nonsense. Rather, the focalization intended by Magritte works and I share the evocations of the physicist Albert Baez, who commented on the picture as follows:

> By confronting us with a massive rock in mid air – something we know cannot happen – we are somehow forced to wonder *why* doesn't the rock come plunging down into the sea? We know, of course, that it should. But why should it? ... What fails to happen in the painting reminds me of the mystery of what actually does happen in the real world. (Torczyner 1979: 99)

Now, the interesting thing is that Magritte himself does not think in terms of meaning, just as Sperber's theory would have predicted. Magritte asserts emphatically that his pictures do not have any meaning, and in a letter to Pierre Demarne he writes:

> I particularly like this idea that my paintings *say nothing*. ... It is possible that one may be moved while looking at a painting, but to deduce by this that the picture 'expresses' that emotion is like saying that, for example, a cake 'expresses' the ideas and emotions of those of us who see it or eat it, or again, that the cake 'expresses' the thoughts of the chef while baking a good cake. ... To try to interpret ... is to misunderstand an inspired image and to

substitute for it a gratuitous interpretation, which, in turn, can become the subject of an endless series of superfluous interpretations. (Torczyner 1979: 132)

A logical consequence of this view is Magritte's practice of giving his pictures names that are as symbolic as the images themselves. Thus Magritte clearly recognized what Sperber was later to show, that is to say, any interpretation or exegesis of a symbol is itself symbolic and requires or implies further interpretation or exegesis (see Sperber 1975: 23). Shortly before his death Magritte found the formulation with which he summed up the matter most precisely: 'The titles go with my painting as well as they can,' he said in 1966 in an interview with Guy Mertens. 'They are not keys. They are only false keys.'

Magritte has written that ultimately he cannot explain how the right displacement which causes focalization and the resulting evocation comes about. He achieves it in moments of extreme lucidity which he calls 'presence of mind'.

As I consider Magritte's texts to be of the greatest interest to the student of symbolism let me cite him here at length as he explains how he painted the picture *Time Transfixed* in which a locomotive comes steaming out of a dining-room fireplace:

> I decided to paint the image of a locomotive. Starting from that possibility, the problem presented itself as follows: how to paint this image so that it would evoke mystery – that is, the mystery to which we are forbidden to give a meaning, lest we utter naive or scientific absurdities; mystery *that has no meaning* but that must not be confused with the non-sense that madmen who are trying hard to be funny find so gratifying. The image of a locomotive is *immediately* familiar; its mystery is not perceived. In order for its mystery to be evoked, another *immediately* familiar image without mystery – the image of a dining-room fireplace – was joined with the image of the locomotive. … There are neither *mysterious* nor unmysterious creatures. The power of thought is demonstrated by unveiling or evoking the mystery in creatures that seem familiar to us [out of error or habit].
>
> I thought of joining the locomotive image with the image of a dining-room fireplace in a moment of 'presence of mind'. By that I mean the moment of lucidity that no method can bring forth.

Only the power of thought manifests itself at this time. We can be proud of this power, feel proud or excited that it exists. Nonetheless, we do not count for anything, but are limited to witnessing the manifestation of thought. When I say 'I thought of joining etc. ...' exactitude demands that I say 'presence of mind exerted itself and showed me how the image of a locomotive should be shown so that this presence of mind would be apparent'. Archimedes' 'Eureka!' is an example of the mind's unpredictable presence. (Torczyner 1979: 60)

In a lecture delivered at the London Gallery in 1937 Magritte let us have a glimpse of the more mechanical side of this 'presence of mind' when he said:

> Certain images have a secret affinity. This also holds true for the objects these images represent. Let us search for what should be said. We know the bird in a cage. Our interest is increased if we replace the bird with a fish, or with a slipper. These images are strange. Unfortunately, they are arbitrary and fortuitous. However, it is possible to arrive at a new image that will stand up better beneath the spectator's gaze. A large egg in the cage seems to offer the required solution. (Torczyner 1979: 138)

This solution impressed itself on him as follows:

> One night in 1936 I awoke in a room in which someone had put a cage with a sleeping bird. A wonderful aberration made me see the cage with the bird gone and replaced by an egg. There and then, I grasped a new and astonishing poetic secret, for the shock I felt had been caused precisely by the affinity of the two objects, the cage and the egg. (Torczyner 1979: 121)

This is how the 'presence of mind' finds the displacement which is capable of achieving strong focalization.

The displacement may be of different kinds (which have, incidentally, all been found empirically by anthropologists who have studied ritual and symbolism). It may be a displacement consisting of an object or objects transferred into unfamiliar environments (a Louis-Philippe table on an ice-floe, a piano in the desert); it may be a displacement that involves the 'encounter between two completely unrelated objects' (the locomotive and the dining-room fireplace); it may be a displacement that involves a secret affinity between the objects (the cage and the egg); and the element of displacement may be contained in the creation of new objects, in the transformation of known objects, in the alteration of the substance of familiar objects, in the use of false labelling of an image and its objects, etc. All these modes of displacement have one crucial element in common. The choice of things displaced is made from among objects that are close to the members of the cultural and social formation of which Magritte himself is a part. Only this gives the displacements their great effectiveness. In truly surrealist fashion Magritte has summed up this truth by saying: 'A burning child affects us much more than the self-destruction of a distant planet' (Torczyner 1979: 121).

There is thus more to the process of focalization than Sperber has brought to light. At the basis of it lies a complex process of creative thought which constructs statements in such a way that lasting focalization can come about. These statements can neither be accepted as meaning something in the strict sense nor can they be dismissed as nonsense. The reaction oscillates between acceptance and rejection and in that very process they affect us strongly. Deep layers of experience are exploited when statements are constructed that are meant to cause focalization and evocation. At the same time, universal physiological and psychological factors play a role as well as specific cultural and historical factors. Furthermore, the construction of these seemingly meaningless and yet so compelling statements is intentional. It is motivated and, in Magritte's case, its most general aim was, as he himself said, to create mystery. In a text which I have already cited above, he said that the central problem of his art was to paint a familiar object in such a way that it evoked mystery. In a more general statement about art and psychology he formulated the view again: 'Art, as I conceive it, is resistant to psychoanalysis. It evokes the mystery one should not mistake for some sort of a problem, however difficult' (Torczyner 1979: 62).

Where does this creation of mystery fit into Sperber's theory of symbolism as a cognitive mechanism? As I see it, it does not and cannot have a place in it, because the intention and the motivation which create the structure of symbolic statements are ultimately social. Symbolic construction is an art, not an art in itself and for itself, but an art to affect others, an art with an aim and a goal, and it is as such that it has to be explained.

2.3 From evocation to implicature (Grice)

In the preceding subsection I have examined focalization and displacement. By doing so, I have found that symbolic statements, even though they may seem meaningless, are none the less aimed at focusing the attention towards an intended goal. I also found that it is this goal and the motivation behind it which give symbolic statements their specific structure.

Sperber's theory cannot explain the specific directedness of symbolism, which is caused by the motivation underlying symbolic creativity. It is simply not enough to look at symbols in terms of what they may evoke. Something has already happened before there can be any evocation. That is, even though I may express myself so badly that nothing in particular is evoked in the memory of my interlocutor, I still may mean to say something. In order to include this vital point in our analysis we must widen our view and include not only evocation, but also motivation and purpose. In short, we must take into account the full communication triad of sender, transmitter and receiver. This immediately puts the problem of meaning into a new light. Now we can suddenly have both the presence of meaning and the apparent absence of it, for what the sender means when articulating a message does not necessarily have to be what the receiver understands when he deciphers it. In fact, the sender may deliberately construct a message in such a way that it is ambiguous and may be both understood and misunderstood, each, of course, in its own time.

It is here that motivation takes on its full force and symbolism shows itself to be not a matter of absent meaning, but rather a matter of indirect and multivocal meaning. Without the possibility of creating indirect and multivocal meaning, symbolic production would cease immediately. The possibility of saying something indirectly and multivocally animates the sender to engage in that type of creative thought which we call symbolic and which generates an infinite variety of symbolic statements which pervade everyday life in the form of politeness, flattery, irony, jokes, slogans, puns, etc. All the messages that pass to and fro in these delicate fields have in common that they say something and say it not, that they reveal and also hide. They can only have this dynamic character because their meaning is not absolute but situational and is defined in terms of time. The time involved may be no more than a fraction of a second (as in an easy pun); it may involve hours, even weeks (as when someone suddenly understands a joke which was told to him some time ago); or it may be that a latent meaning never gets detected (as in some forms of gentle irony). When the mind constructs a statement with multiple meanings or when it is confronted with such, it moves from one meaning to the other. This leads it from the unfulfilled conditions for the truth or acceptability of the statement to the conditions that would fulfill that truth. And then again, it may continue and realize that the conditions for the truth of the statement have been multiply fulfilled. Or, to put it more simple, the mind may realize that the statement 'says' several different things at once. This movement of thought is what we experience as so exciting and gratifying in symbolism. Therefore, if we want to advance our understanding of symbolism, we must advance our understanding of the logic by which statements with indirect and multivocal meanings are constructed. This task leads us immediately into linguistics.

On a very basic level, general linguistic theory is interested in the problem of meanings in that it tries to eliminate the misunderstanding of semantic ambiguity (Bechert *et al.* (eds) 1970). Thus it distinguishes between lexical ambiguity as it occurs in 'pound', 'lock' and 'down', for example, and structural ambiguity as it occurs, for example, in the sentence 'All the men won't go to war' (adapted from Smith and Wilson 1979: 63). But to learn more about the creation of indirect and multivocal meanings with which we are concerned here, we have to turn to pragmatic linguistics which studies 'the purposes, effects, and implications of the actual use by a speaker of a meaningful piece of language' (Flew 1979: 265).

Since Austin's *How to Do Things with Words* (Austin 1962) and Searle's *Speech Acts* (Searle 1969), Paul Grice has been one of the most influential thinkers in pragmatics (Grice 1971; 1975). As his contributions and especially his notion of the 'conversational implicature' are of great importance for the anthropologist's study of culture, I present them here in detail.

If one inquires 'into the general conditions that, in one way or other, apply to conversation as such, irrespective of its subject matter' (Grice 1975: 43), one often finds that a speaker deliberately says something which is not, in fact, what he means. To describe what happens in such cases, Grice has introduced, 'as terms of art, the verb *implicate* and the related nouns *implicature* (cf. implying) and *implicatum* (cf. what is implied)' (1975: 43–4). He gives a rather wayward example to illustrate what he means by these terms. I, therefore, cite instead a slightly adapted version of Cole's 'clear case of conversational implicature'.

A duke addresses his butler:
(1) Duke: It's cold in here.
(2) Butler: I'll close the window, sir.
It is clear that the butler has understood the duke's meanderings on meteorology as an imposive. Hence his reply in (2). It would be counter-intuitive, however, to claim that the logical structure of (1) is that underlying (3):
(3) Close the window.
(3) is the result of a deduction, or inference from (1) (Cole 1975: 260)

Cole then goes on and reconstructs what may have taken place in the butler's mind on hearing (1):

The butler realizes that his occupational goal is to cater to his master's wants. Upon hearing and understanding the literal sense of (1), the butler asks himself why the duke is telling him about the temperature. Dismissing as improbable that the duke is merely commenting on the end of the summer, the butler concludes that the duke is uncomfortable and that he, the butler, had better correct this state of affairs. Thus, he replies as in (2). (1975: 260)

These kinds of conversational implicatures are only possible because conversations are governed by what Grice has called the co-operative principle. When they converse with one another, people do not randomly utter disconnected remarks. Rather, their utterances follow, as Grice says, 'a common purpose or set of purposes, or at least a mutually accepted direction' (1975: 45). This directedness necessitates that at each stage in a conversation 'SOME possible conversational moves would be excluded as conversationally unsuitable' (1975: 45). Thus, the participants are expected to follow some kind of general principle of co-operation. Grice defines it as: 'Make your conversational contribution such as is required, at the stage at which it occurs, by the accepted purpose or direction of the talk exchange in which you are engaged' (1975: 45). Now, to adhere to the principle of co-operation, participants in conversations must follow certain maxims. Grice leaves it open as to how many these might be and how each maxim should be defined, but distinguishes tentatively the following maxims, which he groups under four major categories of quantity, quality, relation and manner.

Interestingly, he shows that these maxims are found not only in conversation but have their analogue in all varieties of purposive behaviour and transactions. Grice suggests the following analogues for the conversational maxims which he has distinguished:

1. *Quantity*. If you are assisting me to mend a car, I expect your contribution to be neither more nor less than is required; if, for example, at a particular stage I need four screws, I expect you to hand me four, rather than two or six.

2. *Quality*. I expect your contributions to be genuine and not spurious. If I need sugar as an ingredient in the cake you are assisting me to make, I do not expect you to hand me salt; if I need a spoon, I do not expect a trick spoon made of rubber.

3. *Relation*. I expect a partner's contribution to be appropriate to immediate needs at each stage of the transaction; if I am mixing ingredients for a cake, I do not expect to be handed a good book, or even an oven cloth (though this might be an appropriate contribution at a later stage).

4. *Manner*. I expect a partner to make it clear what contribution he is making, and to execute his performance with reasonable dispatch. (1975: 47)

Applied to conversations, Grice defines these maxims as follows:
1. *Quantity*.

1. Make your contribution as informative as is required (for the current purpose of the exchange).

   2. Do not make your contribution more informative than is
     required. (1975: 45)

2. *Quality*.

   Under the category of QUALITY falls a supermaxim – 'Try to make
   your contribution one that is true' – and two more specific
   maxims:
   1. Do not say what you believe to be false.
   2. Do not say that for which you lack adequate evidence. (1975:
     46)

3. *Relation*.

   Be relevant! (1975: 46)

4. *Manner*. This category relates 'not to what is said but, rather, to
HOW what is said is to be said'. The supermaxim is 'Be perspicuous'
and it divides into various maxims, as:

   1. Avoid obscurity of expression.
   2. Avoid ambiguity.
   3. Be brief (avoid unnecessary prolixity).
   4. Be orderly. (1975: 46)

Now, the point of enumerating all these maxims is not to show
what happens when they are obeyed, but, rather, to see what happens
when they are violated. They may be violated simply to mislead a
participant in a conversational exchange, but often the matter is
more complicated. Someone may deliberately and blatantly violate a
maxim, not to mislead, but to get some other message through. This
is the point where Grice's theory of the implicature becomes
extremely interesting for the study of indirectness and multivocality,
and for symbolization in general. An implicature is generated by
'flouting' or 'exploiting' a maxim. Grice describes the process as
follows:

   On the assumption that the speaker is able to fulfil the maxim and
   to do so without violating another maxim . . . is not opting out, and

is not, in view of the blatancy of his performance, trying to mislead, the hearer is faced with a minor problem: How can his saying what he did say be reconciled with the supposition that he is observing the overall COOPERATIVE PRINCIPLE? This situation is one that characteristically gives rise to a conversational implicature; and when a conversational implicature is generated in this way, I shall say that a maxim is being EXPLOITED. (Grice's emphasis, 1975: 49)

Grice goes on then to define the logical pattern of an implicature:

A man who, by (in, when) saying (or making as if to say) that p has implicated that *q*, may be said to have conversationally implicated that *q* PROVIDED that (1) he is to be presumed to be observing the conversational maxims, or at least the cooperative principle; (2) the supposition that he is aware that, or thinks that, *q* is required in order to make his saying or making as if to say p (or doing so in those terms) is consistent with this presumption; and (3) the speaker thinks (and would expect the hearer to think that the speaker thinks) that it is within the competence of the hearer to work out, or grasp intuitively, that the supposition mentioned in (2) is required. (1975: 49–50)

This then is the logic of implicature. The same logic must, as I see it, lie behind the generation of symbolic statements, Metaphors, metonymies, euphemisms, meioses, hyperboles and all the other forms involving indirectness and multivocality may be explained as implicatures. They all share the same complicated nature brought about by a process – to use the terminology of communication theory which I have suggested above – in which the sender deliberately flouts certain maxims of communication in order to create an implicature and tries to exploit some deep-seated social principle of co-operation with the aim of producing a figure of speech.

I will go into this important point later in detail and make intensive use of it, but for the moment, let us return to Sperber. He views figures of speech (e.g. 'The lion is king of the animals') as 'defective conceptual representations' which the symbolic mechanism puts into quotes in order to cope with them. This exemplifies, as I have said above, the perspective of the receiver, and it is from this perspective alone that symbolism appears to be solely a cognitive mechanism, that is, a mechanism that leads to evocation and a certain activation of the memory and a concomitant acquisition of a particular kind of knowledge. However, as soon as one widens one's perspective and also includes the sender, the picture changes: one now has both 'implication' and 'evocation'. 'Evocation' marks the perspective of the receiver, who, as Sperber has shown, focalizes his attention on the defectiveness of a statement and on the conditions which may account for this defectiveness. Obviously, one cannot generalize from the perspective of either sender or receiver alone. But this is what Sperber has done and what has led him to the hypothesis that symbolism is simply a cognitive mechanism. There is certainly a cognitive element in symbolism, yet this does not exhaust the phenomenon.

As Grice's theory of the implicature shows, symbolization has a social basis. Only when both the sender and the receiver are taken into account does this important fact become visible. It may be that as an ethnographer one is often confronted with a whole lot of statements which are said to be custom and seem to have no author. But does this justify our remaining for ever on the receiving side of things, for ever with the spectators, never with the creators? I think not. If we want to understand cultural forms we must know how they are brought about. This is why Grice's account of the generation of a conversational implicature is so useful. We can apply his findings and use them to analyze symbolism wherever we find it.

To take Sperber's example:

The lion is king of the animals.

According to Sperber this statement is defective. The cognitive answer to this defectiveness consists of putting the statement into quotes. Upon this, the mind focuses on the displacement contained in the statement (i.e. on 'king') and this in turn triggers off a series of evocations which vary according to whoever is confronted with the statement and in what context. According to Grice, the statement carries a nicely constructed implicature. It involves a detailed anticipation by the speaker of the reflective competence of his interlocutor on the basis of a common social and cultural ground shared by both. Over time, figures of speech may become conventionalized, but even that does not stop the speaker from having some quite definite meanings in mind when he utters a statement such as this and a concomitant conviction that his interlocutor is able to grasp the meanings he has implicated. There thus exists a crucial difference between the Sperberian and the Gricean approaches: while the first abandons meaning as a useful concept and confines itself to an understanding of symbolism as a cognitive mechanism, the latter shows how multiple meaning is generated and opens the way to an understanding of the logic of indirect communication. Sperber's category of evocation is an introspective and self-centred notion in which the external world and one's fellow human beings figure only as some intangible traces in the memory. Grice's category of implicature, on the other hand, is an anticipatory notion that includes alter as well as ego and mobilizes a jointly shared knowledge about the world in motivated and practical speech acts. Thus, to think about implicature is to think about social processes, because the notion of implicature presupposes, as we have seen, the existence of social norms such as those contained in the co-operative principle and the conversational maxims.

2.4 Irony as a test case of symbolization (Sperber)

At one point in the outline of his theory, Sperber comes very close to the Gricean notion of implicature and the interactionist view of symbolism which this entails. In order once again to show Sperber's train of thought and to be able to point out exactly where he goes wrong, let me recall his argument in detail. The point in question is a paragraph where he examines irony as a test case of his theory. He asks us to compare the following four sentences:

(1) Jerome buys *The Parisian* even though he is not interested in sensationalism!
(2) Arthur buys *The Parisian* even though he doesn't need lavatory paper! ...
(3) *The Parisian* isn't worth buying except for reading sensationalism.
(4) *The Parisian* isn't worth buying except to use as lavatory paper.
(1975: 123–4)

The crucial sentence is (2) which carries a *sous-entendu* that is ironic. Statement (3) which is the *sous-entendu* of (1) does not attract attention and evokes 'nothing beyond what it states' (1975: 124). Statement (2), however, feigns a surprise and is 'suggestive and evokes imaginary conditions in which the surprise would be real' (1975: 124). It is constructed in such a way that the speaker 'provokes in the listener the construction of a particular conceptual representation' (1975: 124) that is not 'close at hand', as it were, but rather 'far out'. In statements (1) and (3), there is an immediate and obvious link between the utterance itself and the knowledge that is shared between the interlocutors and can be mobilized to make sense of the statement without much effort. However, at the moment when this link is not obvious any more we enter the realm of symbolism. Sperber describes this shift from the plain to the symbolic statement as follows (note how close he is at this point to Grice's theory of the implicature and the violation of conversational maxims by which an implicature is brought about):

> One never makes explicit all that one wishes to convey, not because one wants to hide something, but on the contrary because on the basis of a partially explicit statement the remainder may be automatically reconstructed. Yet, precisely for that reconstruction to occur without problems, everything which is new and not self-evident must be stated, and the hearer should not be left with the effort of discovering it. The conceptual representation of an utterance thus has a canonical form: the most immediate implications of the statement uttered contain the new information with respect to the shared knowledge of the interlocutors; the more distant implications ... and the *sous-entendu* correspond to already-shared information. When this correspondence between the degree of explicitness and the degree of novelty of the information is not respected, one of the conditions on conceptual representation of utterances is itself violated and the representation is put in quotes. (1975: 125)

Statement (2) is put in quotes and is interpreted as (4), but statement (4) still remains paradoxical (one does not buy an expensive paper to use it in the lavatory) and in turn has to be put into quotes. Only when the original ironic statement has thus been doubly put into quotes can it be read as

(5) '*The Parisian* isn't worth reading.' (1975: 126)

Sperber's final analysis runs as follows:

> Utterance (2) doubly violates the rules of conceptual interpretation of utterances, which establishes a direct correspondence between the degree of explicitness and the degree of informativeness (and in particular, of controversiality) of statements. The fact that *sous-entendu* (4) is more informative than utterance (2) blocks the interpretation of (2). One certainly understands the meaning of (2); one understands that (2) implies (4), but one has no way of immediately interpreting the fact that the more informative statement has only been implied. Whence we get a putting in quotes of (2) with a commentary such as that in (6):
>
> (6) '(2)' is there to suggest (4).
>
> But *sous-entendu* (4) cannot be linked to encyclopaedic knowledge without its own *sous-entendu* (5), and this *sous-entendu* is itself more informative than the statement that implied it. Whence we get a second putting into quotes as in (7):
>
> (7) '"(2)" is there to suggest (4)' is there to suggest (5).
>
> Corresponding to this dual putting in quotes is a dual focalization, firstly on (4), then on (5) or, more exactly, on the fact that these statements – even though implied – are more informative than the explicit utterance that implied them, directly or indirectly. In other words, the focalisation is on the two occurrences in which the canonical condition of conceptual representation of utterances has been violated. This dual focalization sets up two interconnected evocational fields. (1975: 126–7)

Now, the interesting point in this analysis is the fact that it is so detailed that we can detect exactly the limits of the theory of evocation and the point where it is bound to go wrong. Let us look at the ironical statement again:

(2) Arthur buys *The Parisian* even though he doesn't need lavatory paper

Sperber analyses it as

> (7) '"(2)" is there to suggest (4)' is there to suggest (5). (1975: 126–7)

That is: (5) *The Parisian* isn't worth reading.

How was this delicate ironic sentence constructed? Obviously the speaker was motivated, otherwise he would not have uttered such a complex statement. His motive seems to be hostile: he is attacking something or someone. According to Sperber's evocation theory the first thing that comes to mind is the possibility that he is attacking *The Parisian*. But has he really uttered (2) in order to offend *The Parisian*? A closer look at the statement shows us that this is not so. If he had intended to slander the newspaper he would have phrased the ironic statement differently. He would have said, for example:

> (8) Arthur says he finds nothing wrong with *The Parisian*. There is always one good use one can make of it!

Which use Arthur meant would have to be reconstructed by the interlocutor (i.e. the use of *The Parisian* as lavatory paper). As long as he shares the same background knowledge as the speaker and has similar sentiments, the listener understands what has been implied. Indeed, this understanding has been anticipated by the speaker and is part of a conspiracy by the speaker, the listener and Arthur against *The Parisian*. Thus the quality of *The Parisian* is not really at issue in statement (2) and if the hostility is not primarily directed towards the newspaper then it must be aimed at Arthur himself. Seen in this light it appears that (2) does not mean (5), although it makes use of that evocation, but rather implies

> (9) Arthur is stupid!

Or, even worse and by a kind of metonymic reasoning,

> (10) Arthur is 'shitty'!

The speaker seemingly attacks the newspaper but his utterance is really aimed at Arthur. The speaker may not pronounce (9) or (10) directly if he wants to avoid a breach of norms or even an open conflict. Therefore he must hide them behind the protective armour of statements that both say something and say it not. Such is the motive that must have generated the ironic figure: that is, the speaker is hostile to Arthur. However, because he does not want to attack him bluntly he discredits Arthur indirectly by discrediting *The Parisian*.

Sperber completely overlooks this 'hierarchy of hostilities', as one might call it, which characterizes statement (2). According to his theory the hearer focuses on the defectiveness of (2) and puts it in quotes. This evokes statement (4) and by way of further focalization and a further putting in quotes he arrives at statement (5). Here his interpretation ends, and indeed nothing forces him to push on, to forget about the hearer's preoccupations and find out what the speaker must have meant. Evocation is by its very nature such a diffuse and meandering process that it is easily content with whatever apparent solution it may find, even if that solution stops half-way and does not answer the problem completely. Thus it is ill-suited as a tool to cope with the multiple meanings which are involved in symbolic statements. An interpretation of (2) which is based on the notion that the speaker was motivated and meant something very specific does not, however, end with (5). It ends, as we have seen, with statements (9) or (10), which spell out what the speaker must have implied when he initially uttered (2). To understand what is meant by (2) – so as to react appropriately to (2) – one has to work out what one's interlocutor implies when saying (2). This necessitates that one puts oneself in the position of the speaker and grasps the purpose for which he uttered (2). The process is much more one of empathy than of evocation and an unchecked evocation (which would be nothing but an extreme preoccupation) may in fact become a major obstacle to the proper understanding of an implicature.

I have already pointed out repeatedly that according to the structure of the sentence the main motivation underlying (2) must be the speaker's hostility towards Arthur. How deep or how superficial this hostility is we cannot know, nor have we any idea whether the uttering of (2) was simply occasioned by an insignificant coincidence or whether it is in fact just one step in an ongoing and systematic attempt by the speaker to harm Arthur. But we know that there is some hostility because, as we have seen above, if the speaker had wanted to aim his hostility at *The Parisian* rather than at Arthur he would have formulated (2) differently; for example, as in (8).

Besides the motivation of hostility there exists, furthermore, a second motivation which is closely bound up with the first and yet has an opposite quality: by uttering (2) the speaker expresses hostility to Arthur while at the same time he tries to ingratiate himself with his interlocutor. He slanders Arthur by slandering *The Parisian*, and he does this not directly but by way of a figure of speech. If his interlocutor does not accept the remark he may answer with a similarly ironic statement, pretend not to have understood or in some other way opt out. On the other hand, if he accepts the remark, then immediately something happens which goes beyond the simple exchange of information or opinion. Now the interlocutors not only understand each other, but also enter a kind of complicity that excludes all outsiders who do not share the knowledge which would allow them to understand the figure of speech and who do not share the values which would allow them to agree with what has been said.

It is interesting to note that Sperber is keenly aware of this complicity motive as it is involved in irony. However, instead of following the direction in which the facts are pointing, that is instead of including social and motivational factors in the explanation of symbolism, he sticks to an exclusively cognitive view and uses the notion of evocation *ad absurdum*. To substantiate this point let me quote a decisive passage where he looks, as it were, at the right things the wrong way round:

> We suggested that the initial aim of symbolic evocation was always to reconstruct by recollection or by imagination the background of information which, if it had been available in the active memory, would have allowed the analysis to be completed and the relevance of the defective conceptual representation to be established. Considering the example – (2) – in the light of this hypothesis, we may delimit a dual evocational field. The field corresponding to the focalization of (5) comprises not only everything that the hearer knows to the discredit of *The Parisian* but also, and above all, everything that would permit consideration of this knowledge as knowledge shared with the speaker. It is not sufficient to imagine the conditions in which (5) would be true; it is crucial to imagine the conditions in which this truth would be so evident and so evidently shared by the interlocutors that it would have been legitimate to imply it. Whence an evocation not only of all the contempt felt by some people for *The Parisian*, but also, crucially, a complicity of the interlocutors in this contempt. ... What is

precisely evoked by (2) in the final analysis is a tacit agreement between the speaker and hearer alone, in which others such as Arthur do not share; a complicity from which those who buy *The Parisian* either to read or to put in the lavatory are excluded. The two evocational fields linked to (4) and to (5) combine, then, to evoke the distance and the superiority of the interlocutors *vis-à-vis* both *The Parisian* and its unsophisticated public. (1975: 127–8).

As I have said above, by developing the complicity motive underlying irony Sperber is certainly pointing to the heart of the matter. But he looks at the facts the wrong way round and his argument needs to be put back on its feet. The crucial aspect of an ironical statement simply does not lie in what it evokes but in what the speaker implies. It is the speaker who structures the statement and gives it its specific directedness (or 'point' or 'edge', etc.). This is his risk and if the utterance meets with success it also becomes his gain. To look at irony only in terms of evocation is to miss this point! When the speaker uttered (2) he quite definitely meant what has been spelt out as statements (9) and (10). But he did not utter either (9) or (10). He constructed (2) in the very way he did because he did not want to say (9) or (10) directly. He wanted the attack to be light and not heavy; he wanted to express hostility and yet retain some benevolence; he wanted to involve himself and yet retain full command of the situation; he wanted to hide and yet reveal what he meant, etc. These are the contrarities that furnish the dialectic which underlies the creation and the finesse of (2) and which give the statement its particular effectiveness.

One can generalize, I think, and say that far from being 'waste products of the conceptual industry' (1975: 113), ironic statements are extremely precise, though complex, tools of communication and social interaction. They do not lead to the existence of remote symbols which seem to have no author and the meaning of which can only be dealt with in terms of evocation. On the contrary, ironic statements are situational. They are uttered in contexts that vanish as soon as they appear and they are inextricably bound up with the speech acts themselves. They quite specifically mean something and to view them only in terms of evocation is to forfeit an explanation of their genesis and of their very structure. What is most important for an understanding of irony (and similar structures of multiple meaning) is not the symbolic mechanism which, according to Sperber, allows one to process it, but rather the social and cognitive factors that generated the ironic statement in the first place.

To put this in the terminology of communication theory, only if one focuses on the sender first can one grasp the particular character of an ironic statement. It is he who, to use Grice's terminology, 'exploits the cooperative principle' and 'forces the implicature' which may lead to the complicity between the interlocutors that Sperber has observed. I say 'may', because an ironic statement need not necessarily lead to complicity. The relationship between the interlocutors (the sender and the receiver) is asymmetric. The speaker who utters statement (2) is on the offensive and runs the risk of exposure. In fact, it is the very risk which leads him not to use a direct and open form of attack which might make it difficult to withdraw should this be necessary. Thus he chooses irony as a hidden form of attack and takes only a limited risk. On the other hand, the interlocutor who receives the ironic statement (2) runs hardly any risk at all (at least under normal circumstances). Either he rejects the implications of (2) by what I have called opting out, or he accepts them and thereby enters the complicity instigated by the speaker. There exists, thus, a hiatus between the sender and the receiver which entails both the risk of a loss and the promise of a gain for the sender. This hiatus and the asymmetry which it creates constitute the necessary condition and, in turn, the cogent motive for symbolization.

3 Symbolization as a social practice

Having investigated the cognitive basis of symbolization, my aim is now to discover how in everyday life people make use of symbolization, motivated use, that is. I want to see why and how they switch from straightforward, univocal communication to an indirect, multivocal and roundabout way of saying things. My interest is thus, at first sight, close to linguistics, especially to speech-act theory and rhetoric, but in fact my orientation is quite different. Ultimately I want to understand symbolism in ritual, and only because I think that an explanation must eventually go back to the grass roots, to the practice of symbolization in everyday life, do I go into the details of language usage and its relation to social interaction.

In a study entitled 'Universals of language usage: politeness phenomena' (1978) Penelope Brown and Stephen Levinson have provided us with detailed empirical material and with a theoretical framework which directly help our attempt to understand the social basis of symbolization. The authors do not make such a claim and the notion of the symbolic does itself not enter their analysis, but this makes their contribution only the more interesting because it acts as an independent yardstick by which we can assess the factors which cause symbolic phenomena. Brown and Levinson are both linguists as well as anthropologists. Penelope Brown has done fieldwork in the community of Tenejapa in Chiapas, Mexico while Stephen Levinson has worked in a village in Tamilnadu, South India. This double orientation has provided their approach with a fortunate blend of a sense for cultural detail (their linguistic heritage) and an awareness of the general social relationships that lie at the basis of culture (the heritage of social anthropology). As the title of the study says, Brown and Levinson are dealing with politeness phenomena, which, they claim, can be universally detected in language usage. More precisely: Brown and Levinson explore how specific social situations put specific constraints on the choices between different alternatives of language construction. They are concerned with 'social pressures on grammar', and this is why I can make such good use of their findings: they have in fact shown how social pressures generate symbolism. Or, as they do not themselves discuss symbolism, I should say that with the help of their theory I will be able to demonstrate how social pressures generate symbolization.

I will work through Brown and Levinson's text in three successive stages. Firstly, in section 3.1 I will give a description of Brown and Levinson's general approach and provide an outline of their theory. In 3.2 I show how this theory may be used to explain in detail why and how everyday life is pervaded by the social practice of symbolization. The empirical material I use from this point onwards is taken from the observations which I have made in Hamar communities in southern Ethiopia. Brown and Levinson make use of comparative data from English, Indian and Mexican cultures. I here add examples from an Ethiopian culture, and this will not only serve to substantiate my argument but also will add to our general stock of comparative data in this field, a stock which is, by the way, rather small when it comes to non-literate societies. Furthermore, Brown and Levinson's theory will, as I have said already, be submitted to an independent test by using my empirical findings (and, of course, vice versa) which were all made prior to their study. In order to emphasize this independence and the surprising fit between my observations and Brown and Levinson's theory, I will wherever possible quote my already published material, and also Jean Lydall's material, on Hamar (Lydall and Strecker 1979a, 1979b; Strecker 1979a). Finally, the examples serve to build up an empirical basis for further steps in my argument.

In section 3.3 I extend and modify Brown and Levinson's model of strategy selection, and later I apply the new version of the model to a study of social domination. I show that the strategies of politeness, which Brown and Levinson have analyzed so well, may in fact also be used as strategies of social domination. For quotation I use the original version of Brown and Levinson's paper which was first published in 1978 as part of Esther N. Goody (ed.), *Questions and politeness*. This paper was reissued as a separate book in 1987, a few months before my present thesis was getting into print (Brown and Levinson 1987). The new edition has an extensive introduction in which the authors review much of the recent work on politeness theory.

3.1 Brown and Levinson's theory of politeness

It is interesting to note that Brown and Levinson pursue an approach which is at once similar and diametrically opposed to that of Sperber. Like Sperber they are interested in functionalist explanations and search for factors that lie outside purely linguistic systems and yet act at the same time as unmistakable constraints on the patterns of language construction. However, unlike Sperber, Brown and Levinson expressly do not locate such factors in the 'principles of cognitive processing, or the interaction of language with other mental faculties' (1978: 261). Rather, they point out that 'remarkably little attention has been given to *social* [Brown and Levinson's emphasis] pressures on grammar' (1978: 261) and they state that on the question of how social factors affect language usage they 'find no arguments of a scope paralleling that of the now fashionable internal functionalism' (1978: 261).

The inclusion of social functions in an explanation of linguistic phenomena is essential, because in some areas explanation by means of cognitive functions alone leads to a situation 'where linguistic rules seem to increase rather than decrease the complexity of sentence-processing' (1978: 262). When such a point is reached, the only alternative is to leave what Brown and Levinson call the 'internal' cognitive functionalist explanation (to which, as we have seen, Sperber subscribes with his view of symbolism as a cognitive mechanism) and turn to ' "external" pragmatic theories that seek to link linguistic structures to the organization of communication' (1978: 261).

First and foremost among these pragmatic theories is the one proposed by Grice which I have already outlined above. Indeed, Brown and Levinson say that the whole thrust of their argument is concerned with one 'powerful and pervasive motive' that leads the speaker to violate the conversational maxims and behave linguistically exactly in the way predicted by Grice. This 'powerful and pervasive motive' is politeness.

Language is, in the eyes of Brown and Levinson, a tool that has a double function:

1. Firstly, in everyday interactional practice it is an actor's efficient (and as I will suggest later, almost 'magical') tool for tailoring

social relationships: 'We believe that patterns of message construction, or "ways of putting things", or simply language usage, are part of the very stuff that social relationships are made of (or, as some would prefer, crucial parts of the expressions of social relations)' (1978: 60).

2. Secondly, for the sociological observer language serves as a tool with which he can analyze the quality of social relationships: 'Discovering the principles of language usage may be largely coincident with discovering the principles out of which social relationships, in their interactional aspect, are constructed: dimensions by which individuals manage to relate to others in particular ways' (1978: 60).

Brown and Levinson's politeness theory is based on the following empirical starting points:

1. Every competent adult member of a society has a public self-image which Brown and Levinson call 'face', following Goffman's study of interaction ritual and face-to-face behaviour (Goffman 1959; 1967). In English, the term 'face' immediately conjures up the metaphor of 'losing face' which describes an embarrassment or humiliation. Face has to be attended to in interaction. Every person tries to maintain and enhance his own face and people also generally co-operate in keeping each others' faces because their own face depends on the co-operation of others whom they therefore try not to offend. What in particular constitutes the face of an actor differs from culture to culture but Brown and Levinson claim 'that the mutual knowledge of members' public self-image or face, and the social necessity to orient oneself to it in interaction, are universal' (1978: 67). There are two aspects to face:

   (a) negative face: the basic claim to territories, personal preserves, rights to non-distraction – i.e. to freedom of action and freedom from imposition;
   (b) positive face: the positive consistent self-image or 'personality' (crucially including the desire that this self-image be appreciated and approved of) claimed by interactants. (1978: 66)

In their explanatory model Brown and Levinson treat these two aspects as 'basic wants, which every member knows every other member desires, and which in general it is in the interests of every member to partially satisfy' (1978: 67). Rephrased in terms of wants, face is defined as

negative face: the want of every 'competent adult member' that his actions be unimpeded by others;
positive face: the want of every member that his wants be desirable to at least some others. (1978: 67)

Negative face is maintained by means of various forms of non-imposition, while positive face is maintained by means of a more complicated process. It requires that a person's personal wants and goals are subscribed to by others and are considered desirable. Or, expressed differently, to attend to someone's positive face means to satisfy his wish 'to be ratified, understood, approved of, liked or admired' (1978: 67).

2. The second assumption of the theory is that actors are rational agents and that they employ a form of 'practical reasoning' (Aristotle 1969) which 'guarantees inferences from ends or goals to means that will satisfy those ends' (Brown and Levinson 1978: 69). Such rationality allows an actor the 'maximization, or minimum-cost assessment in the choice of means to an end' and leads him 'not to waste effort to no avail'. Thus, 'if I want a drink', for example, 'and I could use the tap in this room or the tap in the bathroom or the tap in the garden, it would surely be "irrational" to trot out into the garden unnecessarily' (1978: 70).

In terms of message construction the notion of rationality is essential because it alone makes it possible to view verbal exchanges as following linguistic strategies which in turn act as means (or tools) to achieve face-oriented ends, and which are the main topic of Brown and Levinson's study. The central concept for an understanding of these strategies is the 'face-threatening act' (FTA). Some of ego's acts may threaten the face of alter and/or of himself; that is, they may offend the face wants of the addressee and/or of the speaker. Brown and Levinson distinguish between a number of different kinds of FTAs which they class into two categories. These are, firstly, those which primarily threaten the hearer's face and, secondly, those that mainly threaten the speaker's face. This division is again subdivided into those FTAs that offend either positive-face or negative-face wants. Here are a few examples:

1. FTAs on hearer's (H's) negative-face wants are orders and requests; suggestions and advice (the proverb 'If you want to lose a friend, advise him' comes to mind!); reminders; threats; offers; expressions of strong emotions, etc. (1978: 71).
2. FTAs on H's positive-face wants are disapproval of all kinds, such as criticism, contempt, ridicule, complaints, reprimands, etc., and irreverence; bringing of bad news; boasting; raising of divisive topics, etc. (1978: 71–2)
3. FTAs on speaker's (S's) negative face may consist of expressing thanks; acceptance of thanks or apologies; excuses; acceptance of offers; responses to a *faux-pas*; unwilling promises or offers, etc. (1978: 72)
4. FTAs on S's positive face may be apologies; acceptance of a compliment; breakdown of physical control over body and 'emotion leakage' such as non-control of laughter and tears; self-humiliation, etc. (1978: 73)

Now, the crucial point about these FTAs is the fact, or rather the hypothesis, that, given their mutual vulnerability of face, actors will seek to avoid FTAs, and where this is not possible will rationally choose certain strategies to soften and minimize their face-threatening acts. The employment of these strategies leads to the complex and delicate patterns of message construction which constitute the object of inquiry, that is, politeness phenomena.

Brown and Levinson distinguish between four 'super-strategies' for doing FTAs which they sum up in Figure 2 (1978: 74). Excepting strategy 5, one can say that these super-strategies are hierarchically ordered on a continuum of FTA danger. Thus, when there is only a small danger of damaging the face of alter, ego will use strategy 1, but as the risk increases and ego may harm himself by harming alter, then he employs a higher order strategy. The higher the order of strategy, the more effort is put into message codification and this again is inversely related to the clarity of the message.

These three variables are illustrated by means of Figure 3, adapted from Brown and Levinson (1978: 80). Note that the figure excludes strategy 5.

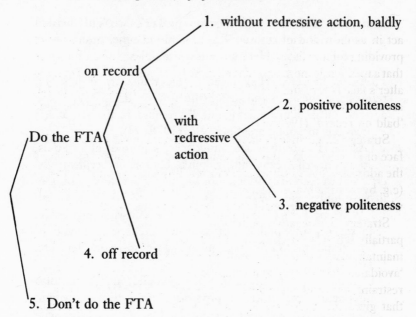

Figure 2   Possible strategies for doing FTAs   (Brown and Levinson 1978: 74)

Effort	Clarity	Danger	Strategy
least	most	least	on record minus redress (strategy 1)
↓	↑	↓	plus redress: positive politeness (strategy 2) negative politeness (strategy 3)
most	least	most	off record (strategy 4)

Figure 3   Factors influencing strategy selection

Strategy 1, 'bald on record without redress', consists of doing an act in as clear and direct a way as possible without the bother of providing for any face wants of the addressee. If ego and alter agree that a message is more urgent than their face wants or if the danger to alter's face is very small (as, for example, in offers and requests that are obviously in alter's own interest), etc., then the FTA may be done 'bald on record' (1978: 74).

Strategy 2, 'positive politeness', 'is oriented towards the positive face of H' (1978: 75). It is 'approach-based; it "anoints" the face of the addressee by indicating that in some respects, S wants H's wants (e.g. by treating him as a member of an in-group, a friend, a person whose wants and personality traits are known and liked)' (1978: 75).

Strategy 3, 'negative politeness', 'is oriented mainly towards partially satisfying (redressing) H's negative face, his basic want to maintain claims of territory and self-determination' (1978: 75). It is 'avoidance-based' and characterized by self-effacement, formality, restraint, etc., and generally can be seen as a 'softening mechanism that gives the addressee an "out", a face-saving line of escape, permitting him to feel that his response is not coerced' (1978: 75).

Strategy 4, 'off record', consists of constructing an FTA in such a way that 'there is more than one unambiguously attributable intention so that the actor cannot be held to have committed himself to one particular intent' (1978: 74).

> Linguistic realizations of off-record strategies include metaphor and irony, rhetorical questions, understatement, tautologies, all kinds of hints as to what a speaker wants or means to communicate, without doing so directly, so that the meaning is to some degree negotiable. (1978: 74)

There are, then, four main 'super-strategies'. The linguistic realizations operate, respectively, as a kind of 'social accelerator and social brake for decreasing or increasing social distance in relationships' (1978: 98). Brown and Levinson are anxious to point out that they do not claim strategies for doing FTAs to be the only motivation for the linguistic realizations which they entail. 'The want to be poetic, or to avoid responsibility (as in the evasions of a servant or the vagueness of a Delphic oracle), or to play with language' may 'stimulate the use of the off-record strategy' (1978: 98).

Nevertheless, face wants are universal and all-pervasive and we find in them one of the social factors without which the 'general abundance of syntactic and lexical apparatus in a grammar seems *undermotivated* [my emphasis] by either systemic or cognitive distinctions and psychological processing factors' (1978: 99). To understand fully the choice of particular strategies by an actor one has to know how he 'computes the weightiness of an FTA.' Brown and Levinson have described the calculus for such a computation as:

$$W_x = D(S,H) + P(H,S) + R_x$$

The values are defined as follows:

> W_x is the numerical value that measures the weightiness of the FTAx, $D(S,H)$ is the value that measures the social distance between S and H, $P(H,S)$ is a measure of the power that H has over S, and R_x is a value that measures the degree to which theFTAx is rated as an imposition in that culture. We assume that each of these values can be measured on a scale of 1 to n, where n is some small number. Our formula assumes that the function that assigns a value to W_x on the basis of the three social parameters does so on a simple summative basis. Such an assumption seems to work surprisingly well, but we allow that in fact some more complex composition of values may be involved. In any case, the function must capture the fact that all three dimensions P, D and R, contribute to the seriousness of an FTA, and thus to a determination of the level of politeness with which, other things being equal, an FTA will be communicated. (1987: 81)

D (social distance) is a 'symmetric social dimension of similarity/difference' (1978: 81) between S (speaker) and H (addressee) and it may be assessed in reference to the frequency of interaction and the flow of material and non-material goods (i.e. psychological transference, words, etc.) between them.

P (social power) is an asymmetric relationship which manifests itself in the fact that 'H can impose his own plans and his own self-evaluation (face) at the expense of S's plans and self-evaluation' (1978: 82). Both (or either), a differential access to material control and to metaphysical control are the source for the differential P of the actors.

R (ranking of impositions) defines the degree to which impositions are 'considered to interfere with an agent's wants of self-determination or of approval (his negative- and positive-face wants)' (1978: 82). R is measured in terms of expenditure involving services and goods.

When an actor thus attempts a particular FTA, he calculates the risks to his own and his interlocutor's face by evaluating D, P and R. The interesting point now is the fact that by doing so he automatically compounds the three variables into a 'single index of risk' (1978: 86) which does not reveal whether P, D or R is responsible for the particular W_x value. The 'single index of risk', that is W_x, is the motive for selecting one strategy rather than another and using one linguistic realization rather than another which, in turn, encodes the degree to which a speaker considers a particular FTA to be dangerous. Though the degree of danger gets encoded, it remains ambiguous which of the variables P, D or R is in fact responsible for the high value of W_x. But if it is open to question whether D, P or R is responsible for any specific W_x value, then a speaker must be able to exploit an FTA and use it to define D, P or R in his own interest and to his own benefit. Indeed, if P, D and R were always rigidly defined there would be no need for any complex 'scheming' and all the strategies would collapse into one, that is strategy 1 (bald on record). If, on the other hand, P, D and R are not absolutely fixed, then there can be something gained or lost socially by doing an FTA. As we are concerned here with some of Brown and Levinson's most interesting observations, which, furthermore, have important implications for our understanding of symbolism, let me quote them at length:

Any FTA utterance will encode the estimated danger of the FTA, but it does not necessarily display which of the social variables is primarily responsible for the assessed weight of W_x. S and H will both have some estimate of these variables, and S may choose to try to re-rank the expectable weighting of one of the variables at the expense of the others.

In trying to re-rank R, S may take advantage of mutual-knowledge assumptions between S and H of their respective social distance D and social power P, and S may choose to act *as though* R_x is smaller than he in fact knows (and knows that H knows) it really is. He can do this by saying, for example, 'Hey, Harry, how about lending me your new car!' and hoping that the positive-politeness optimism will convince Harry that it is not a very big or unreasonable request. This is risky, as Harry may decide that it is D or P that the addressee is manipulating, rather than R, and take offence. But the fact that there are three possible variables to manipulate means that the choice of which one is manipulated is off record, and the speaker could argue (if challenged by Harry) that he didn't mean to imply that D or P was small, simply that R was small. Similarly for the other factors. (1978: 233)

A diachronic or 'biographical' factor completes the theory as illustrated by Brown and Levinson's outline of the exploitative re-ranking of P:

A speaker can use a bald-on-record FTA to claim (by implicature) that he is powerful over H, and does not fear his retaliation. This is risky, but if he gets away with it (H doesn't retaliate, for whatever reason), S succeeds in actually altering the public definition of his relationship to H; that is, his successful exploitation becomes part of the history of interaction, and thereby alters the agreed values of D or P. (1978: 233)

It is in this way that

the linguistic realizations of positive- and negative-politeness strategies may operate as a social accelerator and a social brake, respectively, to modify the direction of interaction at any point in time. Interactants, in any situation where the possibility of change in their social relationship exists, are constantly assessing the current 'score' – the mutual-knowledge assessments of D and P, for example – and may make minute adjustments at any point in order to re-establish a satisfactory balance or to move the interaction in the desired direction towards greater closeness or greater distance. (1978: 236)

In passages such as the ones which I have quoted here, the authors indeed come close to their goal of giving us a 'piece of descriptive apparatus for the recording of interactional quality in some more sophisticated way than the use of gross labels like "respect" and "familiarity", with which anthropologists have hitherto seemed content' (1978: 247).

I think that the same apparatus is also applicable to the analysis of the social practice of symbolization. Therefore I will now work through the strategies of politeness outlined by Brown and Levinson one by one. This will involve empirical observations, many of them made among the Hamar of southern Ethiopia, which in their details are perhaps not always easy to follow. But, as in so many other fields, in symbolic theory it is precisely the details which matter.

3.2 Symbolization within the strategies of politeness

Let me recapitulate a few crucial points: politeness theory constitutes an effort to explain linguistic forms by social pressures and social constraints. The theory shows how patterns of message construction are related to the quality of social relationships and thus it establishes a necessary connection between general wants and linguistic means. The general wants relate to the maintenance of face, and the means by which face wants can be satisfied are linguistic realizations of politeness.

Being endowed with rationality, a speaker selects from among several alternatives that linguistic form which has the highest satisfactoriness value in relation to his ultimate communicative goal, and employs specific strategies of politeness which 'intrinsically afford certain pay-offs and advantages' (Brown and Levinson 1978: 76). These strategies are hierarchically ordered, ranging from those that are employed in situations of low risk to those that are employed in situations of high risk. The choice of any particular strategy is determined by the way in which a speaker perceives a situation: by applying a certain strategy the speaker reveals his interpretation of the situation and in so doing he affects the situation itself. Thus there is a feed-back involved which turns linguistic realizations (the output of politeness strategies) into tools with which a speaker can deliberately and to his advantage shape the social relationships in which he is involved. In particular he is able to manipulate the important variables of social power, distance and imposition.

All this adds up to a powerful theory of 'politeness as a social mechanism'. As Brown and Levinson have convincingly shown, politeness carries a motive and it is this motive which gives the linguistic realizations their structure, down to innumerable details of message construction.

3.2.1 SUPER-STRATEGY I: BALD ON RECORD WITHOUT REDRESS

To speak baldly on record means to speak in conformity with Grice's conversational maxims which have been outlined above. That is (a) to speak the truth, (b) to say no more and no less than required, (c) to be relevant and (d) to be perspicuous, that is to express oneself as clearly as possible. Now, the interesting aspect of politeness strategies consists in the fact that many of them do not conform to the maxims but instead flout and exploit them. In short, politeness strategies make extensive use of implicature rather than unequivocal message construction. Only in a limited number of situations do politeness realizations adhere to the maxims and can be called bald on record. The direct imperative provides the most striking instance. It may be uttered without redress in a number of circumstances of which Brown and Levinson name the following:

(1) When maximum efficiency is very important, and this is known to both parties involved.
(2) When channel noise is high.
(3) When the focus of interaction is task-oriented.
(4) When the speaker is so powerful that he does not have to attend to the listener's face.
(5) When the FTA is primarily in the listener's interest.

Two further cases involve an intriguing complication:

(6) When it is intended to communicate 'metaphorical urgency'. In certain situations any redress of an FTA would decrease the communicated urgency. Thus, 'Please help me' is not as urgent as 'Help!' (1978: 101–2).
(7) When both parties anticipate each other's wants and try to show that they don't want to impinge upon each other. In such situations, 'it is polite, in a broad sense, for S to alleviate H's anxieties by pre-emptively inviting H to impinge on S's

preserve' (1978: 104). Welcomings, farewells and offers are examples of such pre-emptive invitations. The dialectic involved is as follows: 'If H is reluctant to impinge, he will be the less reluctant the firmer the invitation is. So, provided that no other face wants are infringed, the firmer the invitation, the more polite it is' (1978: 104). We have here, so to say, the 'flouting of an expected flouting' and are back to a statement that outwardly looks as if it was simply adhering to the conversational maxims while in fact it contains a developed string of implications.

Examples of this kind do not affect the general argument that bald-on-record strategies can be described as adhering to the maxims. What they do, however, is to warn us that what looks plain on the surface may still hide implications that are not easily accessible and involve (as in (1), (4) and (5) above) a tacitly shared knowledge of the situation and an interpretation of that situation as encoded in the use of the strategy of bald on record. Or, to put it differently, bald-on-record strategies are always employed with a mutually shared knowledge about the other alternative strategies which are more polite. As the same applies not only to the actor but also to the analyst I proceed at once to the next strategy of positive politeness.

3.2.2 SUPER-STRATEGY II: POSITIVE POLITENESS

Positive politeness is a strategy that aims at satisfying face wants 'by communicating that one's own wants (or some of them) are in some respects similar to the addressee's wants' (1978: 106). The strategy is very widely cast and does not restrict itself to the imposition contained in the FTA. Any appreciation of the listener's wants may be brought into play in order to 'anoint', as Brown and Levinson call it, the addressee's face so that he gets assured of his public self-image and does not feel threatened when confronted by the imposition contained in an FTA.

Often the 'appreciation' and the 'anointing' of an addressee's face is not done directly, openly and bluntly but indirectly and subtly or, as I would say, by means of symbolization. Brown and Levinson do not follow up this important point. They realize it, however, as, for

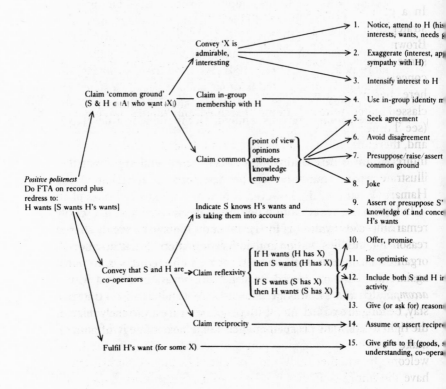

Figure 4   Chart of strategies: positive politeness   (Brown and Levinson 1978: 107)

example, when they say that 'Positive-politeness utterances are used as a kind of *metaphorical* [my emphasis] extension of intimacy' (1978: 108). Thus positive-politeness strategies may consist of combining statements which (a) adhere to the maxims in that the speaker does an FTA on record and (b) flout the maxims in order to achieve some sort of redress and therefore make the FTA more easily acceptable. Brown and Levinson distinguish fifteen different realizations of the overall strategy of positive politeness. In order to facilitate my discussion I reproduce in Figure 4 the chart with which the authors have summed up the strategies.

Strategy 1: Notice, attend to H (his interests, wants, needs, goods)

In a general sense strategy 1 subsumes all the other fourteen strategies of positive politeness because all of them 'attend to H'. But Brown and Levinson think of this strategy in the more restricted sense of noticing someone expressly and showing him that one is concerned with his condition. The authors do not mention greetings here, but many forms of greeting-behaviour should, I think, be classed under strategy 1. Being 'threshold' and 'liminal' phenomena (see Turner 1967: 93), greetings contain potential danger to face and, therefore, one should expect them to encode either directly or indirectly the relationship between the guest and the host. To illustrate what I mean let me provide some observations from Hamar.

In Hamar the 'metaphoric extension of intimacy' (i.e. strategy 1) is remarkably slow in coming forth when a visitor is to be greeted. The reason for this lies in the individualistic pattern of Hamar social organization, where small domestic groups are on perpetual guard against each other. Therefore greeting only occurs after a *fait accompli*, that is, when it is already established that a guest is going to stay, be lodged and fed, etc. With people who are not closely related the right to hospitality is an open question. I have found it difficult to make out what clues allow a potential guest to judge whether he is welcome or whether he would do better to continue on his way. I have the impression that if people want a guest to stay they will encourage him to do so step by step. When a male guest arrives he will first, without comment, sit down on the small stool he always carries, either in the shade of a tree if it is during the heat of the day, or close to the kraal fence if it is early morning or evening. No one in the homestead will seem to notice him at this stage (an irritating experience, by the way, for a European visitor who has been culturally conditioned to expect his face wants to be attended to immediately). But after a while the visitor may realize that a woman, somewhere not too close to him and yet not too far from him, has begun to sweep the ground. This is the first indication that he is not going to be snubbed. If, after all, he has come only for some limited business he now makes a move and asks for a drink of water, asks to talk to someone about a goat that has gone astray, or says whatever else he has come about. In this way he indicates that he does not wish to be invited to stay for long, and so the hosts know now not to invite him more expressly and he avoids having to refuse such an invitation which would be to commit an FTA. If, however, he wants to stay he simply continues to wait in silence for the next sign which will probably be the woman spreading out a cow hide on the spot she has just swept clean. She nods to him and he takes off his sandals and settles down on the cow hide. There he rests for a while and then at last the proper greeting takes place. One by one the male members of the homestead stroll casually over to where the guest rests. Each one sits down on his stool neither too close nor too far from him, and after pausing for a moment, addresses him. As they do so, they employ strategy 4 which Brown and Levinson define as 'use in-group identity markers' (1978: 112). That is, they greet the guest with a term of address to which the guest responds with an appropriate term of address. Hamar abounds with terms of address, both reciprocal and non-reciprocal. Reciprocal terms reflect symmetrical relationships, non-reciprocal terms reflect asymmetrical relation-ships. The relationship between brothers-in-law is a symmetrical one, and so they address each other reciprocally as *soddo*. The relationship between a man and his sister's son, on the other hand, is considered asymmetrical and so non-reciprocal terms of address are used; the sister's son addresses as *abo* his mother's brother, who addresses the sister's son as *yäxa*. Besides terms of address which reflect relationships based on kinship or affinity, there are others relating to age, initiation, hunting achievements, livestock transfers, etc.

To call someone by a term of address is like 'anointing' his face. It means lifting his individual self to the position of a social person and including him and oneself in the same social domain. Thus, the term of address does more than simply denote the guest as a specific individual. Rather, it implies, in the light of the situation in which the term is uttered, something that is eminently social about the visitor. Indeed, the term is something of an implicature. By addressing someone not by his personal name but by the name of a social category or relationship to which he belongs, the conversational maxim of quantity is flouted and an implicature results in the guise of a synecdoche in which a part is expressed by the whole. This is where the symbolic character of the address shows itself. True, the implicature is conventional, but this does not stop manifold and calculated evocations occurring when the terms of address are used in the practice of everyday life. Sometimes the evocations come to light more clearly than in other situations, but latently they are always there. Let me exemplify this by means of the term *bel* which is of great importance in Hamar as well as among neighbouring peoples.

1. On the first of May 1973 together with my friend Baldambe and some other Hamar men I visited the Arbore, a neighbouring non-Hamar group. We had come to speak to Surra who was then one of the leading men of the Arbore, and we hoped we could discuss with him the ending of a feud that had recently developed between the Arbore and the Hamar. When we arrived the following happened:

> We stand in a semi-circle but Surra looks only at me on the left. He does not look at any of my Hamar companions, not even at Baldambe. I take his hand and greet him, but when Wadu puts out his hand, Surra rejects it. Then Baldambe stretches out his hand slowly, and in a sweet voice addresses Surra as *bel*. This is the first time I have seen the term *bel* (bond-friend) in action. The term is like magic, it appeals to an existing link of friendship which, being personal, cannot be destroyed by public affairs, not even by the state of war which currently exists between the Hamar and the Arbore. So Surra takes his hand, saying that he will accept Baldambe's hand and no other. (Lydall and Strecker 1979a: 105)

What has happened here between Baldambe and Surra is exactly what Brown and Levinson mean when they speak of the strategy of positive politeness. Appealing to safe common ground the use of *bel* could indeed act like magic and solve a problem of face which otherwise might have been insurpassable. And let us note that the original problem was itself caused by the fact that both sides belonged to different grounds. Baldambe as part of the Hamar and Surra as part of the Arbore were at war (first synecdoche), but Baldambe and Surra as part of a culturally valued and sanctioned *bel* relationship were at peace. Thus, one synecdoche was played against the other.

2. Once, before I left Dambaiti after a long stay in Hamar, I gave goats as gifts to the womenfolk in Dambaiti (for a portrait of these women see Strecker 1979a). I handed each of them a female goat. I

offered each goat as the Hamar do by holding it under my left arm, lifting its right foreleg with my right hand and offering it to the right hand of Ginonda, Aikenda, Gardu or whoever I was giving the animal to. While I did this, I called them, as is Hamar custom, *bel*, upon which they addressed me also as *bel*. The next morning (I am quoting now from my diary)

> when I crossed Dambaiti *boaka* (an open space in front of the homestead) Gardu was calling someone *bel* with that soft, vibrating and affectionate sound which so often I have heard when some of the women call Baldambe. Well, that morning for the first time the *bel* was meant for me. Gardu smiled as she saw the effect of the word on me, knowing very well the power of the term.

Its power was, of course, its ability to evoke in me in an instant a recollection of a large number of exceedingly pleasant and touching events which until then I had witnessed only as an outsider, and which had never become a true part of myself.

To return to the visitor in Hamar who we left sitting on his cow hide. He will get addressed by reciprocal and non-reciprocal terms exactly as Brown and Levinson have predicted. That is, their theory says that, because of their 'face-anointing' character, reciprocal terms should be used between people whose relationship involves a relatively large social distance (D) or in situations where D is small but the rating of the imposition (R) is high. Furthermore, when the speaker's (S's) social power (P) is great compared to the addressee's (H's) then no effort at positive politeness and hence no use of reciprocal terms of address should be expected. This is precisely what happens to our man in Hamar. Everyone who is related rather distantly to him tries whenever possible to employ such reciprocal terms as *soddo*, *kubu*, *misso*, *bel*, *bargae*, etc. and everyone who is related more closely to him but wants to do an FTA in the near future does the same (e.g. between close kinsmen the term *imbanas* (father's child) is often used). However, people who have such power over him that they have no reason to be concerned with his face, call and greet him by his personal name. Thus, a senior person greets a junior person by his *gali* name, a name which is given soon after birth (for a description of the naming ceremony see Lydall and Strecker 1979a: 18, 142ff, and Lydall and Strecker 1979b: 48–50, 63–4) or his *gar* name, which is given at initiation to men (1979b: 93) and the junior replies simply *woi*, which can be translated as an affirmative – 'yes'. Should the junior initiate the greeting he speaks to the senior using teknonymy, that is, by referring to the senior's oldest male or female child; for example, *Berimba* (father of Beri). In this way a hierarchy related to age and procreation is emphasized. The mechanism works even when the addressee is himself already a father of children. Senior persons who are related closely to him will still call him by his *gali* name but junior persons and those who stand at a greater social distance tend to call him by the name of his oldest child or by the reciprocal terms described above.

With this I conclude, for the time being, my excursion into Hamar greeting practices. The greeting falls, as we will see later, into a yet wider pattern of social relationships. But at the moment it suffices to note that greeting as a realization of strategy 1 is not necessarily confined to on-record statements. Rather, as the example of Hamar forms of address shows, the positive-politeness strategy of 'noticing and attending to H' may itself be speaking of hidden things, may be indirectly telling something about the relationship pertaining between the speaker and the addressee and subtly encoding an interpretation of the situation which is at once persuasive and elusive; in short, it may contain an element of symbolization.

Strategy 2: Exaggerate (interest, approval, sympathy with H)

Exaggeration is a form of symbolization in so far as it violates the conversational maxim of quantity and thereby forces an implicature. Brown and Levinson consider under this heading exaggeration by means of intonation and stress rather than by means of hyperbole, which they regard instead as a form of 'going off record' (see below, p. 114). Prosodic features may on occasion imply an added meaning but any symbolization involved is very slight. The function of intonation and stress is rather to emphasize the openly intended meaning of a statement, as in the example:

'What a fantástic gárden you have!' (1978: 109)

Note, however, that such an exaggeration of approval may in itself amount to an FTA. If it is reciprocated by an answer like:

'Oh, not at all, I have just let the weeds grow.'

then the face-wants of the initial admirer of the garden will in turn be satisfied and the FTA of the initial statement will be cancelled. But if the addressee does not respond in this way and simply accepts the statement, then the speaker has truly given something away. Perhaps he is rich (emotionally and socially) and can afford to give things away. Isn't flattery one of the cheapest commodities with which to go and make one's fortune? The Hamar say *apho daetsee*, by which they mean that words are not heavy to carry, one can always take enough of them along wherever one goes to hand them out and use them whenever it seems useful. But then, the Hamar also say, *kissa apho sholba ne*, 'his words are light, he is not trustworthy'. Both phrases mirror an awareness of the danger that resides in words. Properly used, they are a blessing, lightly or wrongly used they are self-defeating. Accordingly, fully integrated and socially secure persons in Hamar will not employ strategy 2 but abhor it. Only people who are desperate, as, for example, a mother who tries to find food for her children in times of drought or an old man who has no kin to support him, may occasionally make use of some reckless flattery in the hope that it may work and help them to get what is wanted so badly. In short, nobody uses strategy 2 if they still have something to lose. A rhyme by Wilhelm Busch comes to mind which sums up the situation:

Ist der Ruf erst ruiniert, lebt man völlig ungeniert.
('Once one's public image has been ruined, one begins to live completely uninhibited.')

There is also something else which works against the use of strategy 2 in Hamar. Remember the guest who arrives. He does not initiate the greeting as we westerners would expect him to. Furthermore, we westerners would bring some gifts and offer them to the host in order to oblige him. We trust in what Marcel Mauss has called 'the power of the gift' which 'compels the making of counter-gifts' (Mauss 1954: 37). Hamar society teaches us a different lesson.

A visitor who arrives as guest (*shoshi*), and not as a marriage go-between or someone who explicitly enters into transactions concerned with bond-friendship, does not, as a rule, bring gifts. On the contrary, once he has been accepted as guest and once he has been greeted, he begins to demand things, food (good food) and drink (good drink), tobacco, etc., and then, when the time of his departure draws near, gifts to take away. This pattern is so striking that Jean Lydall made the suggestion that Hamar is not a society based on a principle of give but on a principle of take (1979a: 19). Indeed, the pattern is the reverse of ours:

Western

| Guest initiates greeting and is greeted immediately. | Brings gifts. | Behaves modestly and does not impinge on host. |

Hamar

| Guest does not initiate greeting but waits to be greeted. | Does not bring gifts. | Behaves demandingly, impinges on host, takes away gifts. |

Obviously, strategy 2 fits into the pattern of western culture but does not fit well into the pattern of Hamar. In Hamar the visitor is advised not to flatter his host but rather to use FTAs in order to persuade the host that he, the guest, is a big man and has great power and that he, the host, had better give him what he, the guest, demands. In other words, his strategy is to be demanding rather than to flatter. But just as flattery in western society must not be done too obviously lest it lose its impact, so the demands of the guest in Hamar must not go too far and must not be too blunt lest the strategy works against the one who uses it. Also, one must not underestimate the fineness of the feelings involved. On the surface the behaviour of the guest might perhaps look as if he was intimidating the host. But his very presumptuousness and his demanding way eventually make it easier for the host to give and show himself to be generous. Thus, in the end, it is better for the host to have a strong and powerful guest who bullies him into giving than to have a weak guest who does not dare to demand and consequently does not receive anything which would spread the fame and public esteem of the giver.

Strategy 3: Intensify interest to H

Brown and Levinson have made the perceptive observation that 'making a good story' may be viewed as a realization of positive politeness 'as it pulls H right into the middle of the events being discussed, *metaphorically at any rate* [my emphasis], thereby increasing their intrinsic interest to him' (1978: 111). What they mean is that a stylistically rich or elaborate performance has always, so to speak, something behind it, a second message that is not and must not be expressed directly. The message might be very general, saying something like 'I, the speaker, accept you, the listener. I am interested in you, I respect your wants, etc.', or it might be more specific and relate to a particular situation which will be indirectly affected by the 'making of a good story'.

In fact, something of an implicature may be involved, because by investing a comparatively high effort in message construction the speaker induces the addressee to ask himself why the special effort was made, the answer being that S was indirectly trying to honour and enhance H's face. In this sense then strategy 3 can be seen as leading to innumerable forms of ritual and symbolism which all ultimately intensify interest to H by making a good story for him or by helping to make one.

Hamar conversations abound with stylistic features that intensify the interest to H and, as they throw light on Brown and Levinson's observation, I examine some of these features here in detail.

Echoing: Often a listener reassures the face of a person while he is speaking. He does this either by uttering certain appreciative 'hmm' sounds (the Hamar have a special name for this), or, more dramatically, he echoes (repeats) parts of what the speaker has said. Here is an example:

Baldambe:	Yesterday the men of Merrie's settlement came bringing a goat.
Choke:	Brought it.
Baldambe:	And they arrived with it at the gateway over there.
Choke:	Arrived.
Baldambe:	At the gateway the goat was given to Elata.
Choke:	Was given.
Baldambe:	He was made to bless them.
Choke:	Was made to bless.
Baldambe:	To hide away the sickness.
Choke:	To hide it away.

Baldambe: After that, coffee was drunk.
Choke: Was drunk.
(Strecker 1979a: 15)

Typically the echoing is done by someone who is junior to the speaker or of his own age. Rarely would an older person echo what a younger one has said. As age and authority or, in Brown and Levinson's terminology, age and social power (P), are related, the use of echoing encodes a message that indirectly says: 'I accept you and do not challenge you, in fact I want to be close to you.' Sometimes the echoing is also a device for establishing a strong link between S and H to the detriment of a third party who gets excluded from the 'in-group' of those who echo each other (see below).

Directly quoted speech: The use of directly quoted speech is all-pervasive in Hamar. In one sense it may be viewed as a reflex of the dominance of face-to-face relations. People share so much know-ledge in common that they may use directly quoted speech very often where we, in our western world which is divided into many 'stages' and countless 'sets of actors', would get lost. To understand the sequencing of directly quoted speeches one has to know the original speakers who are supposed to have said this or that. To mention each speaker each time he is quoted would be antithetical to the main object of using directly quoted speech which is to re-create what one has witnessed and communicate it as a drama. Here is an example of this kind of dramatization taken from Hamar.

Two Hamar women are talking about the hardship that comes to the herdsman when he has lost his teeth:

Bargi: (imitating the speech of the toothless) Only gums are left. 'Leave the meat deep inside the pot and let it soften.'
Aikenda: *Nyarsh!* When they said: 'Let the meat soften deep inside the pot', we ...
Bargi: ... we laughed: 'Why do you leave home then, where your wife can feed you with porridge?' '*Ye*, we have nothing with which we can bite.'
(Strecker 1979a: 137)

In this and in similar ways directly quoted speech is constantly employed in Hamar and it reflects, among other things, the constant and close interest which people have in each other.

Onomatopoeic words and imitation of natural sounds: The technique of using onomatopoeic words and imitating natural sounds can be viewed as a variety of direct quotation of speech. It is part of the general strategy of re-creating and dramatizing which 'pulls H right into the middle of the events being discussed' (Brown and Levinson 1978: 111). As my present example shows, onomatopoeic words also lend themselves to the technique of echoing:

> Baldambe and Choke are standing early one morning in front of the homestead, and look at the clouds in the sky to divine the fate of Hamar raiders.
>
> Choke: And when the raiders are on their way, the clouds show us their footprints: *ba-ta-ta-ta-ta-ta-ta*, white and spreading out like my hand ...
>
> Baldambe: Yes, *misso*, I know all this. They have attacked, look at all this dust, look at the flashing light: *rara-ra-ra-- barcha-barcha-barcha.*
>
> Choke: (joining him) *Ra-ra-ra-ra-ra-ra-ra-ra-ra-ra.*
> (Strecker 1979a: 33)

Imitation of people's voices, dialect, jargon: This technique can again be viewed as just one more variety of dramatization. Brown and Levinson do not mention it under strategy 3, but under strategy 4, which uses 'in-group identity markers'. Indeed, the technique may do two jobs at once. If S switches to the dialect and/or jargon of H he automatically implies the intimacy which is the aim of all positive politeness, and at the same time he may use the dialect, jargon and possibly the imitation of actual people's voices as a means to enliven his talk. In Hamar all kinds of switches can be observed but none is as powerful as that employed among age-mates. The age-set system of the Hamar does not function any more today (for a description of the system see Lydall and Strecker 1979b: 122ff), but age has remained one of the dominant factors in social organization and there exists a strong sense of identity between people of similar age, which may be expressed in language use. Men move collectively through the life-cycle. When they are young they play together. Later when they have grown up a bit, they herd goats, sheep and cattle together and, very importantly, they dance together. After this, more joint herding follows which at times includes strenuous labour at the waterholes, moving the herds from one grazing area to another and also scouting and fighting to defend the herds against raiders, going raiding together, hunting, etc. In short, age-mates share many experiences together and this is expressed in the language. In a way every age not only has its own stories to tell, it also tells them in its own way with its own vocabulary, prosodics and, occasionally, even its own syntax.

Language usage does indeed mirror the social structure here. It does not do so, however, in a mindless way. Rather, the speakers are well aware that by means of language usage they can, between the lines so to speak, express that they belong together, that they share something which is unique to them and sets them apart from others. This exclusion or inclusion (depending on the point from which one views the process) must not be expressed openly or defined literally, it must remain hidden if it is to have any effect.

Summary words and the rhetorical use of 'ama': There are numerous further ways in which the Hamar dramatize their speech as a means of positive politeness, but in order to be brief let me finish my illustrations with a description of how the Hamar use two further techniques which Brown and Levinson mention: the switch from past to present tense and the 'use of tag questions or expressions that draw H as a participant into the conversation, such as "you know?", "see what I mean?", "isn't it?"' (1978: 112).

The switch to present tense and the use of the tag expressions are often combined. As the speaker builds up his story and as he reaches a climax (there are, of course, several moments of climax in any longer story), his sentences become shorter and more compressed, with the content of whole sentences or phrases compacted into single words. Jean Lydall has described these words as 'expressive words and compound descriptive verbs' (Lydall 1976). One of her examples (which I modify here slightly) could well be taken from the climax of the description of a hunt:

Hamar:	*Lansi*	*agadem*	*zap;*	*torsh;*		*limm;*	*dosh.*
Literal:	Then	that	grab;	jab through the heart;		lifeless;	dead.
English:	\multicolumn{7}{l}{Then they grab it; jab a spear through its heart;}

English: Then they grab it; jab a spear through its heart;
           it sinks down lifeless and is dead.

The four summary words, *zap*, *torsh*, *limm*, and *dosh*, could have been presented in combination with rhetorical tag expressions. For example, like this:

> *lansi agadem – zap ama*; (small pause) *torsh ama*; (small pause) *limm ama*; *dosh.*

Ama means 'say' and the speaker alludes here to the Hamar practice of echoing the speaker's most emphatic words. That is to say, often a speaker asks a listener to repeat specific words he has uttered. Choke, for example, once asked me to echo him as follows:

Choke: Were they really two or were they three? I think they must have been two. My friend, their water gourd, say 'they took'.

I.S.:   Took.

Choke: Then from here all the way to the plain of the dry mud, the water of Marano, say 'they reached'.

I.S.:   Reached.

Choke: Fresh water, say 'they fetched'.

I.S.:   Fetched.

Choke: The mountain of Dibis, say 'they climbed'.

I.S.:   Climbed.

Choke: There they found plenty of cattle. These cattle, say 'they took'.

I.S.:   Took.

Choke: Say 'they drove away'.

I.S.:   Drove away.

(Strecker 1979a: 66–7)

In another variant of the same technique the speaker does not give any part of his speech away and the use of *ama* remains only a rhetorical invitation which no one is meant to follow. Thus we get the variation which I have indicated above:

Then they, say 'grab it'; say 'jab a spear through its heart'; say 'it sinks down lifeless'; dead.

The 'giving of the word': One final point relating to strategy 3 may be of interest here. I have said above that the relationship between guest and host in Hamar may be characterized as

Guest is kept waiting, greeted late.	Guest does not bring gifts.	Guest demands gifts.

We may now add a fourth variable, the 'giving of the word'. By handing the word to the guest, one certainly employs a strategy of positive politeness. One does not, as Brown and Levinson put it, 'anoint' the guest's face but rather lets him 'put on his own make-up' and present his self-image in the light in which he wants it to be seen. As I made my observations on this point long before I ever heard of positive and negative face, FTAs, etc., let me quote my original observations at length:

The central focus of Hamar domestic social discourse is the coffee pot. The men sit in a semi-circle around the fire on which the heavy round clay pot is placed, and from which they are served with large bowls of steaming coffee. The coffee is made with the whole beans, husks and all, and is so weak that it would not be recognized as coffee by an uninitiated western observer. Large quantities are drunk, perhaps more to replace bodily water loss in the hot climate than for its stimulant value. The bowls are large half-calabashes. A good visitor in Hamar is expected to arrive at a homestead either early in the morning or early in the evening, at the time when (ideally) his host's wife has put on a pot of coffee.

He is invited to sit down on a cow hide and then, when the coffee is served, the host will ask him: 'Tell me the country' (*pen gia*). The guest answers: 'No, no, I have heard no bad', or he uses a metaphor like: 'No, no, the wind has not whistled' and he adds: 'Tell me yours.' Upon this the host replies: 'No, no, the country is well.' Then there follows a pause after which the guest slowly begins to tell the news which he has brought. He always has something new to tell because he will unfailingly begin his talk by telling what he himself has done, from where he came and which way he took, etc., and into this account of his private actions he weaves the public 'news of the country', the description of rituals and oracles he encountered, the news of raids in which he participated or of which he heard, the rains that have fallen or failed to fall, the state of the pasture and the fields.... No one interrupts him while he talks. There is only a certain 'echoing' by the host to whom he addresses himself, and there are spontaneous reactions of the audience, e.g. laughter and exclamations of disbelief and anger.

The length of a *pen gia* varies depending on the extent of dramatic events happening in the country, on the speech competence of the speaker, on the sympathy and interest of the audience, and other factors. Over a period of three years, I have listened to countless *pen gia* which extended over more than half an hour, sometimes even over more than an hour, and I was always struck by the excellent memory of the speaker, his sense of detail, his minute reconstruction of time sequences and, above all, his dramatic reconstruction of social arguments. The *pen gia* is a complex process which contains several elements that directly and indirectly relate to social control:

1. The most important element in the situation is certainly that the speaker is telling factual news. Responding to ecological and external political pressures, the Hamar have developed a fragmented, dispersed and highly individualized society. These loose organizational features would not help them survive, if they did not constantly pass vital information from one fragment of the society to the other. It is this manifest function which has turned the *pen gia* into an institution in Hamar.

2. A second important element is that the speaker is evaluating news. He is not only passing on factual information, but also evaluating. When his rational and moral evaluations concern his fellow countrymen (or women) the *pen gia* turns into an explicit agent of social control. In Hamar, as in many face-to-face societies, each word said in favour or disfavour of a particular individual affects that person's social credit and with it his chances to achieve the goals to which he aspires, i.e. to collect large herds, to perform memorable rituals, etc. ... On one level the *pen gia* is, therefore, institutionalized gossip. The element of social control in gossip is well known to comparative anthropology and it is interesting to note that the Hamar often themselves refer to the

pen gia as gossip. They call it *mermer* if the *pen gia* contains neutral gossip; they call it *wupha* if the *pen gia* contains gossip of malice and slander.

3. The *pen gia* always reflects back on the speaker. If he tells the news well, he gains social esteem, if he speaks badly, he loses it. This is well understood by the Hamar. So much so that many speakers turn the tables and use their *pen gia* offensively, trying to impress upon the listeners their general social competence by means of magnificent speech performance. This can reach bizarre, even pathological dimensions. I have witnessed *pen gia* which had a therapeutic element. During such therapeutic *pen gia* the sympathetically listening audience allowed the speaker to embark on 'far-out' monologues in which he tried to develop – for himself and for the audience – a unified image of his self and of his actions. I think that this need for self-repair results from the frustrations which Hamar anarchic social structure creates in the individual. A Hamar who is wronged by one of his countrymen usually has no immediate means of direct redress. His only avenue is talk – talk not only to muster social support to repair broken social relations, but also to repair his disturbed inner self.

4. To tell the news the speaker uses numerous stylistic features and a host of bodily motions. He does not so much talk about events, but rather tries to re-create them for the audience dramatically. But important as this artistic element is, it is enjoyed only implicitly and with divided hearts, for the Hamar know too well that the speaker's verbal art is closely related to aggression and social domination. So, whenever a speaker excels in poetics, the delight in the pure artistic forms is sometimes counterpointed by the cruelty of the message.
(Strecker 1976: 587–9)

This description of the *pen gia* contains already a number of observations to which I will return later in detail (for example, the 'cruelty' of symbolic statements) but here I am concerned only with the anticipatory logic of the 'I know that you know' type which is involved in the custom of the *pen gia* and which hands the word to the guest so that he may attend to his face for himself. In as much as this logic remains hidden and derives its effectiveness only by remaining hidden, we may say that we have entered the field of symbolization. 'Intimacy' has been 'metaphorically extended', not in the way Brown and Levinson have pointed out, that is, by 'making a good story' which is delicately adjusted to H's face wants, but by handing the word to H in a conventionalized manner in order that H, who now becomes S, may tend to his face for himself. This goes with what I have said about Hamar culture above: in Hamar you do not flatter someone else. To flatter others is the strategy of the desperate. Normally a person flatters, and is expected to flatter, no one but himself. He does this, however, in an indirect way, that is by implication.

Strategy 4: Use in-group identity markers

This has been dealt with under strategies 2 and 3 above, when dealing with exaggeration and intensification of interest.

Strategy 5: Seek agreement

I now turn to strategy 5, which Brown and Levinson define as 'seek ways in which it is possible to agree with H' (1978: 115).

Interestingly, they point out that one way to do this consists of a technique which is in many respects similar to the one which I have termed 'echoing'. Brown and Levinson describe the technique as follows. Agreement may be stressed by repeating part or all of what the preceding speaker has said in a conversation. In addition to demonstrating that one has heard correctly what was said (satisfying strategy 1: notice, attend to H), repeating is used to stress emotional agreement with the utterance (or to stress interest and surprise). For example:

A: I had a flat tyre on the way home.
B: Oh God, a flat tyre! (1978: 118)

Besides repetition, Brown and Levinson mention the use of 'safe topics' as a way of seeking agreement. The archetypal safe topic is, as we all know, the weather. We use it to reassure each other indirectly that any FTA that may ensue is not the cause but rather the effect of the social relationship pertaining between us. Thus, indirectness may be involved in strategy 5. However, its main effectiveness lies in going unequivocally on record as agreeing with one's interlocutor.

Strategy 6: Avoid disagreement

For this strategy Brown and Levinson name three main realizations.

(1) Token agreement and pseudo-agreement occur where S pretends to agree with H and twists his words 'so as to appear to agree' (1978: 119).

(2) White lies occur 'where S, when confronted with the necessity to state an opinion wants to lie ... rather than damage H's positive face' (1978: 120–1).

(3) Neither (1) nor (2) leaves room for any elaborate symbolization, but (3), the 'hedging of opinions', does.

'Hedging' is defined as being deliberately vague about one's own opinions. Thus, if S employs a straightforward strategy which goes on record, and, having done so, has second thoughts about it, realizing that what he has said might be too strong, he then adds a hedge, as in the following example:

'It's really beautiful, in a way.' (Brown and Levinson 1978: 121)

Or S utters an FTA and combines it with a hedge so that any implied criticism, complaint, or whatever the FTA may be, will get blurred. Furthermore, such hedges are often used to signal or mark a metaphor as in Brown and Levinson's example:

'That knife sort of "chews" bread.' (1978: 122)

This 'marking' is possible because the hedge shares something with the metaphor; it is 'open' and its calculated vagueness opens the way for a perception of the metaphor which in turn has its *raison d'être* in that it may evoke more than one meaning. As I will have to return to a discussion of hedges when I come to examine negative politeness, I break off here and turn to the extremely intriguing strategy which centres on the 'common ground' that S and H may share.

Strategy 7: Presuppose/raise/assert common ground

The practice of strategy 7 is basic to all societies in which face-to-face relationships predominate. One could say that in such societies common ground is already given and cannot, therefore, be 'asserted'. Yet a closer look at Hamar shows us that this is not so. Even in a society such as Hamar, people are differentiated enough to make certain realizations of strategy 7 possible. The most important of them is what Brown and Levinson have called the 'point-of-view operation'. The underlying principle of this operation has been analysed by Fillmore (1971) who has shown how 'sentences are anchored to certain aspects of their contexts of utterance, including the role of participants in the speech event and their spatio-temporal and social location' (Brown and Levinson 1978: 123). Thus, sentences are normally anchored in such a way that 'the speaker is the central person, the time of speaking . . . is the central time, and the place where the speaker is at coding time is the central place' (1978: 123).

When the speaker switches away from the normal anchorage, Brown and Levinson call this a 'point-of-view operation'. This operation may have a positive-politeness function by reducing the distance between S's and H's points of view. Examples of this kind are, personal-centre switch (S speaks as if H were S), time switch (the switch from past to present, for example) and place switch (like the switch from the past to the present, so the switch from distal to proximal demonstratives conveys increased involvement). In Hamar a combination of personal-centre switch and place switch is very common and has the form of a synecdoche, where a part switches to become the whole. At public speeches, for example, a speaker will get up and exclaim,

> 'I have been wounded, I have been killed, let me take my spear and avenge myself!'

Of course, the speaker himself is well and alive, otherwise he would not be speaking. He is also probably so old that he will not himself fight physically any more. What he says must therefore be understood figuratively. The figure is clearly an application of strategy 7: it aims at emphatically including S and H in the same social domain. The domain has been hurt (i.e. some other Hamar in another place has been hurt and hence S himself has been hurt). This synecdochical identification of S with his social domain works on many levels of social segmentation and when it comes to territorial affiliation a man (or woman) may well say,

'You, Kadja [a territorial segment] are well fed, but I, Angude [a territorial segment] am hungry. Give me something to eat.'

One of the most important situations in which this synecdochical switch may be employed is the frequent lamentation that happens in Hamar and which I have interpreted as an 'attempt to absolve oneself of responsibility for what is happening and *yet to retain a recognizable* claim on the control of public affairs' (Lydall and Strecker 1979a: 254). By saying, 'I have been wounded, I have been killed' when others not he himself have been hurt, the speaker indicates his concern for the others. But in so far as he himself was not hurt he must have been away and possibly excluded in political and economic terms from those who were hurt and therefore cannot be held responsible for the misfortune that befell them. The implicit reproach is left to be worked out by those who listen to the lamentation, that is, the reproach which says, 'Had you only included me more in your life and given me a say in your decisions then you would be well now.' An unmistakable element of indirect message construction (i.e. symbolization) is involved here: the personal-centre switch causes, to paraphrase Sperber, a conceptual representation which is somehow 'defective' (i.e. a synecdoche) and hence 'evocative' or, in the terminology of Grice, the personal-centre switch 'forces an implicature' which raises an awareness of the concomitant togetherness and separateness of S and H, it draws attention to the fact that (and now we have reached Brown and Levinson's terminology) H and S are separate and yet share common ground.

Strategy 8: Joke

In a hidden yet powerful way the use of jokes is a tool to express and shape intimacy. As Brown and Levinson point out, 'Since jokes are based on mutual shared background knowledge and values, jokes may be used to stress that shared background or those shared values' (1978: 129). Similarly, Freud, the great theoretician of the joke, has drawn attention to the fact that 'a joke would lose all its efficiency if the path back from the allusion to the genuine thing could not be followed *easily*' (my emphasis; Freud 1978: 208). The more immediate and appropriate the response to a joke is, the greater the intimacy. On the other hand extreme embarrassment (often exploited in comedy) may be caused by the wrong joke at the wrong time in the wrong place, or an insult may be implied in the refusal to accept someone's joke. Jokes may, therefore, be risky and, according to Brown and Levinson's theory, one would expect them to be employed only in situations of low FTA danger. Except, that is, when this expectation again is dialectically exploited and the jokes are used indirectly to symbolize a wide social distance rather than closeness.

As far as I am aware, this complicated use of strategy 8 does not exist in Hamar. Rather, the joke is used in its more straightforward form to 'decrease social distance' in the way Brown and Levinson's theory predicts. The situations in which I personally experienced this use of jokes in Hamar were on the occasions immediately after my 'age-mates' had brought home their new wives. Choke and Bali (for a portrait of these two friends see Lydall and Strecker 1979a: chapter 7) both invited me shortly after bringing home their wives, to visit them at their homes. I had already been living a long time in Hamar by then and had witnessed the behavioural patterns which are observed on such occasions, yet I was struck again each time by the complex nature of what happened. Thus, when I visited Choke after he had brought home his young wife, the following drama ensued:

> I arrived in the evening at Choke's homestead and settled down on my stool somewhat awkwardly several paces away from the entrance to the house. My presence was noticed, Choke was called, and after he had arrived we kept sitting together talking quietly and intimately, but not much. Meanwhile a girlish-looking young woman (Choke's new wife) began to sweep the ground in front of the house and soon after she had spread out cow hides there, we settled down and rested. Then, perhaps an hour later, the coffee was ready and we entered the house. There were just the three of us, Choke, his young wife and myself. Now, like all newly married couples, Choke and his wife hardly looked at each other. Choke put on a very haughty attitude towards his wife and she a very humble and subdued attitude towards him. After I had been given my bowl of coffee, Choke's wife sat for literally minutes extending a bowl of steaming coffee to Choke. Being perfectly aware of the fact that she was holding out the bowl for him, he nevertheless kept talking to me and disregarded her until

eventually without turning his head he extended his right hand towards her and she placed the bowl into it. Thus there was a deep hierarchical cleavage between Choke and his wife and a close egalitarian intimacy between Choke and myself. How, in the light of this fact, was I then to view the relationship between myself and Choke's wife? Intuitively I was avoiding her because of my conflicting feelings (I would have liked to say to Choke: 'Come on, stop playing the tough guy', but this would have offended him and I would have risked spoiling his relationship with the new wife which depended partly on a good and close *misso* [hunting-friend] relationship between Choke and myself). But this avoidance was the wrong strategy and Choke reminded me soon of the fact that several of the things which are not allowed between a husband and his wife (especially when the latter is new) are wanted and welcome between a wife and her husband's friend. Seeing my inhibition, Choke said: 'You two are *misso* in the same way as you and I are *misso*; joke with her, tease her and demand that she feeds you well and gives you presents.' So I let go my inhibitions and the young woman and I talked freely with each other and even laughed and joked. As we did this, I realized how the isolation into which Choke's behaviour had pushed the young wife was now counteracted by our joking and the intimacy it brings forth. Both Choke's behaviour towards his wife and her behaviour towards me were, of course, prescribed by custom. None of us could do away with these prescriptions, the only thing we could do was to handle them 'tactfully' which meant in practice that Choke tried not to humiliate his wife too much and that his wife, in turn, did not antagonize him by overdoing the licence she had towards me, her *misso*. To end this account, let me mention that Choke's wife has had her first child by now, a daughter whom Choke has called Ziini (mosquito) which, if the initial consonant is pronounced slightly slurred, sounds like 'Jeannie', that is the endearing form for 'Jean' under which Jean Lydall is known in Hamar when she is not referred to or addressed as Theoinda (mother of Theo). In a purely Hamar context the name becomes Ziini and in conjunction with the foreign guests it becomes Jeannie. No doubt, this is another example of Choke's use of positive-politeness strategies.

Strategies 9–14: Convey that S and H are co-operators

To simplify the exposition I treat strategies 9–14 together. They all derive, as Brown and Levinson put it, 'from the want to convey that the speaker and the addressee are co-operatively involved in the relevant activity. If S and H are co-operating, then they share goals in some domain, and thus to convey that they are co-operators can serve to redress H's positive-face want' (1978: 130). Note that Brown and Levinson use the word 'convey' here and not 'say'. What they mean is that in the strategies, as in the preceding ones, the content of the message is not bluntly stated but indicated. This is what makes the message 'polite' and, as I am trying to point out, also symbolic. The strategies, as listed in Figure 4 above, are:

Strategy 9: Assert or presuppose S's knowledge of and concern for H's wants.
Strategy 10: Offer, promise.
Strategy 11: Be optimistic.
Strategy 12: Include both S and H in the activity.
Strategy 13: Give (or ask for) reasons.
Strategy 14: Assume or assert reciprocity

The strategies all share the interesting aspect that they are based on an implicit presumptuousness which Brown and Levinson aptly characterize as a point-of-view flip in which S daringly assumes that 'H wants S's wants for S (or for S and H) and will help him to obtain them' (1978: 131).

From what I have said about the 'take' character of Hamar society, one would expect that strategies 9–14 abound in Hamar, and indeed they do. Remember the Hamar guest who comes to visit. Brown and Levinson mention an example of strategy 11 which could well have come from our Hamar guest if one substitutes 'tobacco' for cookie and drops the 'thanks':

'I'll just help myself to a cookie then – thanks!'

(1978: 131)

Also very common in Hamar are variations of the statement Brown and Levinson give for strategy 12:

'Let's have a cookie then (i.e. *me*).' (1978: 132)

Furthermore, the use of rhetorical questions, which may sometimes be considered an application of strategy 13, is all-pervasive in Hamar. Brown and Levinson analyze the power of rhetorical questions as part of the off-record strategy, but it is also a tool of positive politeness. This point is implied in Brown and Levinson's reasoning when they write: 'By including H ... in his practical reasoning, and assuming reflexivity (H wants S's wants), H is thereby led to see the reasonableness of S's FTA (or so S hopes)' (1978: 133). Thus, S makes 'indirect suggestions which demand rather than give reasons' (1978: 133), yet at the same time he doesn't want to hear the reasons, as in sentences like:

'Why not lend me your cottage for the weekend?'

(1978: 133)

A sentence which Brown and Levinson quote from Tzeltal could well have been pronounced in Hamar:

'Why didn't you watch, as you burned your field?' (Complaining that the fire encroached on S's field)

(1978: 134)

Much of what can be said about the strategies which convey that S and H are co-operators has either aleady been touched upon when dealing with 'sharing of common ground', etc., or will be topical when I discuss the negative-politeness strategies below. I break off here, therefore, and conclude my examination of positive-politeness strategies with a short word about the giving of gifts.

Strategy 15: Give gifts to H (goods, sympathy, understanding, co-operation)

Brown and Levinson introduce the giving of tangible gifts as an on-record example of showing interest that one is concerned with alter's face. But can the giving of gifts really be regarded as on record? Indeed the material transaction undeniably takes place and in this sense is on record, but what it 'says' is far from definite and in this sense the material transaction is off record. This is precisely what gives the gift its power. Something has definitely been transmitted but what it means has not been spelt out. Thus the gift has a multiplex nature which may express intimacy (positive politeness), social distance (negative politeness) and a whole variety of things which are all communicated indirectly.

Since the giving of gifts is not a linguistic realization of an FTA strategy, I am not concerned with it here.

3.2.3 SUPER-STRATEGY III: NEGATIVE POLITENESS

While positive politeness is a mechanism to achieve intimacy or at least to reduce social distance, negative politeness is the opposite: a tool to increase or at least to keep the social distance between S and H. Brown and Levinson examine negative politeness predominantly as on-record strategies, but much of the face redress which negative politeness strategies aim at is achieved by indirect means. So we have both on-record and off-record aspects to negative politeness. Both contribute to the same goal, to helping S communicate to H that S does not want to impede H's freedom in any way, that S has 'respect' for H and is reluctant to offend H's negative-face wants. This is what negative politeness is all about. Interestingly, Brown and Levinson mention, as a prototype of negative politeness, the rituals of avoidance which Durkheim has called 'negative rites' (1978: 124). However, they never return to the implicit suggestion that there may exist a relationship between politeness phenomena and ritual, a relation which, I think, does exist, and which has in part prompted me to embark on this essay.

Strategy 1: Be conventionally indirect

The strategy encodes a clash of wants. The speaker is faced 'with opposing tensions: the desire to give H an "out" by being indirect, and the desire to go on record' (1978: 137). That is, S does not want to look as if he is trying to coerce H nor does he want to impose on H by 'making him work' at tackling an obscure (i.e. indirect, off-record) statement. As a solution he comes up with the compromise of conventional indirectness: 'In this way the utterance goes on record, and the speaker indicates his desire to have gone off record (to have conveyed the same thing indirectly)' (1978: 137). Typically, much verbal effort is spent in constructing such messages and they all contain an element of symbolization in so far as the 'face-preserving work' is conspicuously elaborate, to the point even of being clumsy.

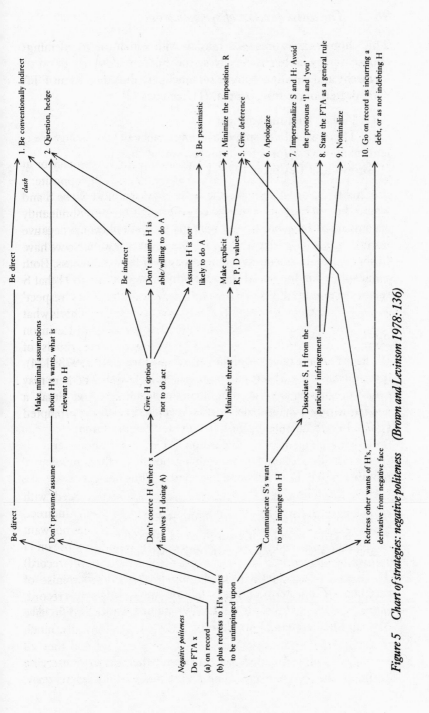

Figure 5   Chart of strategies: negative politeness   (Brown and Levinson 1978: 136)

This clumsiness expresses a burden with which the interlocutors choose to encumber themselves, the burden of social distance, hierarchy and isolation. Simple sentences are thus transformed into complicated ones: for example, (1) becomes (2):

(1) Please, lend me your car.
(2) There wouldn't I suppose be any chance of your being able to lend me your car for a few minutes, would there?
(Brown and Levinson 1978: 147)

Preferably, in order to make the latter message more complete, it would be uttered in a confused and slightly excited manner, accompanied by a blush, and perhaps by a stumble which would mirror the social ladder from which the speaker is afraid to tumble. In short, the laboriousness of the structure of the sentence becomes a metaphor for the social distance which the speaker is trying to retain despite his FTA.

Strategy 2: Question, hedge

We have here the opposite of the seventh positive-politeness strategy (presuppose/raise/assert common ground). The strategy carefully avoids presuming anything other than the negative-face wants of H, and Brown and Levinson define it as 'keeping ritual distance from H' (1978: 149). The wording indicates already that the authors sense an underlying element of symbolization. They do not, however, fully spell it out. The reason for the symbolization lies in the compounded motivation to neither presume nor coerce. Thus one gets sentences such as the following:

'I am pretty sure you are not quite right.'
(i.e. S criticizes H being sure that H is wrong;
example adapted from Brown and Levinson 1978: 150)

To give a more topical example which also provides a telling variation of the term 'hedge', let me quote an article in the *International Herald Tribune* (6.11.1979) entitled 'Panel Says Nuclear Mishap Deliberately Downplayed':

'No', the official added, 'as I just said, there appears to be no significant core damage.' The report said that, by inserting the

'weasel word significant' the official left the impression there had
been no damage to the core even though he earlier had provided
contrary information to Pennsylvania Lt. Governor William
Scranton.

One could find further metaphors and speak, for example, of
chameleon words, but what is it that makes these weasel words,
chameleon words or hedges such ideal tools for deception?

According to Brown and Levinson, they do their job by modifying
'the degree of membership of a predicate or noun phrase in a set'.
The weasel words make sure that this membership is '*partial*, or true
only in certain respects, or that it is *more* true and complete than
perhaps might be expected' (1978: 150). But, and this is the crux of
the matter, the weasel words do not specify the extent to which
something is 'true only in certain respects' nor the degree to which
something is complete or incomplete. Thus, the decisive aspect of
the message depends on some tacit knowledge which S and H share
or, for that matter, do not share. As the example of the official who
employed the word 'significant' shows, the use of a weasel word
(hedge) may be based precisely on the calculation of a disjuncture
between the knowledge of S and H. In such a case S uses the weasel
word because he knows that H cannot possibly give a precise
meaning to it. And even more importantly, even if H should, after all,
work out what is implied, or rather what is deliberately not being said
(i.e. hidden), he still cannot pin S down. S has made himself
immune, he cannot be held to task for having said what H may
impute him to have meant. Thus weasel words make the speaker safe
and at the same time they nurture the process which Sperber has
described as 'evocation'. In the field of politeness their main task
is, as I understand Brown and Levinson, to avoid commitment, and
disarm interactional threats (1978: 151). As these formulations
describe very well how symbolization is a socially motivated process
let me quote the authors here in full:

To ask someone to do something is to presuppose that they can
and are willing to do it, and have not already done it; to promise to
do something is to admit that one hasn't already done it, to assume
that the addressee wants it done and would prefer you to do it –
and so on ... Consequently, to hedge these assumptions – that is,

to avoid commitment to them – is a primary and fundamental method of disarming routine interactional threats ... In an exactly parallel way, conversational principles are the source of strong background assumptions about co-operation, informativeness, truthfulness, relevance, and clarity, which on many occasions need to be softened for reasons of face. (1978: 151).

I think Brown and Levinson could not have put the matter better if they had been speaking about symbolization. Symbolism, as I see it, is, among other things, a primary and fundamental method of disarming interactional threats. Not, however, just of 'routine' threats, but, as we will see later, of exceptional threats as well. It is at those points where threats are greatest that symbolism flourishes most richly.

Finally, it may be interesting to note that neither the method of hedging (strategy 2) nor the method of elaborate and burdensome 'face-preserving work' (strategy 1) seems to be frequently used in Hamar. This corroborates Brown and Levinson's finding that negative politeness, at least in its more emphatic forms, is related to systems which are pronouncedly hierarchical (having great D and P differentials), while the strategies of positive politeness are more characteristic of egalitarian societies and social groups. Yet, as we will soon see, other forms of negative politeness are by no means absent in Hamar.

Strategy 3: Be pessimistic

Again this strategy has its opposite among the strategies of positive politeness (see 'Be optimistic'). Its main aim is not to presume that H is willing to co-operate but rather to assume that he probably is not. Thus, S goes on record as giving H the option not to do the act which S is asking him to do. Brown and Levinson distinguish between several realizations of this strategy. They all have some of the 'burdensomeness' which we have already observed in strategies 1 and 2. An example given by the authors (1978: 179) reads:

$$\text{I don't} \begin{Bmatrix} \text{imagine} \\ \text{suppose} \end{Bmatrix} \text{there'd be any} \begin{Bmatrix} \text{chance} \\ \text{possibility} \\ \text{hope} \end{Bmatrix} \text{of you} \ldots$$

Our Hamar guest who demands presents from his host may put his words in a similar way – the only difference being that the sentence would not end with 'you' but rather with 'anyone'. That is, it would take the more general form of a lamentation such as I have already referred to above. Furthermore, the Hamar guest would not stick to one strategy alone but would rather move from one strategy to another, even to the extent of 'jumping' from negative to positive politeness and back again. I will deal with the question of the sequence of strategies below.

Strategy 4: Minimize the imposition, R_x

Although Brown and Levinson do not say so, minimization seems to work very much by way of off-record realizations and hedges (which, as we have seen, must also be considered as essentially off record). Here are two of their examples which indicate this (1978: 182):

(a) I *just* dropped by for a minute to ask if you ...
(b) Could I have a *taste* (c.i. slice) of that cake?

('c.i.' is Brown and Levinson's abbreviation for their technical expression 'conversationally implicates').

When S minimizes R_x he thereby indicates that the imposition should be regarded as small but preferably does not say so in such a way that he may be taken literally. To say so expressly would, indeed, be antithetical to any aim of politeness because it would reduce H's motivation to comply with the request. For example, it would be extremely rude to go on record by saying:

'I ask you this favour because to grant it to me does not mean any loss to you.'

Such a sentence could only be uttered in conjunction with other statements which counteract its negative effect.

The point which is perhaps most interesting about strategy 4 is the fact that the minimization of an imposition may be 'expensive' in social terms and may involve some unpleasant 'concessions' on S's part. That is, when S delicately indicates to H that, if H feels inclined to do so, he could pretend that the imposition is really as small as S has made it out to be, then S implicitly humbles himself. He acknowledges H's superior social power, or rather he allows the situation to turn into one in which H loses materially but gains socially. In other words a quiet complicity ensues in which S offers some of his P to gain R and where H allows S to devalue R in order to increase his own P value, that is his P value relative to S. All this is formulated in terms that are off record and yet S and H know exactly what is at issue.

The next strategy demonstrates another variation of the logic of minimization.

Strategy 5: Give deference

In a similar way but to a greater extent than the preceding strategies, this one manipulates values of social distance and social power. The speaker conveys that in his perception H has a high P value and, therefore, must not feel threatened by any of S's FTAs. S simply does not have the means to coerce H. The only thing he can do is to make the best of his weakness and use it to induce H to respond to the FTA favourably. The same logic operates as in the minimization of an imposition described above. That is, S gets what he wants by identifying with the aggressor, by humbling himself and selling his possible claim to a P value equal to that of H or by assuring H of the status quo.

Note that this process is the reverse of what happens in positive politeness where S raises H (for example, by flattery as discussed above). In negative politeness S lowers himself. This is linguistically partly encoded in the awkward and clumsy message construction which I have described above. Brown and Levinson (1978: 184) give a fine specimen of such 'humiliative' forms: An Urdu speaking Delhi Muslim is said to have uttered:

'Please bring your ennobling presence to the hut of this dustlike person sometime.'

One of the most striking and most universal forms of the deference strategy is the use of honorifics, such as the English 'Sir'. Brown and Levinson develop an interesting extension of the theory of honorifics, not only distinguishing between S (speaker) and H (addressee) but also taking into account the setting, the bystander and the referent. Thus they show how S can indicate respect for H 'by using . . . referent honorifics about something associated with H'.

What is meant by this becomes clear when one looks at the following examples:

(1) We look forward very much to $\left\{ \begin{array}{c} \text{dining} \\ \text{eating} \end{array} \right\}$ with you.

(2) The library wishes to extend its thanks for your careful selection of

$\left\{ \begin{array}{c} \text{volumes} \\ \text{books} \end{array} \right\}$ from your uncle $\left\{ \begin{array}{c} \text{Dr Snugg's} \\ \text{Snugg's} \end{array} \right\}$ bequest.

Brown and Levinson
(1978: 186)

When a message is constructed in such a way that an alternative word for one of those used (e.g. 'dining' for 'eating') can be perceived, then we have a process which Brown and Levinson call a 'calculation by triangulation'. They illustrate this process by the diagram shown in Figure 6.

Figure 6: Triangulation

At issue is the speaker-addressee relationship (S-H). This relationship may be indirectly expressed by referent honorifics. If H is closely associated with R, and S gives R a high value, then by doing so he also 'lifts' H. That is, he shows 'respect' towards H. On the other side, if he lowers R, then he also lowers H. Brown and Levinson give, as an example of the latter, S calling H's house a hovel, and by so doing indicating that the S-H relationship has a low value of respect. The opposite case to this would be when someone refers to someone else's house as a 'palace' and thus gives the relation between himself and the addressee a high value of respect.

Although the authors deal with this very interesting indirect form under the heading of 'negative politeness', its off-record, and hence symbolic, character is indisputable. In fact, whenever a referent honorific is felt as such, and thereby becomes a true tool of politeness, something of an implicature is involved. 'Why does he say "dine"?' H asks himself. 'Aha, he is honouring me (or us) and the situation.' For referent honorifics to work, an alternative must always be available. This comes out most clearly in one field where the technique is most pervasively employed: irony. In irony the speaker, knowing that he should employ a referent honorific to imply high respect value, uses the opposite, a low one, or vice versa. Here is an example of an imaginary tramp saying to another:

Where shall we dine, mate, here on the curb or on that barrel over there?
(Both have, let's say, a piece of bread to share.)

Let us return to the use of the direct application of honorifics. It is indeed surprising how universal they are and how they unfailingly point out where in the social structure FTA danger is greatest. As this is, once again, an opportunity to demonstrate how useful Brown and Levinson's theory is as a tool for the description of the quality of social relationships, let me show what it reveals in Hamar.

Although they otherwise make little use of deference strategies, the Hamar have a single honorific. The term is *geshoa.* Jean Lydall and I have translated *geshoa* as 'master'. The stem *gesh* is found in the adjective 'old' and the verb 'to herd, look after, bring up'; and likewise a *geshoa* is someone who is old and is bringing up others. He has authority over others. The prototype of 'master' is the hereditary ritual leader or 'chief' called *bitta* (there are two of them). He is the 'oldest' or the 'foremost'. Hamar *bitta* means 'first' or 'foremost'. When people come to him and ask to perform rituals they address him, accordingly, as 'master':

A young female goat is collected from Rach and a male goat is collected from Ba Balambala. Both goats are brought with the gourd to the *bitta.*
'May the "*master*" [my emphasis] come forth from the house, may he come out. The gourd has come. Sweep the gateway.'
(Lydall and Strecker 1979b: 13)

The same deference which is shown to the *bitta* on a public level, is afforded to the head of the homestead in his own social domain. Every head of a homestead in Hamar is a kind of miniature *bitta* and as such he may be referred to or addressed as *geshoa.* Women refer to their husbands respectfully as *geshoa,* otherwise they call them their male, *angi*. Also, very importantly, ancestors are typically referred to and addressed in rituals as 'master':

> Now when the dead man performs these rituals and the sheep-skin which has been hung over the doorway of his house is pulled up, he gets well and the dancing stops.
> 'Today the *"master"* [my emphasis] is well.' (1979b: 45)

> '*Eh!* All right, we will leave the master alone. We won't bury him yet ...'

> 'Pull the master out of the house, make him recover.' (1979b: 47)

We have, then, one single honorific in Hamar and, significantly, it is employed in situations of greatest FTA danger (a curse by the *bitta* kills you; to offend the ancestors makes you ill). Or, to express the same in structural terms: the honorific is associated with the two most crucial hierarchical cleavages within Hamar society, the cleavages between young and old and male and female. The honorific term '*geshoa*' serves as a 'distancing device' which creates and reinforces not just high D values but also, and more importantly, unequal P values. By way of conclusion Figure 7 sums up the argument.

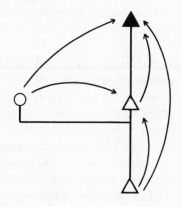

Figure 7   Use of geshoa as honorific

Strategy 6: Apologize

The strategy is by its very nature so heavily dependent on clear on-record realizations that the potential for indirect, hidden and symbolic communication is very limited. Therefore, I omit its discussion here altogether to return to it later when I examine ritual forms of face-redress. The ritual of reconciliation, in Hamar called *kash*, is an example of such indirect face-redress (see Lydall and Strecker 1979a: 94–5, 195–7).

Strategy 7: Impersonalize S and H

The manifold realizations of this strategy are so subtle and make such effective use of hidden implications, that is, they contain so many symbolic elements, that I would be inclined to count many of them as off-record strategies were it not for the fact that by doing so the aspect of 'attention to negative face-wants' would be in danger of getting lost. Why, when we use imperatives, do we say,

'Take that out!'

rather than

'You take that out!'?

A normal speaker would never think that he is using a strategy here. And yet he is. He is reducing the face-threatening act by omitting the addressee. As Brown and Levinson put it: 'One way of indicating that S doesn't want to impinge on H is to phrase the FTA as if the agent were other than S, or at least possibly not S or not S alone, and the addressee were other than H, or only inclusive of H. This results in a variety of ways of avoiding the pronouns "I" and "you"' (1978: 195). The authors examine several linguistic realizations in which this aim is achieved (in performatives, imperatives, impersonal verbs, etc.). To my view, the impersonalization of S and H is a form of 'point-of-view operation'. The logic of this operation has already been discussed above in connection with the positive-politeness strategy of 'presuppose/raise/assert common ground' so I need not go into details here again. Let me only repeat that the point-of-view operation involves an exploitation of the deictic anchorage which encodes the special point of reference of the place and time of utterance. Now, just as all point-of-view operations may be used to 'nail' H down and assert common ground between S and H (which in turn forces H to comply to a demand, listen to a criticism, etc.; that is, accept an FTA) so, inversely, the point-of-view operation may be a means to not 'nail' H down. It may give him, as Brown and Levinson put it, an 'out'. This is precisely what happens when S impersonalizes himself and/or H.

Consider the following examples:

(1) It is expected that such-and-such a thing will be done.
(2) One expects that such-and-such a thing will be done.
(3) We expect that such-and-such a thing will be done.

Contrast these examples with the next one:

(4) I expect you to do such-and-such a thing.

The utterances (1), (2) and (3) contain a calculated vagueness. The speaker has either switched the deictic anchorage away from himself or he has let the anchorage come, so to say, adrift. Deictically the utterance 'One expects ...' is afloat. One does not, strictly speaking, know any more where one is and who is doing the FTA to whom. Who are the 'it', 'one' and 'we' of (1), (2) and (3)? They are all the allies, all the customs and moral rules that count in S's society and implicitly support his cause.

At the back of any linguistic realization impersonalizing S and H there lie two things: firstly the desire not to single out literally either the addressee or the speaker and thus to provide S with an 'out' if the FTA is found unacceptable and, secondly, the hidden threat that although S may be inferior to H and comparatively weak, he nevertheless has the (hidden and unspecified) support of an intangible collective, the 'society', behind him. My observations in Hamar confirm this combination of 'defence and attack' in impersonalization. The pluralization of the 'you' and 'I' pronouns (which, by the way, is just as universal as the use of honorifics which I have discussed as a realization of the deference strategy above) is a case in point. It is used in Hamar as follows.

The usage is asymmetrical. While the plural 'I' occurs, the plural 'you' is not used as a means of impersonalization. This goes well with the general asymmetry which I have already stressed above. The Hamar guest does not bring gifts, as we have seen, but rather takes them away. He also does not flatter his host but rather flatters himself, etc. The same applies to his use of impersonalization. He generously substitutes a collective self ('we') for his individual self ('I') but he never grants alter ('you') the same benefit, that is the second-person plural pronoun 'you' (German *'Ihr'*). A man who speaks at a public meeting or on a ritual occasion, for example, will often speak of himself as *wossi* ('we') instead of *inta* ('I'). And then, when he wants to emphasize his importance (and the importance of the situation) even further, he may speak of himself as *wossil*, linking an 'L' to the last syllable which gives the pronoun an added meaning of authority and exclusiveness. The emphatic suffix 'L' provides four alternative ways for ego to present himself: 'inta' first-person singular pronoun); 'intal' (emphatic for 'inta'); 'wossi' first-person plural pronoun) and 'wossil' (emphatic 'wossi'). The pluralization makes visible the defence involved and the suffix 'L' reveals the attack but, as I have said above, if the suffix 'L' is dropped the attack does not disappear altogether, it only vanishes from the surface.

Strategy 8: State the FTA as a general rule

Brown and Levinson introduce this strategy with the following words:

> One way of dissociating S and H from the particular imposition in the FTA, and hence a way of communicating that S doesn't want to impinge but is merely forced to by circumstances, is to state the FTA as an instance of some general social rule, regulation, or obligation. (1978: 211)

We have here a development from the preceding strategies. What is being stressed is the support of society and tradition to back up an FTA. The specific, individual and arbitrary FTA is turned into a general, socially approved and necessary act.

While doing fieldwork in Hamar I made some observations which, I think, throw an interesting light on the genesis of strategy 8. These observations relate to three different events: an argument about a cow; a flirtation between a young man and an elderly woman; and a night at the Hamar cattle camps. As I witnessed these events I progressively came to understand the logic of 'stating the FTA as a general rule' which, as we will see, involves a switch not only from personal to collective but also from present to historical authority.

Case 1: The argument about a cow

This morning there is an argument between Haila ... and Kalle. Haila should have cleared up an old argument today by bringing a young sheep to Kalle for which the latter would have given Haila a cow that he owed him. The sheep would have signified that the cow was to be Haila's indisputable property and that Kalle would have no right to any of its offspring. But Haila has not brought the sheep. Does he want to receive the cow as the sign of the establishment of a bond-friend relationship with Kalle? The men of Dambaiti who gather at Kalle's homestead urge him to act as if this were the case. I record the interminable argument and conclude that it furnishes yet another example of how ritual, language and social control are interwoven, being the stuff of day-to-day politics. Language protects a disputant, like a suit of armour. Anyone who wants something from someone else has to talk himself through a barrier of reasonable and argumentative men. If someone attacks wrongly he exposes himself and furnishes an opportunity for third parties to embark on long lectures and speeches. Kula the 'black', Alma and Banko, who are close friends and age-mates of Haila, have not come this morning. This seems to be significant; knowing Haila's weak position, perhaps they were not eager to speak against him. When Banko visits me later, I ask him why he did not come and he answers that someone came to see him about a debt. Yet not long afterwards Wadu joins me and lets the cat out of the bag. The trusty tape recorder records that, in actual fact, Banko advised Haila what to do this morning. But Haila did not accept Banko's advice, so Banko washed his hands of the affair. Banko says that Haila is often intractable and relates how he had recently offended Balle by taking some goats that Balle owed him, by force. In this connection, it is interesting to note that Balle was one of the principal critics of Haila. The importance of precedents is becoming increasingly clear to me. When someone is being criticized, the talk moves back and forth between general formulations of basic moral axioms and specific cases in the past which serve as examples. (Lydall and Strecker 1979a: 212–13)

Case 2: A flirt

Duka invites Choke for coffee early in the morning. This is typical of her: she likes to present her perfection to young men. In her playful way Ginonda does exactly the same, virtually flirting with Choke in a charming way. Choke says to her: 'I'll cut your field for you, if you pay me in the evening.' Ginonda laughs and answers: 'You mean the way the old woman paid that man in Ulde?' Choke joins her laughter; she does not have to say more, for she refers to a story which they both know well. Only I am left in the dark. This often happens and I get the impression that there are many such tales, almost mythical in nature, which summarize what one may want to say in a specific situation. Or are these stories more like precedents epitomizing fundamental human experiences? (1979a: 242–43)

Case 3: At the cattle camps

At night while Bali speaks to us sitting on our cow hides, more and more young men join us and listen with quiet intensity. I get the same feeling I had the other night when Banko stood silently before us. An audience materializes almost inaudibly, making the speaker feel that he is saying something which they value highly. And then slowly the members of the audience sitting in the darkness start to speak themselves. Their speeches are long and are listened to by the assembled company. They constantly invoke the 'old', the 'fathers', the 'older brothers' and refer to the 'precedents' of which I have talked above. There is a confidence and trust in the old and the established which has never seemed to me quite so marked before (although I realize now that it has always been there). I suddenly realize that here may lie one of the keys to understanding Hamar 'conservatism' and (paradoxically?) its 'anarchy'. The cattle camps play a big part in the socialization of the young men. Here, to a large extent, they are free from the strict domination of the elders. Here they have to make their own decisions, and these decisions are made on the basis of precedents, by referring to what the great men of the past would have done in such-and-such a situation. By invoking a precedent the speaker almost becomes the historical person himself, so by invoking historical authority they reject the present authority of others. One might argue that Hamar anarchy is a result of the fact that everybody rejects a living person's decision if it is based on purely individual and contemporary judgement. Outright individual cleverness and power are taboo and no one may openly aspire to them. Instead one must make a precedent of an incident in the historic past which will be acknowledged by others as offering the appropriate answer to a specific problem in the present. (1979a: 249–50)

I think the three cases speak for themselves and show the logic which lies behind the strategy of stating an FTA as a general rule. The strategy is perhaps especially important in egalitarian and non-literate societies where there are no centralized institutions of arbitration and adjudication and where most, if not all, social control is exercised in a seemingly free social field. In such societies ego is well advised to back up his FTAs with the power of tradition or, more precisely, with the power of the precedents which I found so important in the three cases quoted above. To refer to precedents dissociates ego and alter from the imposition in the FTA which, if it is linked to the individual actors themselves would be found unacceptable.

At the same time the precedent (or general rule) also lends more credibility to the imposition. It makes the particular imposition a part of an actual or potential chain of preceding impositions and their associated arguments in exactly the way demonstrated by Haila's case and the elders' argument about the cow. In most cases the elders do not have to be summoned and the problems get solved before they ever develop into open conflict. This is what strategy 8 is about: it offers, so to say, a prophylactic treatment which anticipates the possibility of conflicts and, therefore, does everything to prevent them.

Finally, the observations about precedents and their use in FTAs point to the fact that in strategy 8 an indirect, symbolic element may be involved. That is to say, the strategy may be used to do an FTA in an evasive way, 'to say something and say it not'.

Choke's and Ginonda's flirtation is a case in point. Why did Ginonda laugh when Choke said to her, 'I'll cut your field for you, if you pay me in the evening'? At first sight there seems nothing funny about the sentence. Not, that is, until one shares the knowledge that what Choke has said is in fact quite unusual. If someone helps someone else in the fields he is paid during the day, at noon, when the sun is hot and one cannot work for the time being. Food and drink, *hailano*, is given to him and it is less a payment than an expression of gratitude for the help one has received and is willing to return one day in kind. Now, by saying that he wants his *hailano* in the evening (used here, by the way, as a euphemism for 'night') Choke forces an implicature, that is an indirect interpretation of his sentence to mean: 'I'll cut your field for you if you let me sleep with you at night.' But, as will soon become evident, Choke is also implicitly quoting a precedent, some tacit knowledge that goes deeper than the facts concerning the *hailano*. This comes out when one looks at Ginonda's answer. 'You mean the way the old woman paid that man in Ulde,' she says. On first sight she seems to answer the FTA by softening it. She switches it away from herself and Choke to the 'old woman' and 'that man in Ulde'. But if one looks closer one realizes that she softens what has already been softened. Choke had already anticipated her reply, not just her 'literal' reply but her very switch. We therefore have a double creation of ambiguity within the field of one single precedent: firstly Choke formulates his invitation to sleep with Ginonda in such a way that he cannot strictly speaking be held to task for having made such an invitation and, secondly, Ginonda answers in such a way that she indicates that she has understood what Choke has meant but cannot be nailed down as having read a rude meaning into Choke's statement. In this way the precedent makes them both safe: for there are, after all, many old women and many men in Ulde and people tell many quite different stories about them.

Strategy 9: Nominalize

When a speaker employs the strategy of nominalization, he tries to switch attention away from the actor who is doing the FTA. Compare the following two examples:

(1) I am pleased to be able to inform you ...

(2) It is $\left\{ \begin{array}{l} \text{pleasing (to me)} \\ \text{pleasant} \\ \text{my pleasure} \end{array} \right\}$ to be able to inform you ...

(Brown and Levinson 1978: 213)

Reading the different sentences one realizes immediately that they become increasingly more formal. Brown and Levinson explain this as follows: 'Intuitively, the more nouny an expression, the more removed an actor is from doing or feeling or being something; instead of the predicate being something attributed to the actor, the actor becomes an attribute (e.g. adjective) of the action. As far as FTAs are concerned, with the progressive removal of the active 'doing' part of an expression, the less dangerous it seems to be – it is not *objects* that are dangerous, it is their trajectories' (1978: 213). We have then here, as in so many other strategies of positive and negative politeness, realizations that hide subtle off-record structures beneath their conventional on-record surface . If I understand rightly, nominalization hides a metonymy, that is 'the substitution of one "cause" (in Aristotle's sense of the word) for another: cause for effect (efficient for final cause), container for contained (formal for material), and such variants as instrument for agent, agent for act, etc.' (Sapir 1977: 19–20).

In Brown and Levinson's example the 'I am pleased' of (1) has been replaced by the 'It is my pleasure' of (2c). In this way attention gets shifted away from S who now focuses on 'pleasure' as if it was a real agent. In (1) it is I who am informing you. In (2c) 'pleasure' seems to have taken my place. One cause has been substituted for another.

Something analogous seems to happen when nominalization occurs where a noun is substituted for a verb or, as Brown and Levinson put it, 'instead of the predicate being something attributed to an actor, the actor becomes an attribute (e.g. adjective) of the action' (see quotation above). In this way the actor hides behind the action which acquires some kind of fatal necessity of its own, because its originator has vanished from the picture. This in turn gives rise to evocations like those provoked by the strategies of 'impersonalization' and 'stating the FTA as a general rule', which are powerful because they muster the anonymous support of society and its morality.

In Hamar nominalization abounds, especially in requests, criticisms, admonitions, etc.; that is, in situations involving an FTA.

Strategy 10: Go on record as incurring a debt, or as not indebting H

Brown and Levinson put special emphasis on the fact that this strategy goes on record in that the speaker is 'explicitly claiming his indebtedness to H, or ... disclaiming any indebtedness of H' (1978: 215). Yet, as my interest in the strategies concentrates on the element of symbolization involved, let me once again point out that even in this, the last of the on-record strategies, one can detect equivocality.

Here are two of Brown and Levinson's examples:

(1) I'd be eternally grateful if you would ...
(2) I'll never be able to repay you if ...
(1978: 215)

As one can see, the two statements go in one sense on record and in another sense off record. They go on record in that they state that S would be incurring a debt if H would do him the favour he has asked for. On the other side, the expressions go of record when it comes to the precise nature of the debt incurred. They use the rhetoric form of hyperbole which must not be understood literally but figuratively, and it is this figurative element in the request which makes it felt as being 'polite' rather than face threatening. To visualize just what is at issue, imagine someone who does not use any technique of indirectness and, sticking to the literal truth, says (to paraphrase the example given above):

'I would be grateful for five days if you would lend me your car for an hour.'

3.2.4 SUPER-STRATEGY IV: OFF-RECORD STRATEGIES

When looking at symbolization within the strategies of positive and negative politeness, I have already made constant use of the notion of 'going off record'. In fact, the notion has been crucial for me to show how there is a social need for symbolization. To go off record is one of the most pervasive strategies in social interaction whenever actors want to avoid harsh confrontation and the possibility of conflict, and when they want to persuade others, to influence them so that they do what they cannot be openly coerced to do. All this is done by means of indirect message construction.

In my view, off-record strategies should not be separated from positive-politeness and negative-politeness strategies as they have been by Brown and Levinson. What seems to me more promising is to see (as I have done so far) how positive and negative politeness go off record to achieve their respective aims of intimacy and social distance. The question of how far social distancing (exclusion) and how far social incorporation (inclusion) is achieved will therefore remain foremost in my mind as I now examine the off-record strategies which Brown and Levinson have distinguished. But before I do so, let me once again outline the logic of going off record.

The motive for going off record is, as we have seen, 'to say something and say it not'. Brown and Levinson put it as follows:

> A communicative act is done off record if it is done in such a way that it is not possible to attribute only one clear communicative intention to the act. In other words, the actor leaves himself an 'out' by providing himself with a number of defensible inter-pretations; he cannot be held to have committed himself to just one particular interpretation of his act. Thus if a speaker wants to do an FTA, but wants to avoid the responsibility for doing it, he can do it off record, and leave it up to the addressee to decide how to interpret it. (1978: 216)

Here, I think, it becomes obvious that off-recordness constitutes an integral part of symbolism. What Brown and Levinson say is that those 'defective conceptual representations' which Sperber has confined exclusively to the sphere of cognition (where they activate the memory) can do a specific job in social interaction: they allow S to say something indirectly which he must not say directly. Constructing the 'defective conceptual representations' deliberately in such a way that they force an implicature (in the Gricean sense) S leads H to ask himself what is meant and not what is said and thus embarks on an exploration of the implied, and possibly multiple, hidden meanings within the statement. All the off-record strategies are derived from a violation of the Gricean maxims. Brown and Levinson list the off-record strategies as in Figure 8 (1978: 219).

Strategies 1–3: Give hints, give association clues, presuppose

As can be seen from figure 8, the first three strategies derive from a violation of the relevance maxim. The speaker 'says something that is not explicitly relevant' and thus 'invites H to search for an interpretation of the possible relevance' (1978: 218). A hint may

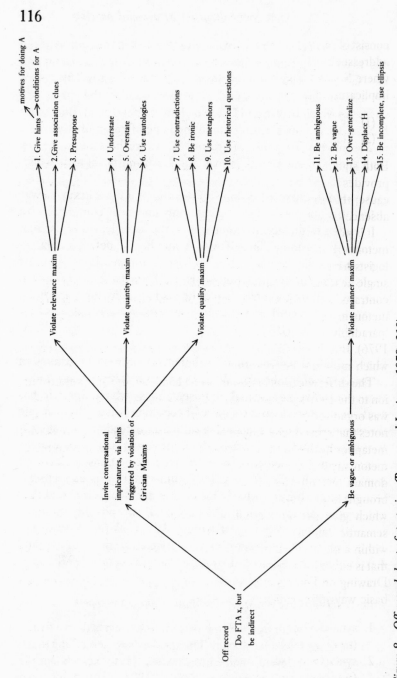

Figure 8 Off-record chart of strategies: (Brown and Levinson 1978: 219)

consist of raising the issue of something which the speaker wants the addressee to do, as in the examples which Brown and Levinson give where S states a motive or reason for doing act (1) and by way of implicature this indirectly leads H to do (1):

(1) 'It's cold in here.' (c.i. Shut the window.)
(2) 'This soup's a bit bland.' (c.i. Pass the salt.)

Both statements hide a metonymy and it is this metonymy which provides the path to the meaning. An effect is being substituted for a cause; that is, coldness for an open window and blandness for the absence of salt.

It is perhaps telling to bring to mind here the difference between metonymy and synecdoche. Following Jacobson (1956), anthropologists have tended to merge synecdoche and metonymy under the single heading of metonymy in order to provide for a category which contrasts well with the key notion of symbolism: metaphor. Thus, metonymy may stand for 'syntagmatic continuity' and metaphor for 'paradigmatic replacement' (see Lévi-Strauss 1963; 1966; Leach 1976). But there is a difference between metonymy and synecdoche which must not be forgotten.

The difference has been very well elucidated in Sapir's contribution to the 1970 symposium on 'The Social Use of Metaphor', which was organized by the American Anthropological Association. Sapir notes that synecdoche and metonymy are tropes which contrast with metaphor by the fact that the 'two terms involved in synecdoche and metonymy are drawn from what is felt to be the same semantic domain' while in metaphor 'two separate domains are necessarily brought into juxtaposition' (1977: 12–13). In synecdoche the terms which give rise to a trope are hierarchically arranged within a semantic domain. To create a synecdoche involves 'a replacement within a hierarchical classification. An initial term replaces another that is either more general or more particular than itself' (1977: 13). Drawing on Dubois *et al.* (1970), Sapir distinguishes between two basic ways of creating synecdoches:

1. synecdoches produced by an anatomical mode of classification (tree= branches, leaves, trunk, roots, etc.);
2. synecdoches produced by a taxonomical mode of classification (tree= poplar, oak, willow, birch, etc.).

Using both principles of production one arrives at four types of synecdoche each of which has different rhetorical qualities. The synecdoches where a type stands for a kind, or a part stands for a whole, are, according to Sapir, the ones which generate the largest variety of tropes. In the discussions which follow below I will try to adhere to Sapir's definition of synecdoche. But note that Sapir himself points out that 'the criteria that classify two terms *vis-à-vis* each other may be very precise as in biological classifications or quite loose and idiosyncratic' (1977: 13). In the latter case dispute may arise whether a particular trope is to be interpreted as a synecdoche or not.

While synecdoches have to do with replacements in hierarchical classifications, metonymic expressions have to do with replacements within causal pairs. Examples are:

1. cause for effect (efficient for final cause);
2. container for contained (formal for material);
3. instrument for agent;
4. agent for act, etc.

Sapir makes the interesting point that metonymy can be seen as the 'logical inverse of a metaphor' in that it emphasizes the entire domain shared by the two terms which constitute the trope. Thus, 'when we say Homer (agent) for *Iliad* (act) we extend the world of the poem (*Iliad*) not only to its author but also to his other work (the *Odyssey*) and his times' (1977: 21). This extension and direction of thought implicit both in metonymy and synecdoche turn them into effective tools for hinting at desired acts or affairs.

In Hamar the strategy of hinting abounds. But we do not only have the metonymic hint. There are also others, synecdochic hints, for example, and hints that work by means of metaphor. The second strategy which Brown and Levinson define as 'give association clues' may in fact be counted as one of them. The difference between 'hinting' and 'giving association clues' lies in the fact that while the first exploits a causal connection, the latter relies on a relationship of association between the topic of an utterance and the act which is required of the addressee.

The association may be quite inexplicable but it must have, in terms of S and H's knowledge and/or experience, a regular occurrence. This regularity alone provides the key for a decoding of the statement. Brown and Levinson give the following example:

'Oh God, I've got a headache again.' (1978: 220)

This utterance, they say, 'may be used to convey a request to borrow H's swimming costume, *if* S and H mutually know that they both have an association between S having a headache and S wanting to borrow H's swimsuit in order to swim off his headache' (1978: 220). The example stands half-way between a true metonymic hint and a synecdochic hint. It resembles a metonymy in that it states 'motives or reasons for doing A' and it resembles a synecdoche in that the causal relationship between the headache and the need for a swimsuit is rather obscure, both events simply occurring together. The subsequent example (1978: 221), however, is much more of a synecdoche:

'My house isn't very far away ... [intervening material] ... There's the path that leads to my house.' (c.i. Please visit me.)

Here the speaker is pointing to a spatial configuration of living space where one part (the path) is related to another (the house), and to enter the path is in some way like entering the door (part) of the house (whole). Examples like the above, which, incidentally, comes from Madagascar are frequent in Hamar and probably in all social groups. I think this is because to be a host is to gain honour and prestige. So to invite someone, one is asking to be honoured and given prestige. This is true even though the guest is treated as if he/she were the honourable one. One does not hear people say 'What a wonderful guest!' but rather 'What a wonderful host!' One's reputation improves by being a good host, not by being a good guest. This is why the one who invites lessens the face threat of the invitation by using hints which allow both parties an 'out' if one of them does not wish to accept the invitation. In Hamar most invitations are done indirectly in this way, as in the example that occurs at the end of *Conversations in Dambaiti* where a neighbour invites my friend Baldambe and me by saying:

'There is some more coffee in my house.' (Strecker 1979a: 206)

Now, what has happened in this and in Brown and Levinson's example is that, in truly synecdochic fashion, the speaker has replaced one term by another within the same domain (in contrast to metaphoric juxtaposition which makes use of separate domains) and by doing so has drawn attention to the association between the two terms. The listener (H) is led to think about the association between himself and the coffee (in the example from Hamar) or the path and the house of S (in the example from Madagascar), and he comes to the logical conclusion that he is invited to visit S. Now, if he is inclined to follow the invitation, he answers with an offer to come which, compared to the risk of S who made the invitation in the first place, constitutes a mild FTA. If, on the other hand, he does not want to accept the invitation, he can simply refuse to acknowledge or even to make the mental effort of working out the implicature. The latter point is crucial as it shows that all hints embody some degree of positive politeness. They imply that S and H are, to a certain extent co-operators (see the positive-politeness strategies 9–14 above). Indeed, the very willingness to recognize and tackle an implicature is an expression of goodwill and readiness for co-operation. And, inversely, the lack of willingness to recognize and tackle an implicature is an expression of social distance and antagonism.

To substantiate this point and in order to throw light on the working of hints (be they metonymic, synecdochic or metaphoric) in Hamar, let me quote my observations here at length. Note that they were made and written down long before I began to think about the argument which is the subject of this essay.

The observations centre on *assaue* which is one of the many terms which the Hamar employ to characterize the different ways in which people may converse with one another.

The term *assaue* is hard to translate. The German term *Besprechung* comes closer to it than the English term 'discussion', because the *assaue* has more a practical than an intellectual element. In Hamar, where hardly any social relationship can be axiomatically trusted, the *assaue* has an important interpersonal control function and people meet constantly to conduct *assaue*. If nobody else is present, an *assaue* may be held next to the coffee pot, but usually the men who want to talk business take their stools and dissociate themselves from unwanted listeners by settling down in the shade of a tree outside the settlement. During the first phases of my fieldwork, I had been observing such *assaue* situations only from a distance, and the secretive air which surrounded them and the low voices of the speakers had created the feeling that something special, almost asocial, was going on.

When later I intruded on the *assaue* situations, I was surprised to find hardly any change in the style of speaking.

All the *assaue* which I witnessed had almost the same tenor and the same social distance as have the semi-public conversations around the coffee pot. I had expected that certain forms of etiquette would have been dropped and that there would have been a loosening of talk and a tendency to be more outspoken. Nothing like this took place – if anything, the speaking was rather more guarded than usual. After some reflection this certainly made sense to me, for in the business discussion and the political plotting that goes on in an *assaue* each participant faces not only the promise of economic and political gain, but also the risk of exposing himself and making himself vulnerable. One feature especially brings out this precariousness of the *assaue* situation: the use of indirect talk and of metaphors to test whether your partner is basically in tune with your own personal interests or not.

Let me explain what happens in Hamar by means of western examples. Assume that X is a manufacturer of bathing clothes and Y the owner of a chain of shops selling such clothing. Now, X wants to sell his goods to Y, but he doesn't want to make an offer at a time when Y is not interested. So he tests him by indirect talk: 'Fine weather today.' If Y answers with a frown and a 'Much too cold', X doesn't rate his chances for selling bathing clothes today very high. If Y, however, answers: 'Yes, very fine indeed', X will push his test another step forward by saying: 'Well, there has been a long-term prediction that this summer will be fine, what do you think of this?'. If Y answers positively, again X knows that his chances for selling his goods are high, and he now enters his business discussion proper.

While the indirect talk must be familiar to the western salesman, I wonder what he might think of the Hamar use of 'far-out' metaphors? Imagine two secondhand car dealers who agreed with one another to help each other by swapping cars whenever they needed. Imagine also that there is a sudden increase in the demand for the Citroen DS and that X owns a number of them while Y owns none. So Y comes to X intending to swap a Mercedes for a Citroen DS. But he does not know whether his friend still feels loyal to their initial agreement to help each other out. He also does not want to force the matter. He, therefore, casually asks him: 'Do you still have a camel in your stable?' The metaphor 'camel' would refer to the Citroen DS which, having pneumatic suspension, always lifts itself slowly (just like a camel) when you start it. Now, the implicit psychological theory for using such 'far-out' metaphors would be that a sympathetic listener would understand the metaphor quickly, while an unsympathetic one would unconsciouly block his perception and would just look perplexed. If his partner gives him such a non-understanding look, Y would say: 'Drop it, pal' and move to another subject.

This is exactly what happens in Hamar. Clearly such psychological testing can work only in close face-to-face groups in which the partners not only know each other's mental capacities, but also share a common stock of idiosyncratic vocabulary, images and concepts. (Strecker 1976: 591–2).

My independent observations correspond surprisingly closely to Brown and Levinson's theory, although I reached the same conclusions as they from an opposite direction. While Brown and Levinson predict off-recordness in situations of high face risk, I predicted an underlying risk where off-recordness occurs. In addition my argument gives support to Brown and Levinson's formula:

$$W_x = D\ (S,H) + P\ (H,S) + R_x$$

Weightiness = Distance (Speaker, Hearer) + Power (Hearer, Speaker) + Rating of FTA as imposition

which computes the weightiness of an FTA. According to the authors, when an actor attempts an FTA he 'compounds the three variables into a single index of risk which does not reveal whether P, D or R is responsible for the particular W_x value' (see page 66 above). This in turn encodes the degree to which the speaker considers a particular FTA to be dangerous. In this way a speaker's perception of the weightiness of an FTA is revealed and can itself become an object of exploitation. This is what I meant when I wrote that 'the use of indirect talk and of metaphors to test whether your partner is basically in tune with your own personal interest or not' is a measure of the precariousness of a speech situation.

In Brown and Levinson's terminology the logic of the process can be explained as follows. Generally, we have an exploitation of mutual knowledge about the fact that each strategy, as soon as it is employed, encodes a certain perceived FTA danger. S and H may, through their talk, haggle, as it were, about the respective P, D and R values. But they may also haggle about W_x itself. H may reject S's evaluation of W_x and indicate that S has misjudged the situation, having computed R, D and P wrongly. This in turn leads to the possibility that S may exploit either the acceptance or the rejection of a particular W_x as an indirect indication of how H perceives the situation. This is exactly what happens when S and H 'test' whether they are 'in tune' with one another. Thus, in one of the examples I have given above, the car dealer who makes the effort to work out what might have been meant by the rather wayward metaphor 'camel' accepts S's W_x to the extent that he understands him. In other words, the understanding of an equivocal statement becomes a sign of one's commitment to the speaker and, more specifially, a proof of one's acceptance of the speaker's definition of the situation (as encoded in the particular realization of the FTA). Such testing moves from off-record to on-record statements, along a continuum which reflects social relationships that range from close intimacy (where H happily accepts and decodes off-record messages) to antagonistic distance (where H refuses to attempt anything but the literal reading of statements).

Hints, then, are more than simply a mechanism for 'taking the responsibility for the FTA away from S' (1978: 221). Where they are understood they again contain an element of positive politeness and imply a complicity between S and H. This complicity may not only consist in a hidden agreement to keep the level of the FTA down, but may also constitute an attempt to hide something from a third party, X. Brown and Levinson mention the euphemism as a variety of the association clue and, indeed, the trope of euphemism is a case in point. It often serves the double function of protecting S from H while at the same time protecting S and H from X.

Symbolic statements may be used to reveal and also to hide something. As the latter point is increasingly coming into the forefront of my inquiry, let me examine the example of euphemism more closely in the light of my Hamar data.

One domain in Hamar in which the use of euphemism abounds is that of food consumption. Food and drink, being very scarce in Hamar, are felt to be dangerous possessions. Therefore one should lessen, if I may say so, the distasteful fact that one is having food. Thus, whenever a Hamar invites another for food or drink, the actual activity of eating and drinking tends to be expressed indirectly, for example: 'Sit down in order to spit on to your heart.' Here the guest has been offered some milk. He takes a small sip first before he really begins to drink, and spits a few drops of milk on to his chest where the heart is. The invitation to 'sit down and spit on to one's heart' refers to this customary blessing. The euphemization goes so far that when drinking, for example, there is a whole string of hierarchically ranked terms in which each hides the other in that the stronger term is expressed by the weaker: honeywine is called 'beer', beer is called 'coffee', coffee is called 'water'. When I first realized this systematic euphemization I intuitively explained it to myself in terms of S protecting himself from H; that is, I interpreted it as pure negative politeness where S was humbling himself *vis-à-vis* H ranking his drink lower on the value scale of drinks than in fact it is. I thought it was simply an evasive tactic based on the logic that even bad honeywine is as good as beer, bad beer as good as coffee, bad coffee as good as water. However, after a while I came to understand that elements of hiding or, more correctly, shielding and exclusion were involved which related to the scarcity of food:

These days the young ones only get a tiny amount of goat's milk every evening and a few roots from trees growing out in the bush. A man like Baldambe gets three or four pieces of dry sorghum a day and a cup of milk if he is lucky. That is all that there is in his daily menu except for coffee which he may drink in the morning and in the evening. So Hamar social organization is certainly based on a tight control of the stomach. At most times of the year, eating is almost a secret activity and this, I think, is the cause of much of the individual isolation in Hamar. It is not just eating which is kept secret, but also the cleaning of grain and the grinding and the cooking. Often these tasks are carried out in the isolation and privacy of the fields, even at times when there is no other work to be done there. The consumption of food even erects barriers between friends, kin and bond-friends; it operates on all levels. (Lydall and Strecker 1979a: 118–19).

General scarcity provides the main motive for the use of

euphemism in the domain of nutrition. Euphemisms act as barriers between people who are and who are not entitled to food in a particular situation. Seen in this light the logic of using 'beer' for honeywine, 'coffee' for beer, etc., lies in an 'I know that you know' reasoning which we have already observed as working in symbolic codification. On first sight, what happens is that S makes sure that any third party who might be present when the invitation is made gets offended as little as possible. It is less offensive to exclude (not invite) a third party from a poor invitation than from one which promises rich enjoyment. Thus, when S says to H that he should come and have some coffee with him, X may save his face by saying to himself that S and H are just having a sip of water although he knows that they are going to pass the gourd of beer around. But this is not all. The euphemisms are stable and conventionalized. Everyone knows the game. How can it still be effective? I think the answer to this lies in the fact that so long as the substitution of one term for another is recognized (beer for honeywine, water for coffee) it will signal FTA danger. And this is recognized when a conversational maxim (in this case the quality maxim) has been violated. An implicature results which leads H to reflect on what is involved. When, in Hamar, S invites H for 'coffee', a third party, X, automatically understands that S has excluded him from an invitation to drink honeywine, but that S does not wish thereby to damage X's face, and thence his own. In this way S and H are shielded from the third party. The exclusion is not openly stressed but rather encoded in a conventional euphemism which draws attention to the riskiness of the situation and gives it an aura of taboo. Acting as a light source, to use Sperber's appropriate metaphor for symbolism, it illuminates a context in such a way that it forces H to work out why S has rated R_x low or has substituted R_y for R_x. The answer is that R_y is not as low as it is made to be but, on the contrary, quite high.

Here are some further examples which demonstrate the use of euphemism in Hamar as a mechanism both to hide and to make taboo:

1. Death generally involves great face risks for everyone concerned with the process of transforming the physical death of a person into a social death. The risks increase, the more important the dead person is socially. We therefore find cross-culturally an extremely high

degree of off-record modes of expression in the statements that are made in connection with the death of the 'king', 'chief' or 'ritual leader' of a society. It comes as no surprise that the death of the Hamar ritual leader (*bitta*) is announced indirectly; that is, by using a euphemism:

> When the *bitta* dies not everyone sees, just a few bright elders get together. They don't say he's dead, no one hears that said.
> 'He's sick, the master is not well, his head hurts' is said to mean he is dead.
> 'Ai, is the *bitta* sick?'
> 'He is sick. The master is sick and he's in his house. Slowly, little by little, at his own pace, he will get better.' (Lydall and Strecker 1979b: 35)

2. Raiding or warfare is another example. Whenever possible the Hamar refer to it indirectly, especially when they themselves have initiated it. Thus, a raid may be called a 'talk', a raider a 'hunter' and 'death' may be referred to as a 'bleeding nose', etc. When I once asked what happens when raiders return home safely, Baldambe and Choke answered as follows:

> I.S.:   What happens when they [the raiders] return safely?
> Baldambe: Now, haven't they returned?
> I.S.:   Returned.
> Baldambe Having returned, one territorial segment ...
> Choke: *The hunters* are well.
> Baldambe: *The hunters* of one territorial segment are well, and the people of one territorial segment have *a bleeding nose*. When *the talk* and the dead are sorted out the men get up and call the women: 'Look the cattle have been brought!'
> Choke   'Dance!'
> (Strecker 1979a: 48–9)

Euphemization may, on one level, be a form of hiding and, on another level, a way of indicating an area of risk and taboo. Having become conventionalized it puts off-recordness on record and expresses, as Brown and Levinson would say, 'opposing tensions' within the speaker (1978: 137). The tensions do not only pertain between S and H but also between S, H and R_x. Indeed, when one has the latter possibility in mind one might describe euphemism as an expression of respect towards R_x rather than towards H.

How can one express, or, rather, why should one express respect towards a thing rather than a person? Does this not involve some kind of animism? Well, it does not if the speaker holds to a very general theory of causation which assumes that in one way or another language, or, more precisely, the speech act affects both the cultural and the natural world. Given such a theory the speaker believes that to name a thing, an act, an agent, etc., involves the risk of malevolent reaction. *Nomen est omen*, the Romans used to say. Similarly the Hamar are convinced that the word is a dangerous thing. Therefore, one should never spell out a negative possibility. One day, for example, when Baldambe and I were travelling in the south of Ethiopia, I said, at one point, that if we had no flat tyre, we might be able to reach the next village before nightfall. A few minutes later we had a flat tyre and Baldambe remarked:

> You asked me how the word, being only a movement of your lips can affect the natural world. Look, here you have the proof of it. Had you been more careful and had you kept the words in your mouth we would not have a flat tyre now.

Belief in the power of the word is very common and wherever it occurs, euphemism, though not a real remedy, is felt as lessening the chances of loss by reducing the exposure of the real thing.

With this I conclude my discussion of the strategies resulting from the violation of the relevance maxim. In various forms we will find the 'hints' again below because in a sense, all maxims may be said to contain a principle of relevance and the violation of any maxim may provide a hint.

I skip strategy 3 (presuppose) because it does not contribute anything new or relevant which would be important to my argument here.

Strategies 4–6: Understate, overstate, use tautologies

These strategies violate the quantity maxim. When he understates, a speaker provides less information than is required and this generates an implicature which H has to work out. The question is, of course, what serves as the frame of reference which provides H with a clue that the quantity maxim has been violated in the first place. In order to be understood as such, understatements have to be closely linked to scales. As Brown and Levinson put it, 'typical ways of constructing understatements are to choose a point on a scalar predicate (e.g. tall, good, nice) that is well below the point that actually describes the state of affairs or to hedge a higher point which will implicate the (lower) actual state of affairs' (1978: 222–3). Examples of this kind are (1978: 223):

(1) A: What do you think of Harry?
    B: Nothing wrong with him. (c.i. I don't think he's very good.)
(2) That dress is quite nice. (c.i. is awful.)

This kind of understating (with or without hedges) operates in FTAs of criticism, compliment, admission, offers, insults and the like. Oddly enough, Brown and Levinson do not compare understatement with euphemism and yet, in my view, both should be considered as a variation of a single strategy. Both are the result of the more embracing strategy of minimization and evasion and belong partly to the field of negative politeness and partly to the realm of positive politeness. Strategy 5 (overstate), on the other hand, is radically different. It does not minimize and evade. On the contrary, here the speaker emphatically commits himself. Thus, the strategy is outrightly one of positive politeness and closely resembles positive politeness strategies 2 and 3 (exaggerate and intensify interest to H) which Brown and Levinson have characterized as achieving their aim by 'making a good story' which communicates that S shares H's wants.

Now, in a very general sense, all cultural production is constantly flouting the quantity maxim. Whether it is the dramatization in the conversations of everyday life, such as we have observed in Hamar, or whether it is in myth, song, poetry, ritual and the like, in 'making a good story', much verbal (or other communicative) effort is made and S does not seem to worry about violating any quantity maxim. Remember how Grice illustrated the quantity maxim (see 2.3 above) with the following analogue:

If you are assisting me to mend a car, I expect your contribution to be neither more nor less than is required; if for example, at a particular stage I need four screws, I expect you to hand me four, rather than two or six.

When S 'overstates', in terms of Grice's example, he hands the man who is mending the car, not four screws, but six or perhaps even a whole boxful. Has anything problematic occurred? I think not, because, as anyone who has ever worked on a car knows, a screw might easily fall to the ground and get lost. Thus, by offering more screws than seem strictly necessary the helper is being 'polite' and documents his concern for the man who is mending the car. Furthermore, he certainly makes sure that his contribution will not fall short of what is required.

Something similar happens in communicative exchanges where S provides more than H would seem to require. The repetitiveness and redundancy of myth and ritual have often been remarked upon; Sperber, for example, as we have seen, has put much stress on the 'repetitive side of cultural symbolism' (Sperber 1975: 145). Also, in song and poetry, the two other major domains of oral tradition, lavish use is made of repetition. All these repetitions and seeming violations of the quantity maxim should be viewed in the light that all 'cultural products' may ultimately be seen in terms of actual dialogues between S and H (collective and individual) who are motivated by the wish to persuade each other (and often enough themselves) of the meaningfulness of their universe of discourse.

To understand this point better, let us now have a closer look at Brown and Levinson's description of the way in which S may overstate. They give examples (1978: 224–5) of the following kind:

(1) There were a míllion people in the Co-op tonight! (an excuse for being late)
(2) I tried to call a húndred times, but there was never any answer. (an apology for not getting in touch)
(3) Why are you álways smoking? (a criticism)

In addition, Brown and Levinson mention the principle of 'the lady doth protest too much' as an example of flouting the quantity maxim, where the use of too many words in a a particular situation indicates that they are used not to reveal but rather to hide something, thus deliberately drawing H's attention to the fact that something is being hinted at 'between the lines'. On the other hand, the authors draw no attention to cases where S flouts the quantity maxim, not to hide something, but to emphasize it, where he makes sure, as it were, 'that he gets his point across' so that his message will under no circumstances get lost.

Hamar conversational practice is full of such devices.

Here are some examples:

1. On a phonological level the quantity maxim may be violated when certain vowels in otherwise on-record words are lengthened to an extreme extent:

   > Bring a biiiiiiig pot of honey to the Bume *bitta*, our country is full of honey. (Lydall and Strecker 1979b: 31)

2. Words may get repeated to an extent that is redundant:

   > Now all the Hamar, Hamar, Hamar, Hamar, Hamar, Hamar, Hamar arrived, BA, LOWAN, GASI ... (1979b: 3)

3 In the form of an anaphora terms may get repeated in their different manifestations and thus their underlying unity may be stressed:

   > The *bitta* was the first to make fire in Hamar and he said: 'I am the *bitta*, the owner of the land am I, the first to take hold of the land. Now may you become my subjects, may you be my dependants, may you be the ones I command. (1979b: 2)

4. Whole sentences may be repeated in the following way:

   > 'From where do you come?'
   > 'I am KARLA, I come from Kara.'
   > 'Eh! What do you want?'
   > 'I want land.'
   > GULET:
   > 'From where do you come?'
   > 'I come with KARLA from Kara.'
   > 'What do you want?'
   > 'I want land.'
   > One section of GULET is Bume:
   > 'From where do you come?'
   > 'I come from Bume.'
   > 'What do you want.'

'I want land.'
One clan is DILA:
'From where do you come?'
'I come from Kara.'
'What do you want?'
'I want land.'
(1979b: 2–3)

5. Such lavish use is made of onomatopoeic words that they seem to border on a violation of the quantity maxim:

> The clouds show us their footprints: ba-ta-ta-ta-ta … Dull-dull, dull-dull, the dust …
> Look at the red flashing light: ra-ra-ra-ra-ra-ra-barcha-barcha-barcha … (Strecker 1979a: 33)

6. The use of directly quoted speech, which Brown and Levinson have shown to be a realization of the strategy of 'intensify interest to H', may also be considered a conspicuously expensive way of transmitting information in which people do not mind wasting words. The technique abounds in Hamar. Take, for example, the repetition of sentences quoted above (example 4).

7. In arguments, precedents may be cited leading to long accounts of historical events and myth-like stories; a metaphor may be developed into an allegory; a moral issue may get encoded in a parable or a fable; a delicate point may be conveyed by telling an anecdote, etc.

All these efforts aim at a description which is emphatic and carries an element of persuasion. The emphatic aspect is plain enough. As we have seen above, Grice has divided the quantity maxim into two parts, which Brown and Levinson in turn have used to distinguish between the two strategies of understatement and overstatement, where the former gives too little and the latter too much information. However, it is clearly a much more serious violation of the maxim if S gives less information than is required rather than if he gives more. Like our man on the road who is mending his car and needs at least four screws but can still mend the car (and probably can mend it better) when he is offered a whole boxful, so the man in Hamar who wants to know what was presented to the Bume (see example above) must at least hear the words 'big pot'. To make sure that H gets the message S can say 'biiiiig pot', or 'big, big, big pot', or 'big pot, large pot, enormous pot' or 'mountain of a pot' and such like. Sometimes the lavish expenditure of words and sounds and images, etc., is not quite what H expected and yet at the same time everything is still on record. S is simply emphatic and seems to be doing his best to get the message across that, for example, a pot is big.

Yet, where does the element of persuasion come from? Where does the something else lie which we sense as lurking somewhere off record in the background? I think it lies in the odd fact that by giving rather too much S eventually forces the implicature that, in fact, he is giving too little information after all. Thus, if a Hamar says 'biiiiig pot' (or for that matter invents a metaphor for its bigness, composes a song or a poem, etc., about the pot's large size) he does not say 'a very big pot', which would not carry an implicature, but says something like 'a pot so big that I cannot really describe it to you but can only invite you to search in your memory and imagine what the pot which I can't adequately describe to you myself, may look like'. In short, the statement 'biiiiig pot' leads to an evocation of all kinds of bigness. Sperber would say that the statement is symbolic in so far as 'the image is not described but evoked'. Or to put it differently, the description is evocative.

Now, I think that the same holds true for the symbolic statements in myth, ritual, song, poetry; they are evocative in that they doubly violate (or at least flagrantly disregard) the quantity maxim: they say too much and they say too little and thus are bound to involve H, entrance him and animate him to complete the message by himself. This, in my view, is ultimately the most powerful form of persuasion.

To conclude my discussion of the strategies that have to do with a flouting of the quantity maxim I need to say a few words about the use of tautologies (strategy 6). Brown and Levinson point out that by uttering 'patent and necessary truths', 'S encourages H to look for an informative interpretation of the non-informative utterance' (1978: 225). The authors give FTA examples where tautologies are used for excuses, criticisms, refusals, complaints, approvals and encouragements. Interestingly, most of the examples are taken from non-western sources, that is, Tamil and Tzeltal. This supports my impression that in western 'scientific' culture, strong pressures work against the use of tautologies, while in societies without such scientific preoccupations tautologies constitute a common and well-accepted way of saying things. At any rate, in Hamar I was struck from the start by the role tautologies play in Hamar discourse.

At first I considered them as marking an impasse, the speaker not wanting or not knowing what to make of something and therefore finding a solution in the cryptic statement of a tautology. However, after a while I began to view it the other way round, as a point of departure, as it were, and a point to which one returns. As such, the tautology is an assertion of authority and an affirmation of the status quo. It is not for the young and inexperienced to utter tautologies but only for the old and wise. Thus, when in 1973 Baldambe gave a lecture for the children of his friends in Berlin, he closed with the words 'bad is bad and good is good' (Strecker 1975). These words were not only the message of the lengthy speech but also the resumé of a long life in which Baldambe had come to realize the limits of relativism.

The young and inquisitive naturally question all 'patent' truth. They say, 'bad is good and good is bad' and try to discover how far they get these contradictions. But having gone through this process there comes the time when certain things really are what they seem and it is this that gets expressed by tautologies in Hamar. Furthermore, the utterance of a tautology is closely related to the dialogic character of Hamar speaking and arguing. Seen in this light its use may sometimes be best interpreted as a form of echoing. Not as the common echoing, however, where H repeats what S has said, but an echoing where S repeats what he himself has said (see page 80).

Strategies 7–10: Use contradictions, be ironic, use metaphors, use rhetorical questions

The quality maxim, 'speak the truth, be sincere' should not be violated, but when a violation happens, S forces H 'to find some implicature that preserves the Quality assumption' (Brown and Levinson 1978: 226). Following Lewis (1969), Brown and Levinson point out that 'no one could even learn a language in a society where there was an assumption that no one told the truth' (1978: 226). Furthermore, 'it is presumably because this principle [of truth] is so foundational that superficial violations of it provide the major figures of speech and many of the tools of rhetoric' (1978: 226). The authors might well have continued by saying that by the same token the violation of the quality maxim furnishes the major tool for symbolization.

The use of contradictions relates to the first part of the maxim which Grice has defined as 'do not say what you believe to be false'. Brown and Levinson give an example where S uses contradiction for an evasive complaint (1978: 226)

A: Are you upset about that?

B: Well, { yes and no.
          { I am and I'm not

Brown and Levinson do not discuss the strategy further and I too find it hard to envisage the use of contradictions as an element of everyday-life language usage. In literary works and in poetry and in other forms of standardized oral tradition they do, however, occur quite frequently. Here, contradictions have the function of acting as implicatures which activate the addressee's imagination. Furthermore, they provide a sense of mystery analogous to the mystery that can be created by displacement (see 2.2 above). Accordingly, the poet may speak of a 'black sun', 'cold flame', 'silent song', etc. A similiar example from Hamar happens in a blessing, where the men chant and use deliberate contradictions, such as in the following phrase:

The flood in the river beds flows downstream when it rains, may it turn back upstream, may it turn. (Lydall and Strecker 1979b: 169)

Of course, the Hamar know that the flood can't turn back. Yet they say it should. This gives their statement the cryptic and mysterious quality which elevates it above ordinary language and triggers off a set of evocations about the conditions under which it would be true that the floods turned back upstream.

Lichtenberg once said that a complete contradiction is as telling to a wise man as to a fool. This makes it indeed an ideal tool for mystification as it can be rather difficult for H to spell out the contradiction explicitly. For a powerful speaker it is socially quite effective to use and say the opposite of what he means. This strategy does, in fact, abound in Hamar (as probably anywhere where symbolization is a common phenomenon). Irony, which Brown and Levinson describe in stragegy 8, is a case in point:

'By saying the *opposite* of what he means ... S can indirectly convey his intended meaning, if there are clues that his intended meaning is conveyed indirectly' (1978: 226). As we have already encountered irony acting as a cornerstone in Sperber's theory of symbolism, it is interesting to note here that Brown and Levinson do not describe irony in terms of evocation, as Sperber has done, but, as I have suggested, in terms of implicature. Citing Cutler (1974), Grice and Perret (1976) they conclude that irony is an output of an off-record strategy that attends to face threat. Alternatively, in cases where the irony is rendered unambiguous in form, it may be the out-put of an on-record strategy, but in all cases irony is organized around the potential face threat posed by the critical content (including evasion of unambiguous responsibility for it) (1978: 268). Irony thus is a prototype of evasion where S says the opposite of what one expects he truly intends.

Brown and Levinson do not discuss strategy 8 further but, surely, irony is not the only way in which S might force an implicature by saying the opposite of what he means. My observations in Hamar show, for example, that in a whole range of criticisms, admonitions, reprimands, etc., a deliberate inversion of truth may be involved. Such inversions of truth are risky and potentially offensive because truth is an important matter and must not be played with at will. Therefore, the strategy of saying the opposite of what one means presumes a power equality or power differential such that S dares to violate the quality maxim because he does not fear a reprisal from H. The data from Hamar strongly suggest this point as the use of the strategy in Hamar is linked to an asymmetry in the respective P values of S and H (see the patterns of strategy distribution above, 3.1), S saying the opposite of what he means only when he has authority over H and not vice versa. In other words, a young Hamar would never say the opposite of what he means to a Hamar elder in order to force an implicature; this would be highly offensive and would challenge the very basis of authority (he may, of course, say the opposite of what he knows is true in order to hide something, but this is an altogether different matter). The elders, on the other side, constantly make use of this technique. Here is a description of what may happen:

There was an interesting point in Baldambe's description of the public meetings at the cattle camps: he and other speakers told the young men that if they went to Galeba or to Bume to kill, the way in front of them would be bright but that if they returned, everything in front of them would be dark. I have often wondered about the role of cynicism in social control. Instead of just saying, 'Don't go', the elders said, 'Go and see what happens.'

Another example of this way of speaking occurred in a case which took place shortly after the public meetings. A Bume boy came into Hamar territory, driven by hunger. He was picked up by some young Hamar men who brought him to an elder. The elder called all the young men of the neighbouring area together and said to them: 'Kill him!' This was his way of emphasizing the taboo on killing him, for hadn't the speaker of Kadja just explicitly forbidden the killing? (Lydall and Strecker 1979a: 183–4)

So 'Kill him!' here means emphatically 'Don't kill him!' I think it is misleading to speak, as I have done, of 'cynicism' in this case. True, an element of 'sneering' is present, but to stress it is to draw attention to the divisive and antagonistic aspect of the implicature which is already evident enough. What is not so evident, however, but more interesting is the fact that by saying the opposite of what they mean the Hamar elders really apply a strategy of positive politeness: they 'claim common ground', 'convey that they are co-operators' and indirectly 'stress shared knowledge'. They do all this and even go off record by the simple technique of using their authority to invert the truth.

At the same time they amplify their FTA, for the inversion ('kill him' instead of 'don't kill him') draws attention to language use itself and to the FTA danger (or rather, in this case, the conspicuously low FTA danger) encoded in this particular linguistic realization. When a Hamar elder says, 'Kill him!' instead of 'Don't kill him!', he knows that the junior knows that this very linguistic realization may not be used by the latter to address the former. Thus the former's inversion of truth is both a direct tool of social control and an indirect means by which he emphasizes the prevailing asymmetry of power.

To document just how important this particular strategy is in Hamar political practice let me quote the description of a speech made at a public meeting (the interested reader may find the speech on a record together with a transcription of the original text, Strecker 1979c): Lomotor, a Hamar spokesman, relates what Maxulo, a spokesman of the neighbouring tribe, the Galeba (i.e. Dasanetch; see Almagor 1978) said at a public meeting. Note that at a public meeting only certain elders may speak who have expressly been given the right to speak at public assemblies, and that the juniors are not allowed to raise their voices except in the collective singing of war songs and the individual shouting of the names of their dance oxen. Maxulo at first asks whether the Hamar spokesmen are still alive:

'Is Shada still alive?'
'He is.'
'Is Ariangule, Boia still alive?'
'He is.'
'Is Lomotor still alive?'
'He is.'
'Is Korre still alive?'
'He is.'
'Is Baido still alive?'
'He is.'
　(Now Lomotor relates how he answered Maxulo.)
'Ye! Why do you ask for these men? They are my age-mates. They are leaders. They are speakers. They are adult men. The ones who yesterday took the spear together with me, called "hai!" and spoke.'
　(Now Maxulo speaks again.)
'Eh, eh. Let these men come. Man, let me speak ... Lomotor, sit down; Nyangole, sit down; Shada, sit down; Korre, sit down; *Only you young ones who spoilt the country, only you should speak* [my emphasis].

The cattle of your father who drink the good water; the ox whose horns have been bent in this way; man, the one on whose neck a decorative collar has been fastened; the one who goes "whu-whu".

"He who looks so well is my father's ox," is it I who sings like this? "Let him grow fat so that my father may eat."

When the bull grazes, shows off his beauty by grunting "eh-eh-eh". When he mounts the cow, and after a while she is milked, then who says: "May your little sister, may my little sister drink milk?" Who says: "My father's cattle, may they eat grass and multiply?" Who says: "My father's goats, may they eat grass and multiply?"

It was you who talked like this and *only you should speak now* [my emphasis].' (Strecker 1979c)

Maxulo's speech also furnishes us with a good example of another form of violating the quality maxim, the use of rhetorical questions. Brown and Levinson write: 'To ask a question with no intention of obtaining an answer is to break a sincerity condition on questions' (1978: 228). If a question deliberately leaves the answer in the air then this forces an implicature. The process is similar to the strategy where S says the opposite of what he means, except that the inversion is put in the form of a question as in the example given by Brown and Levinson:

How was I to know ... ? (c.i. I wasn't)

The authors provide a host of examples from Tamil and Tzeltal which seem to indicate that, as in Hamar, frequent use is made of rhetorical questions in these cultures. In Hamar they are, in fact, all-pervasive and belong, as their name says, to the rhetorical devices through which FTAs are achieved. Thus Lomotor quotes Maxulo as saying:

'Have the people been fathered for the vultures?
Have they been fathered for the hyenas?
Have they been fathered for the sun?
People are fathered for people ...'

(Strecker 1979c)

Each rhetorical question here implies a 'no' and by drawing attention to the 'no' the speaker castigates the men for their senseless killing. Yet he does so by going off record and leaves it to the men to work out the criticism themselves. The degree to which he can do this justifiably indicates and emphasizes the extent to which he and the listeners share common ground. In short, we are back to the positive-politeness element in off-record strategies which I have already noted several times above.

This element of positive politeness comes out even more clearly when one looks at rhetorical questions that imply an affirmation rather than a negation. Such questions can be viewed as simply a variety of the positive-politeness strategy of repeating part or all of

what a speaker has said. To repeat what he has said is, as we have
seen, to anoint a speaker's face. If, for example, a speaker addresses
his audience by saying,

'Comrades, today is Lenin's birthday'

then the comrades would anoint his face if they repeated part or all of
'today is Lenin's birthday'. Now, when he uses a rhetorical question
and says,

'Comrades, today is Lenin's birthday, isn't it?'

the speaker presumes that the listeners are willing to answer back.
He switches from a monologic to a dialogic definition of the
situation. In fact, he does two things at once, he not only presumes
that the listeners will agree with him and thus implicitly honour his
face, but he himself also honours their face. In other words, he
employs those positive-politeness strategies that activate the interest
of H and involve him together with S in the same activity (see the
chart of positive-politeness strategies, page 72).

The question that hangs in the air must be seen, then, as having
three possible and related realizations. Firstly, we may have
rhetorical questions combined with answers from the audience,
secondly, we may have rhetorical questions raised and answered by
the speaker himself and, finally, rhetorical questions may simply be
raised and left unanswered by either the speaker or the audience.
Here is a slightly adapted example from Hamar (Lydall and Strecker
1979b: 33) which shows the three variations in one and the same
context:

'Look at this ox. Isn't its colour white?'
'It is white.'
(S questions and H answers.)
'Is there any black on it? No.'
(S questions and then answers for H.)
'Are there any speckles on it?
Is there brown on it?
(Question without answer).
Well, my stomach is as white as this. I tell you the truth.'

Rhetorical questions thus embody a strategy which not only goes off record but also contains a strong degree of positive politeness. They are a dynamic device which both separates and unites S and H and may be exploited in either direction according to what is demanded in any particular situation. This is perhaps the reason why rhetorical questions have such a wide if not universal occurrence.

Finally, there is that violation of the quality maxim which leads to the linguistic realization of metaphor. Brown and Levinson deal with metaphor only briefly. They write (1978: 227):

> Metaphors are a further category of quality violations, for metaphors are literally false. The use of metaphor is perhaps usually on record, but there is a possibility that exactly which of the connotations of the metaphor S intends may be off record. For example:
>
> Harry's a real fish. (c.i. He $\begin{Bmatrix} \text{drinks} \\ \text{swims} \\ \text{is slimy} \\ \text{is cold-blooded} \end{Bmatrix}$ like a fish.)

The authors add that hedging particles (like 'real' in the above example) may help to indicate the metaphorical status of a statement, but here their discussion ends.

This treatment is, I think, rather short, and Brown and Levinson do not follow up some ideas which they themselves have developed at another point in their argument. When dealing with the strategy of conventional indirectness, they noted 'that there are degrees of conventionalization [in linguistic realizations], and so degrees of compromise in one direction (off-recordness) or the other (on-recordness)' (1978: 137). In my view, these degrees of conventionalization play an important role in the social use of metaphor. To understand a metaphor is, in the terminology of Brown and Levinson, a matter of concurrence between speaker and hearers over the meaning of the metaphor in a particular speech act of the particular speaker in a particular cultural setting. This concurrence works on the basis of shared background knowledge which includes S's and H's knowledge about the degree to which the meaning of the metaphor is conventionalized. As long as there is a high degree of conventionalization of the meaning, as in so many 'dead' metaphors ('the head of the nail', 'the foot of the mountain', etc.), we can expect a high degree of concurrence between S and H. But the more powerful and 'alive' a metaphor is, the more likely it becomes that S and H will in fact not concur about its precise meaning. Therefore the on-record use of metaphor is often problematic; that is, in the sense that it does not express 'just one unambiguously attributable intention with which witnesses would concur' (Brown and Levinson 1978: 73–4). Note that Brown and Levinson have said that 'the use of metaphor is perhaps usually on record, but there is a possibility that exactly which of the connotations of the metaphor S intends may be off record' (1978: 227; see also above). I would go further and say that it is not simply that such a possibility exists but that people in this everyday life constantly make use of the possible lack of concurrence over the meaning of metaphors. This happens both in the sphere of politeness and social domination, and also more generally as means to exercise social influence (see below).

I said earlier, speaking about euphemism, that a euphemism, even when it has become conventionalized, may retain a protective, shielding function and draw attention to the riskiness of a situation. In such cases the implicature which it entails creates an aura which signals a taboo.

Consider the words 'George the Lion'. They reveal that something similar is happening. 'George the Lion' has an aura, but 'George the Strong' has not (or rather less so). The reason why this should be so is that 'George the Lion' contains a violation of the quality maxim which keeps being felt even though, statistically speaking, the interpretations overlap to such an extent that the meaning of the phrase can be said to be 'on record'.

What is interesting, then, about metaphor is the relation between its off-recordness and its on-recordness. The on-recordness is always a matter of empirical, that is, statistical variation, and this variation plays an important part in the social use of metaphor. It allows for the expression and shaping of social relationships of exclusion and inclusion or, to put it more drastically, metaphor allows for complicity. We have already met complicity in irony and in the use of euphemism where it constitutes a prime motive for these linguistic realizations, but even in seemingly harmless uses of metaphor complicity may be present, both as a cause (being deliberate and intended) and as an effect (being an unintended consequence). However, before I explain this in more detail I think we had better remind ourselves first of the central features which define metaphor.

Sapir, in his useful attempt to elucidate the 'anatomy of metaphor' (Sapir 1977), has made a distinction between an internal and an external metaphor. An internal metaphor involves the substitution of one genus for another, as in the example 'George the Lion'. George is not a lion, he has no tail, he has no claws, etc., but by juxtaposing him with a lion S invites H to think about the way in which both are similar and dissimilar. A number of features define 'George' and a number of features define 'lion' and in as much as some of the features overlap, the two terms can be exploited to create a metaphor. Sapir points out an interesting qualification, though, when he writes: 'The overlap must not be too great, for if it is , the two terms will be considered synonymous (*pail* and *bucket*) and the sense of their being simultaneously alike and not alike will be lost' (1977: 6). An internal metaphor therefore lives by the particular balance it strikes between saliency and obscurancy or, as Brown and Levinson would say, its on-recordness and off-recordness. Sapir uses the diagram shown in Figure 9 (which he has taken from Dubois *et al.* 1970: 108, 109) to show the structure of an internal metaphor. The internal metaphor thus consists of two terms that stem from two separate domains 'plus the bundle of shared features' (Sapir 1977: 6). Usually, however, the structure is not symmetrical. As the example shows, we move from D to A and not vice versa. George is likened to a lion but not the lion to George. To grasp this clearly it is helpful to remember that the metaphor is a dialogic device: by means of it S communicates something to H. In our example the topic of discourse is 'George' (what he is, what he does) and not 'lion'. 'George' is, as Sapir puts it, 'continuous' to the topic while 'lion' is 'discontinuous': 'To have a metaphor at all, the discontinuous term (vehicle) must be stated along with the topic and/or the continuous term (tenor)' (1977: 7).

Following Black (1962) and Richards (1936), Sapir shows that metaphor is more than a verbal game. It creates a movement of thought that oscillates between the poles of likeness and non-likeness, coping with the fact that 'two terms are one in that they are alike, two in that they are not alike' (1977: 9). Or, put differently, metaphors contain an internal dialectic that throws light both on what the topic in question is and what it is not. It is this element of

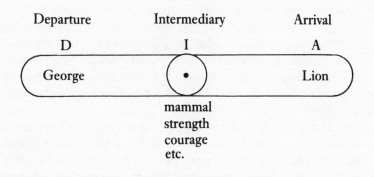

Departure	Intermediary	Arrival
D	I	A
George	•	Lion

mammal
strength
courage
etc.

Figure 9   Structure of an internal metaphor

negation which provides every metaphor with its 'aura' and its
'mystery'. As we are here close to the heart of symbolism, let me
quote Sapir at length as he describes the semantic 'interaction'
which leads to the symbolic impact of metaphor:

> By replacing a term continuous to a topic with one that is
> discontinuous, or by putting the two in juxtaposition, we are
> compelled ... to consider each term in relationship to the other,
> and it is at this point that we are aware of the metaphor. In
> establishing a relationship two processes operate: first, the
> reduction of the terms to their shared features – to what makes
> them alike; secondly, the transference from one to the other, but
> mainly from the discontinuous to the continuous, of what they do
> not share – of what makes them unlike. The first process, which is
> basic, gives the metaphor its specificity. It allows us to foreground
> certain features of this continuous term that are felt as being
> salient to the general topic. On hearing George the Lion we are
> compelled to consider what we know about lions and to select
> those features that would apply to George, thus learning
> something very specific about George. In contrast, the second

process gives a metaphor, for want of a better word, its *colour*. It allows us to consider the continuous term for what it is not, to assume for a moment that, although George is 'really' like a lion only in certain specific ways, he might be a lot more like a lion in just those ways. We are given the means to imagine George as a real lion, straight and simple, even down to his tail (1977: 9).

To complete the circle and see just how powerful this movement of thought is, have a look at Magritte's painting entitled *Une simple histoire d'amour*. It pictures a chair with a lion's tail growing out of it. As I keep gazing at it, claws grow out of the chair's legs, from its back a lion's shoulders emerge, a head becomes visible, a huge mouth opens, teeth show ...

But to return to the on-recordness of metaphor which, as I have said above, is an empirical matter: whether a metaphor is felt as revealing, apt, etc. is (at least partly) a question of how far H shares with S a similar knowledge about the discontinuous term. No one can, indeed, attest to the truth of this matter better than the anthropologist himself. When he conducts fieldwork, his tacit knowledge and the tacit knowledge of the people he has come to study are initially worlds apart. As a result he feels the metaphors which people employ as neither enlightening nor revealing. Rather, they puzzle or simply confuse him. Only when he has learnt a considerable amount about the new world and culture can he begin to cope with its metaphors and feel their adequacy. To give an example from Hamar: the first act of *Conversations in Dambaiti* (Strecker 1979a: 3) opens with a blessing (calling of well-being, *barjo*) where Baldambe (just as Brown and Levinson's theory would predict!) goes off record by employing a simile. He does not say that his brothers and sons should be safe, but

'Let the people walk their different ways as baboons do.'

For someone who does not know anything about baboons, either from hearsay or from observation, the statement remains obscure and is neither apt nor inapt. But if he had seen or heard a description of the ease with which baboons move, especially in dense bush, and if he had heard stories which tell how the baboon always knows in advance what will happen around him, then Baldambe's formulation which refers to his brothers and sons who have gone to war and says they should move like baboons, will be not only apt but also persuasive.

What I have said so far is, of course, not all that can be said about metaphor, and the richness or poverty of a metaphor must ultimately be assessed in terms of its objective structure which encodes all the possible relations that can be construed between the continuous and the discontinuous terms, and the degree to which both terms not only illuminate each other in the process but also throw a light on a 'new entity' (See Sapir 1977: 11–12). Interesting though the problems of the 'objective structure' of metaphors are, they do not affect my present inquiry, which has to do with the social side of metaphor and the social use to which it may be put.

I now turn to external metaphor. Sapir identifies this as Aristotle's definition of analogy where 'one thing is in the same relationship to another as a third is to a fourth' (1977: 22). While the internal metaphor equates genus with genus (A=X), the external metaphor juxtaposes two terms and draws attention to their respective semantic domains. Sperber's example is a case in point (see 2.1 above):

The lion is king of the animals.

This statement (which Sperber called a 'defective conceptual representation' which has to be put into quotes in order to be understood) focuses not directly on the similarities between the lion and the king, but rather on the relationship between the lion and his subjects (the animals) and that between the king and his subjects (people). Here A is to A's domain as X is to X's domain (see Sapir 1977: 23). But we could also read 'George the Lion' in the same way as an external metaphor. The statement remains an internal metaphor only so long as we focus our attention on the bundle of features which both terms share *vis-à-vis* each other (mammal, strength, courage, etc.); if, on the other hand, we relate (first) each term to its own domain and then compare the two pairs, we get an external metaphor, that is George : men :: lion: animals. Both readings are possible and are part of the resourcefulness of a metaphor. Yet, the more interesting cases are those where internal metaphor and external metaphor do not fuse but rather combine to work in conjunction with one another.

Sapir quotes and analyses some examples but I prefer to take my own from Hamar (Lydall and Strecker 1979a: 226):

One night when Baldambe and I were lying on our cow hides in front of our house, watching the stars before we fell asleep, Baldambe, contemplating some deep-seated conflict with his brothers, suddenly exclaimed:

Guderi, nasi kissa zobo,
zobo, nasi kissa guderi!
[The hyena, its son is a lion,
the lion, its son is a hyena.]
(See Lydall and Strecker 1979a: 226)

Two violations of the conversational maxims have occurred here. Baldambe has flouted the relevance maxim (why talk about animals when they can't possibly be at issue?) and the quality maxim (it is false to say that lions beget hyenas). When we put the statements into quotes as Sperber suggests and work out the implicatures as Grice advises, we arrive first at an internal metaphor which leads us to consider both the likeness and difference of lion and hyena. For example, we think of them in their likeness as meat-eaters and their difference as hunters and scavengers. Secondly, we move on to an external metaphor. We realize that we are meant to compare a relationship. The puzzle we have to solve is: what stands in the relation 'father-hyena' to 'son-lion' and 'father-lion' to 'son-hyena'? Answer: human fathers to human sons. Why? The answer is not easy to give and is necessarily an open-ended one. But before I embark on an explanation, let me say that what Baldambe uttered that night was not a unique statement unheard before. On the contrary, it is a proverb which encodes an old knowledge about Hamar social organization and its weakness. It is used whenever people need to comment on certain latent or manifest conflicts within the family. The proverb, a neatly constructed chiasmus, indicates that lions are related to hyenas as fathers are to sons and as sons are to fathers. Lions and hyenas compete over carcasses as fathers and sons compete over cattle. Lions and hyenas are similiar in that both are meat-eaters but stand in contrast in their major roles as hunters and scavengers. Translated into the social relationships of Hamar the proverb seems to say: there is a mutual opposition between F and S. It expresses the identity of members of the same and alternate generations and the opposition between members of adjacent

generations. But this is not all. When I asked Baldambe what
he had meant when he made the statement, his explanation was as
follows. He used the proverb because he wanted to get his anger
about his brothers off his chest without saying precisely what he
meant and without attacking anyone in particular. In Baldambe's
eyes their father Berinas (Gino) had been a true 'lion'. During his
lifetime he had been a strong, self-assured, competent and generous
provider of food. He had been a distinguished hunter, raider and
herdsman, and in his homestead there had been always food which
guests and everyone of the family could share. Baldambe felt that he
and his brothers were not like his father. That is why he said 'The
hyena, its son is a lion; the lion, its son is a hyena' when thinking of
the way in which he and his brothers were quarrelling about the
cattle they had inherited from their father. They were quarrelling
over matters concerning these cattle, he thought, as hyenas quarrel
over the carcass of an animal slain by a lion. Thus, Baldambe was
not so much thinking about the opposition between father and son,
but rather about the competing interests of older and younger
brothers. His father was already long dead and it had been an
argument with his older brothers which had prompted him to
pronounce the proverb. Yet the proverb actually starts with hyena-
father. When I pointed this out to Baldambe, he laughed, agreed and
indicated that it is here where the mystery lies. Out of all the many
'hyenas' born in Hamar, miraculously some will beget sons who will
turn out to be 'lions'. Then, not miraculously at all, the sons of
these 'lions' will again be the usual Hamar 'hyenas' who are greedy
and quarrelsome. Also, many fathers are seen by their sons as
'hyenas' because they do not pass on the cattle which they themselves have inherited from their own fathers and older brothers.
They devour them like 'hyenas' and do not share them with their
sons.

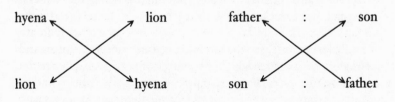

Figure 10   Diagram of a Hamar proverb

There is more to the proverb than what I have said here, but it is time now to return to the mainstream of my argument. Remember, I left off to examine the formal properties of metaphor at the point where it became evident that the use of metaphor may involve social inclusion and exclusion. To stress my point I called it complicity; that is, a kind of secret pact between S and H to use their shared tacit knowledge about the domain of the discontinuous term which makes up a metaphor in order to exclude a third party. To show how strong, in fact, the element of inclusion/exclusion may be, let me quote an observation from Hamar:

> This morning I observe what I was often painfully aware of in England, namely that a close and intensive dialogue can be used to exclude a third party. Last night a travelling Amhara trader arrived in Dambaiti, hoping to get Baldambe to pay back an old debt. It is obvious during the morning conversation by the coffee pot that Baldambe does not want to talk to the trader and he embarks upon a violent and serious conversation with Wadu. Wadu 'echoes' more than usual and Baldambe frowns and complains and laments to an almost grotesque degree. When the trader tries to get a word in, Wadu tells him to keep quiet because their talk is so very serious. Baldambe is clearly in a weak position since he is the debtor. But he plays this down by creating an atmosphere in which something else, of which obviously only he and Wadu know, is infinitely more important than this small, momentary debt. It needs at least two people to play such a game and both partners have to know each other's style of speaking well so that they can understand the implicit meanings of what is said and what is not said, of allusions, of metaphors and so on. Thus, a tight dialogue in which a third party has no place has a double effect: it makes the aspirant participant aware of his impotence whilst at the same time it creates and enhances a feeling of omnipotence in the speakers. (Lydall and Strecker 1979a: 207–8)

I will leave aside for the time being this curious delusion and feeling of omnipotence which the metaphor produces in its creator, and return to it later. Here I am only interested in the other point: the fact that metaphor is a powerful tool for the shaping and operating of social relationships. In the terminology of Brown and Levinson it is a device which acts 'as a social accelerator and a social brake ... to modify the direction of interaction at any point in time' (1978: 236). Thus, Baldambe and Wadu use metaphor (together with other techniques such as echoing) to build up a conspiracy against the trader. They do this not simply to exclude him. Rather, they do it in order to intimidate and isolate him, to make him feel impotent and insecure. The whole process is one long and developed FTA. And yet the trader only feels that he is being threatened. He knows it without being able to point his finger precisely at anything which is threatening him and, more importantly, he cannot take Baldambe and Wadu to task for anything. Haven't they simply discussed something of great importance to them? Wouldn't it in turn be an even bigger imposition for the trader to say that the matter of a small debt should count more than the subject Baldambe and Wadu have been talking about – and of which the trader does not understand anything?

There is a further important point to the example. It shows that the creation of metaphor and figurative speech flourishes especially well in motivated dialogues. In fact, I was often struck in Hamar with how the formulation and the use of apt metaphors was the result of a shared social enterprise, the metaphor emerging, so to say, from a number of separate inputs. Here are three examples which document how this happens (Strecker 1979a: 42, 19, 138). The first is short, the second and third are a little more elaborate:

1. Choke speaks about a herd of sheep that increased to a remarkable size. Maiza, Baldambe's sister, emphasizes what Choke has said by providing the appropriate metaphor:

> Choke: My father's son ... [the sheep] they multipled so much that they became a whole herd.
> Maiza: They were like sand.
> Choke: Like sand, they multiplied so much ...

2. Choke and Baldambe speak about goats which the Hamar have raided from Kenya. As the subject involves a potential danger they develop a number of metaphors in order to go off record:

> Baldambe: One part of the herd has been driven to this place. Why? Probably because there is good grass. He saw them with his own eyes, he saw them, the ones which look like wet clay.

Choke: The ones which are like smooth, hard soil.
Baldambe: The ones like smooth, hard soil ...

An FTA danger, involving praise of the good health and fatness of the animals, is avoided here by the use of metaphors (wet clay, smooth, hard soil). To directly praise the stolen animals means to expose them to the uncontrolled powers that are put into motion by the utterance of words. This is in fact what Choke refers to when, a little later, he adds that it was the raiding which made the goats fat (see Strecker 1979a: 19). One of the original owners, or his neighbour, a visitor or someone else must at the same time have made the mistake of praising the animals too directly and too much. This caused the animals to grow so fat and healthy that it attracted the eyes of the raiders and as the goats were anyway already doomed – that is, destined to get stolen because of the praise – it was easy for the raiders to drive them away. Given this reasoning, it is good to talk about important matters, such as animals, indirectly, in terms of figures like metaphor and the like – and it is very valuable if both S and H help in the attempt.

3. Together with the women and youths of Dambaiti I have spent an evening's coffee session without any other 'elder' present. This is a rare thing to happen and spirits have accordingly been high. As the pleasant hour comes to an end and its special character is commented upon, this is typically done by means of metaphor (note that again an FTA is involved):

Aikenda: Theo-imba's coffee today has ruined everything.
Anti: Today we are elders.
Aikenda: Together with the children we are all elders.
Maiza: Together with the jackals!
Ginonda: (sings with a warm, melodious and lively voice)
         '*Koi!* – my goat everybody knows!
         Hm. – Yahameya.
         From Marmar mountain with rounded horn.
         Ye – trimanana.'
All: (laugh) Hahahaha ... Theo-imba.
I.S.:   Today you are the 'first'.

The first phrase employs the off-record strategy of saying the opposite of what one means: that is, Theo-imba's coffee (the coffee of the ethnographer who is the father of Theo) didn't ruin everything but helped to make the fun possible. Then an antinomy is developed: Anti, a young girl, calls herself and others 'elders', which is then emphasized by Aikenda, who contrasts elders with children (whom she now counts with the elders). Maiza takes this a step further and widens the gap by substituting jackals for children (whom she counts among the 'elders'), and finally I find myself extending the antinomy by calling the girls and women (who have elevated themselves – together with the jackals – to the status of elder) by the highest social status in Hamar, that is the 'first', the ritual leader, the 'chief' (*bitta*). Ginonda, in her clownish way, on top of this develops the metaphor of the jackal and turns it into a song and a story (see Strecker 1479a: 138–9).

These, then, are three examples from Hamar which, I think, clearly show how the construction of metaphors proceeds by a co-operative effort where the various partners in a conversation show that they share common ground and are therefore able to develop to the full the picture hidden behind the metaphor which one of them had initially proposed. In this sense, too, the use of metaphor affirms Grice's theory of the 'co-operative principle' underlying conversational practice. Without at least a partial willingness to co-operate, no metaphorical thinking would ever get off the ground. This willingness in turn allows the metaphor to become a tool of positive politeness: because the metaphor necessitates co-operation it also encodes this and S can use it indirectly to indicate that he thinks he shares common ground with H.

To conclude my discussion of metaphor let me point out that the exclusion/inclusion element does not always have to remain hidden and off record. There are examples where the use of metaphors becomes a quite explicit, even prescribed, marker of specific social situations. I am thinking, at the moment, of the neophytes (*maz*) in the Hamar rite of transition called *ukuli* (see Strecker 1979b). The neophytes are a group of young, partly initiated men who, though taking part in many of the ordinary daily activities, are nevertheless meant to be exclusive and in some way outside society where they are believed to be 'clean' and magically powerful. One of the ways in which this separation from everyday life is achieved is in the use of metaphoric speech. The metaphors which the neophytes use are meant to be so extreme that they cannot be understood by anyone but the *maz* themselves. To some extent their metaphoric speech is a secret language and is, in fact, referred to as 'the language of the *maz*'. (By extension, all indirect speech which is so indirect that it borders on obscurity or is quite unintelligible, is called 'language of the *maz*'.) In the language of the *maz* metaphor is not clandestinely employed to create a complicity *vis-à-vis* society but rather the other way round: society has prescribed that the *maz* should invent and use their own terminology so that they may be publicly recognized as a group apart.

When I had a closer look at the 'language of the *maz*' I found that it mirrors the social pressures that have generated it. That is, whereas metaphoric speech which is motivated by politics, social competition, psychological needs, etc., is extremely rich in Hamar, the figures employed in the 'language of the *maz*' are in contrast quite poor. Sometimes these involve metaphors, as when an axe is called 'the payment of the snake' or when a *maz* calls a big bowl of coffee 'the paw of the lion'. But more often they employ simple synecdoches, preferably of the 'part-for-whole' type, or associations as when they call milk 'fly' (i.e. flies come to where the milk is), and for verb forms they use opposites which, after a while, becomes a rather monotonous device. Yet it does its task all right, especially as it is combined with another device: when a *maz* wants to indicate 'let's go, it will soon get dark' he does not simply turn this into its opposite, saying 'The sun is rising, let's not go', but what is more, he chooses a special emphatic form of negation which is normally only used in interdictions implying a threat. What he says sounds more like: 'The sun is rising, let's not under any circumstances go, or ... ' Understandably the use of such a strong form in even the simplest and seemingly unproblematic exchanges of everyday life has a mystifying effect on any third party, especially on children and women who have never been *maz* themselves. These true outsiders hear the *maz* speak in this odd way and wonder what it is all about. Something seems to be out of place and as a consequence the *maz* seem very mysterious and to belong to a different world.

Strategies 11–15: Be ambiguous, be vague, over-generalize, displace H, be incomplete– use ellipsis

Most of these strategies have already been dealt with above. 'Be ambiguous' and 'be vague' were discussed under headings such as 'be conventionally indirect', 'use hedges', 'give hints', etc. 'Over-generalize' is a variety of the negative-politeness strategy to 'state the FTA as a general rule'. The most interesting aspect of the strategy to 'displace H' has already been elucidated in the context of deixis, point-of-view operations and triangular reasoning when I examined deference strategies and the impersonalization of S and H. Finally, to be incomplete (which contains an element of positive politeness) also needs no further discussion because I have made the relevant points already when dealing with rhetorical questions. I could close this section at this point were it not for one important observation which generally concerns the manner maxim which generates off-record strategies 11–15.

I have already pointed out several times that age in Hamar is associated with an increase in social power (P) and authority. Now, this association of P and age has a striking correlation in the violation of the manner maxim. What roughly happens is that people speak clearly to age-inferiors and speak in a rather muffled, non-fluent, indecisive, vague and elliptic way when they confront older people. And then, the moment they turn around to address a person younger than themselves, their speech becomes articulate, clear and decided. Jean Lydall and I were baffled when we first observed this pattern, especially as the linguistic clumsiness was accentuated by prosodic devices (mumbling, standing awkwardly on one foot, keeping a finger in one's mouth, looking away from H, etc.). It sometimes happened that we first met someone in situations where only older persons (with high P value) were present and this would furnish us with a picture of him, or her, which was totally wrong. Our surprise was, of course, great when we saw someone whom we had only known as inarticulate and almost dumb, suddenly use a quick tongue and reveal a sharp and competent character. This asymmetry in the articulation of speech peters out as a man reaches adult status (by passing through the *ukuli* rite of transition) and as a woman bears children and is accorded adult status. We find here the repetition of a pattern which we have already met above. In Hamar it is offensive for a junior to employ *vis-à-vis* an older person linguistic realizations which are meant to force an implicature. Irony, rhetorical questions and the like are the tools of the powerful and being such they encode the authority of those who may legitimately use them. As a person speaks to a superior in the hierarchy of social power he mumbles and thus negates his very competence of speech. Oddly, this is the only implicature allowed to him, the implicature which says, 'I will not threaten your authority by making you work' (i.e. work out an implicature). In the final analysis the violation of the manner maxim expresses in this context that a young wit may not be pitted against an old one. They are not meant to compete, but are kept separate and do not partake in the same domain of discourse which, by the very nature of language, is also always a domain of power and politics.

3.3 Towards a modification and extension of Brown and Levinson's model

Brown and Levinson's model can be used to show that symbolization may be employed by an actor/speaker as a means of preserving his own and his interlocutor's face in situations of risk. Literal, univocal statements which are 'on record' expose the speaker and make him and the addressee vulnerable. Figurative, indirect and otherwise 'off-record' message construction, on the other hand, provides both the speaker and the addressee with an 'out' where neither can hold the other, or be held by the other, to task for having said or understood something irrevocably. Applied to symbolization this means that it is an ideal tool for evasion. It shields the participants and makes them safe. Or, to view it from a different angle: symbolization reduces the probability of confrontation and thus acts as a mechanism which helps prevent social conflict in situations of risk. The basis for Brown and Levinson's argument is reproduced in Figure 11 (1978:80). The figure shows that as long as the risk or FTA danger is small (i.e. as long as the social distance (D), the power differential (P) and the imposition (R) entailed in an interaction are small) the effort at off-record message construction (symbolization) remains minimal. However, as any one of the variables increases, the FTA also increases and more effort is put into symbolic codification.

As the analyses of the preceding chapter have shown, Brown and Levinson's model needs some modification. To go off record is not

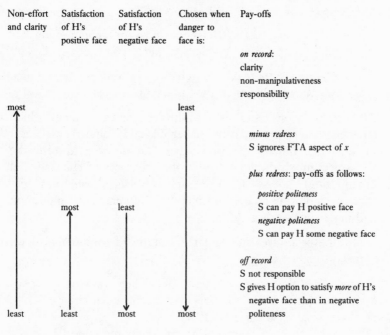

Non-effort and clarity	Satisfaction of H's positive face	Satisfaction of H's negative face	Chosen when danger to face is:	Pay-offs
				on record: clarity non-manipulativeness responsibility
most			least	
				minus redress S ignores FTA aspect of *x*
				plus redress: pay-offs as follows:
	most	least		*positive politeness* S can pay H positive face *negative politeness* S can pay H some negative face
				off record S not responsible S gives H option to satisfy *more* of H's negative face than in negative
least	least	most	most	politeness

Note: see also Figure 3 above.

Figure 11 A priori *factors influencing strategy selection*

only itself a strategy of politeness but, more generally, it is one possible mode which all politeness strategies may adopt. We have, therefore, no progression from on-record statements to off-record statements neatly correlated with an increase of FTA danger. On the contrary, off-record speech abounds in the strategies of positive and negative politeness. Here it acts (as we have seen again and again when discussing the various politeness strategies) as a mechanism of evasion and persuasion. What is more, on-record strategies are often combined with off-record strategies. There exist switches from positive politeness to negative politeness and vice versa. In fact, these switches can be seen to follow logical and/or temporal sequences which constitute a type of super-strategy. Brown and Levinson have not dealt with such sequential switches and yet these switches abound in practice. In order to demonstrate this, let me analyse first an imaginary and then a real conversational exchange involving an FTA.

3.3.1 THE STRATEGY OF SWITCHING STRATEGIES

In Hamar a female guest who has come to ask for some sorghum may well begin with a pessimistic, that is, negative-politeness, statement:

> I don't imagine there'd be any chance of anyone giving me some sorghum. People are just too mean these days.

After this she switches to a positive-politeness strategy which stresses common ground between herself and H – and, if possible, at the same time inflates her own P value. She will stress, accordingly, any aspect in which she is (within the categories of Hamar social organization) superior to H. At first she will probably utter the request employing strategies which both minimize the imposition and impersonalize S and H:

> One never refuses in Hamar a handful of sorghum to one's in-laws.

An analysis of the sentence in terms of its politeness strategies runs as follows: (the Roman numbers refer to the super strategies!)
(1) 'one' – impersonalize H (III.7)
(2) 'never refuses in Hamar' – assert common ground (II.1–8)
(3) 'a handful of sorghum' – minimize imposition (III.4)
(4) 'to one's in-laws' – stress high P value over H (this hides a threat).

There is, in fact, a further strategy involved which is very common in Hamar and might be termed 'invoke custom and tradition' or, more specifically, 'invoke precedents'. Brown and Levinson have described this strategy as 'state the FTA as a general rule'. Thus (2) divides into:

> (a) 'never refuses' – state FTA as general rule (II.7)
> (b) 'in Hamar' – assert common ground (II.4).

Now, depending on factors such as the availability of the commodity, the person who asks, the situation in which the request is made, etc., the answer will vary. If H responds to S's request she usually does so without so many words. In fact, both try to say now as little as possible about the matter. They enter a kind of conspiracy and the transaction is done as secretly as possible. On the other side, if H tries to evade S's requests, her answers will unfailingly make an uninhibited use of politeness strategies, and just as S formulates her requests by a combination of on-record and off-record strategies so does H who now becomes S. Here is an example from *Conversations in Dambaiti* (Strecker 1979a: 168).

Orgo's wife has been drinking coffee in Aikenda's house together with several other women and a few men. As the coffee session and the conversations which go with it come to an end, Orgo's wife asks Ginonda, wife of the most senior man of the homestead, to give her some coffee.

Orgo's wife: (to Ginonda) Now please, my dear, where else could I go? I won't be long and when I return from the water-hole please reach up for me, *korsh-korsh-korsh*. (She indicates the sound of groping for coffee)

Ginonda: Please, if you want to have a look at my platform it is up there. Would it be so bad if you were to step up there and have a look with your own eyes? The gourds are totally empty.

Orgo's wife: But I haven't any, from where could I take it? You don't take the whole sack and pour it out for yourself, you just ask for a little bit to be given to you. Isn't it just your own craziness? Saying to yourself that it would be bad if the father of the homestead returned to an empty house and that you should put on the ritual pot, you go to fetch water without even having found any coffee for it. It's different with some other white women, they go to that one and take with one hand and after this go to another and take with the other hand. Then they prepare the coffee which they have in one hand and keep the other ready for yet another pot.

An analysis shows the following sequencing of strategies:

Orgo's wife:
(1) 'Now please, my dear' – notice, attend to H (II.1)
(2) 'where else could I go?' – claim reflexivity (II.13)
(3) 'I won't be long ... ' – be optimistic (II.11)
(4) 'please reach up for me' – minimize imposition (III.4)
(5) '*korsh-korsh-korsh*' – euphemize, understate (IV.4)

Orgo's wife implies that for Ginonda to give her a handful of coffee is terribly easy. She just has to reach up and take the coffee from the container. The action is made to look like a minimal imposition: it only involves a little *korsh-korsh-korsh*. At the same time the object requested is not named at all. The woman deliberately abstains from mentioning the word coffee. To use it would put her FTA on record and make it more serious than she wants it to be. Thus we get an indirect and at the same time diminutive reference, the *korsh-korsh-korsh* which euphemizes the coffee (see what I have said about the social danger of owning food, p. 123–125).

Ginonda:
(6) 'Please, if you want to have a look ... ' – convey that S and H are co-operators (ironically) (II.9 – 13)
(7) 'The gourds are totally empty' – use white lies (II.6)

In (6) the positive-politeness strategy is employed ironically. Ginonda knows that Orgo's wife knows perfectly well the she is not allowed to 'share the common ground' which Ginonda is offering. The question 'Would it be so bad ... ?' is rhetorical and violates, together with the irony, the quality maxim and is therefore off record (IV.8 and IV.10). The irony is accentuated by the white lie that follows it.

Orgo's wife:
(8) 'But I haven't any, from where could I take it?' – give (and ask) reasons (II.13)
(9) 'You don't take the whole sack ... ' – state FTA as general rule (III. 8)
(10) 'just ask for a little bit' – minimize imposition (III.4)
(11) 'Isn't it just your own craziness?' – give deference (III.5); avoid pronoun 'I' (III.7); use rhetorical question (IV.10)
(12) 'Saying to yourself...' – dissociate S, H from infringement (III. 7–9)
(13) 'It's different with ..?' – claim common ground (II.7); divert aggression (II.2).

Orgo's wife's second set of moves (8–13) need, I think, no further elucidation except that it may be useful to point out two things. Firstly, this time there may be some real invitation for joint reasoning involved in (8) and Ginonda might conceivably answer (and thus solve the problem) by saying, 'Ah, I have heard that a trader recently visited so-and-so's homestead and has brought some coffee.' Secondly, (11) contains not only some deference (Orgo's wife humbling herself by indirectly calling herself crazy) but also a kind of abdication of responsibility for the FTA (thus once again dissociating S and H from the infringement (III.7–9). 'Times are so hard,' Orgo's wife is implying, 'that I am being driven by madness. I am, therefore, not fully responsible for my actions.' In this way she does both; she raises Ginonda's compassion and gives her a way out, indicating that in order to escape she only has to answer, 'Yes, times are really too hard, they drive all of us crazy and we don't know what we are doing ...' Now, by saying (12), Orgo's wife does several things. She tries to involve Ginonda and make her feel responsible. How does she do this? Oddly enough, she uses a strategy of negative politeness first and by means of this strategy she arrives at a point where she can more forcefully launch into a strategy of positive politeness. Thus she dissociates herself from the FTA (negative politeness) by saying that she is not doing it for herself but for the 'father of the homestead' (this also dissociates Ginonda in that she, like Orgo's wife, belongs to the category of people who do not drink coffee by themselves, that is, the women, and who cannot be held ultimately responsible for the FTA of asking for coffee). After this dissociation has occurred, Orgo's wife switches back to positive politeness by pointing out that the coffee is not meant to satisfy personal, physical needs, but spiritual and societal demands. The coffee is meant for the 'ritual pot'. In order to live according to custom Orgo's wife must be able to 'put on the ritual pot'. She herself has done her best to fulfil the custom, she has fetched the water, as she says, and now it is up to Ginonda to also do her best and give her some coffee. In this way Ginonda gets cornered because Orgo's wife has not only established common ground between herself and Ginonda (both being wives who have to provide coffee for their husbands) but she has also mustered the support of custom and consequently the support of the whole society behind her. Finally, (13) constitutes yet another strategy which is very common in Hamar. S establishes common ground with H *vis-à-vis* an imaginary third party whose behaviour contrasts with that of S and H. In one way this is a good technique by which S averts any aggression which might have been aroused in H by the FTA. 'I am not as bad as those 'white' [metaphor for mean] women', says Orgo's wife to Ginonda, implying 'if you have to be angry then, please, not with me but with those who, I agree, deserve to be criticized'. Thus the criticism of the imaginary woman turns into a kind of self-flattery by S. If S is bad, she still is not as bad as the mean woman. And this in turn makes S automatically come closer to H. She manages to establish some common ground which, as we know, is the aim of all positive politeness.

I think this example of conversational analysis shows clearly that, in actual speech exchanges, different strategies of politeness are employed in combination with one another. This gives them their dynamics and their effectiveness and it is in this way that they act as 'accelerators' or 'brakes' in social interaction (see Figure 12).

Figure 12   Sequencing of strategic switches

a) *Speaker*	*Sequence*	*Content of strategy*	*Class of strategy*
Orgo's wife	(1)	notice, attend to H	II.1
	(2)	claim reflexivity	II.13
	(3)	be optimistic	II.11
	(4)	minimize imposition	III.4
	(5)	euphemize, understate	IV.4
Ginonda	(6)	convey co-operation	II.9–13 (off record)
	(7)	use white lies	II.6
Orgo's wife	(8)	give/ask reasons	II.13
	(9)	state FTA as general rule	III.8
	(10)	minimize imposition	III.4
	(11)	give deference rhetorical question	III.5–7 IV.10
	(12)	dissociate S/H from infringement	III.7–9
	(13)	claim common ground divert aggression	II.7 II.?

1   2   3   4   5   6   7

b) *Negative politeness*   *Positive politeness*

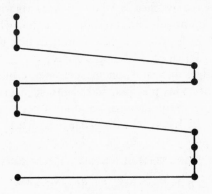

Given the fact that statements vary both in the degree to which they are on record or off record and in the degree to which they are either positively polite (reducing distance to H) or negatively polite (maintaining or increasing distance to H) we now can in principle chart strategic switches in a diagram. As empirical cases such as the one given above are rather complicated let me provide a hypothetical example. It demonstrates a super-strategy involving several switches from on-record negative politeness via off-record negative, and then positive politeness to on-record positive politeness. The switches are represented in Figure 13.

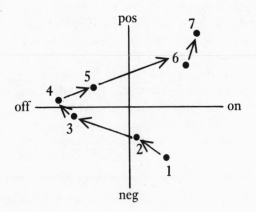

Figure 13 Super-strategy of strategic switches

Reading from 1 to 7, the sequence would exemplify a successful and encouraging series of switches. S, who initially starts with a cautious distance from H, eventually ends up with a statement which encodes an intimacy with H. Reading, however, from 7 to 1 the sequence manifests some defeat and disappointment of S, who at the beginning misjudges the situation in such a way that he cannot progressively 'better' his position, as did the speaker who started with on-record negative politeness, but finds it necessary to retreat step by step until he has reached a distance which H will accept.

3.3.2. THE PATTERNS OF STRATEGY DISTRIBUTION RECONSIDERED.

Brown and Levinson themselves see their approach as going beyond its immediate aim of explaining politeness phenomena. They say that their theory may have an 'explanatory role in the linking of social structure to behavioural patterns in a way the participants themselves do' (1978: 247). To demonstrate this they apply their FTA theory to the problem of 'ethos' and its cultural variability. They derive the term 'ethos' from Bateson's study of the Naven ceremony of the Iatmul (Bateson 1936), but they use it more restrictedly as a 'subset of the behavioural manifestations of Bateson's ethos' and as a notion that characterizes 'interactions, the behaviour of dyads and hence the generalizable aspects of the interaction patterns of groups' (1978: 307). These interactional qualities vary from situation to situation. Sometimes the interaction is warm and easy-going and sometimes it is cold and stiff; sometimes it is loud and bragging and sometimes it is modest and quiet, etc. Now, if such qualities appear frequently and constantly in a wide variety of relationships within a society, then Brown and Levinson speak of a particular 'ethos' within that society. In this way 'stability in social relations provides the explanation of regularities in interactional strategies' and 'ethos' may become the label for the regular 'quality of interaction characterizing groups, or social categories of persons, in a particular society' (1978: 248).

The FTA theory explains 'ethos' as follows. First, it states the three 'universals' of interaction which have already been outlined above but which had better be stated here again:

1. the universality of face, describable as two kinds of wants:
2. the potential universality of rational action devoted to satisfying others' face wants;

3. the universality of the mutual knowledge between interactants of (1) and (2).

The FTA strategies are potentially available to persons in any culture but their specific selection varies in terms of the social variables involved, among them most prominently 'distance' (D), 'power' (P), and 'rating of imposition' (R). Thus, according to the prevailing levels of P, D and R values FTAs are differently assessed in different cultures. For example, one may speak of 'positive-politeness cultures' and of 'negative-politeness cultures': 'in positive-politeness cultures the general level of W_x tends to remain low; impositions are thought of as small, social distance as no insuperable boundary to easy-going interaction, and relative power as never very great. These are the friendly back-slapping cultures, as in the western USA, some New Guinea cultures, and the Mbuti pygmies, for example. In contrast, the negative-politeness cultures are those lands of stand-offish creatures like the British (in the eyes of the Americans), the Japanese (in the eyes of the British)' (1978: 250).

Such cross-cultural differences in ethos assert themselves most drastically by the way in which they lead to cross-cultural misunderstanding where, as already indicated in the above quotation, the French may sound rude to the English, the American boorish to the English and the English pompous to the Americans, etc.

Taking a set of four dyads specified by high and low P and D values attributed to S and H, Brown and Levinson propose a model predicting the patterns of strategy distribution. I reproduce it here, omitting the dyad with high P and high D values because it would look similar to Dyad I.

Patterns of strategy distribution (1978: 255)

Dyad I: high P relations where H has high power over S (and D is low)	H ↑ bald on record (down) ↓ S	negative politeness off record (up)

Dyad II:
high D relations
(+ low P) where H
has no (or low) power
over S, and S and H
have high

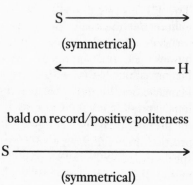

negative politeness/off record

S ─────────────────────→

(symmetrical)

←───────────── H

Dyad III:
low D, low P relations
where H has no (or low)
P over S, and S and H
have low D

bald on record/positive politeness

S ─────────────────────→

(symmetrical)

←───────────── H

When P relations generally carry a high value (Dyad I), as, for example, in India, Brown and Levinson predict both extremes of possible strategies to be in use 'with "bald on record" (and) perhaps positive politeness) going down to inferiors, and negative politeness and indirectness going up to superiors' (1978: 255). Landlord – labourer, or patron – client are typical examples of this kind.

When high D relations abound (Dyad II) as, for example, in Japan, the model predicts a 'symmetrical use of high numbered strategies' (1978: 256) and when low D and low P are emphasized (Dyad III), as, for example, in the USA, 'symmetrical use of bald on record and positive politeness would be expected' (1978: 256).

Having outlined Brown and Levinson's patterns of strategy selection, I will now discuss the patterns and will try to modify the theory.

First pattern

When the addressee (H) has high power (P) over the speaker (S) while at the same time the social distance (D) between H and S is low, Brown and Levinson predict that H will use linguistic realizations which are bald on record and that S will use negative politeness and off-record strategies. The prediction seems plausible, yet when one remembers the Hamar elders who say the opposite of what they mean in order to give their command more weight, Brown and Levinson's prediction is contradicted by the facts. In Hamar, when S has high P he often says the opposite of what he means and uses such indirect forms as rhetorical questions, irony, metaphors, etc., precisely because his authority is greater than H's. The reverse however does not happen. As we have seen (page 135 above) a young Hamar refrains from saying the opposite of what he means to a Hamar elder. He does not dare to force the elder to work out an implicature. This would, indeed, be an unacceptable imposition and the prevailing asymmetry of power is so strong that it has led to the practice of mumbling, where the young Hamar mumbles as he speaks to a superior in the hierarchy of social power and symbolically negates his speech competence. This is, as I have said above, the only implicature which the weak are allowed to force upon the socially powerful; all the other possibilities in the wide range of off-record statements are taboo for them and are the tools of the already powerful.

I propose then to rewrite Dyad I as follows:

Dyad IA:

high P relations where H has high power over S and D is low	bald on record together with on-record and off-record positive politeness (down)	H ↑ ↓ S	mainly on-record negative politeness; sometimes combined with positive politeness and conventional off-recordness (up)

Second pattern

Brown and Levinson predict that the pattern of Dyad I will change little when D is high rather than low. I do not think this is true. To demonstrate this let me recall for a moment the interchange between the duke and the butler which I have quoted above as a 'clear case of a conversational implicature' (page 45). The duke said, 'It's cold in here', whereupon the butler answered, 'I'll close the window, sir'. Now, someone can only use such an off-record statement with any reasonable expectation of success if the D value between himself and the addressee is low. As the duke and the butler are together daily, the duke can be sure that the butler will read the implications of his statement correctly. In a way the duke is being positively polite to his butler when, instead of confronting him with a harsh FTA (the bald-on-record command, 'Shut the window'), he gives him a metonymic hint, the very use of which implies that he 'shares' something with his servant. However, the co-operation which they 'share' is not one of equality. The butler has to serve the master and not vice versa. Therefore the seemingly polite hint is also something else, a reminder to the butler that he has constantly to think about the welfare of his master and that he should have anticipated that an open window might lead to a drop of the temperature and hence cause a lack of comfort to the master. The possibility of such implicit reasoning will diminish as the distance between S and H grows and the extent of shared knowledge decreases. We would therefore expect a dyad more closely resembling Brown and Levinson's Dyad I when high D relations prevail together with high P. The picture gets complicated however by the fact that high P implies the ability to overcome to some extent the lack of shared common ground implied by high D. That is, the powerful may use their power to get to know something about others and then use this knowledge to generate off-record expressions which enable them to further influence others. I therefore propose to characterize this dyad as follows:

Dyad IB:

high P relations	bald on record	H		on-record
where H has high	supported by		↑	negative
power over S	off-record			politeness
and D is high	(down)	↓	S	(up)

Third pattern

Brown and Levinson's second dyad also needs modification. Again my argument is that with the increase of social distance the possibility of using off-record statements in order to force implicatures decreases. Thus when D values are high (and P differentials are low) one would expect predominantly negative politeness with only minimal off-record elements and occasional and tentative switches from negative to positive politeness.

Dyad II:

high D relations and low P where H has no (or low) power over S, and S and H have high D	minimal off-record elements; negative politeness with occasional switches to positive politeness

S ——————————————→

(symmetrical)

←—————————————— H

Fourth pattern

The analyses of the preceding chapter have shown that off-record strategies flourish when D relations are small and differences in social power are comparatively low. Brown and Levinson only include bald-on-record and positive politeness in their dyad which I propose should be modified as follows:

Dyad III:

low D, low P relations where H has no (or low) P over S, and S and H have low D	bald on record; positive politeness with frequent switches to negative politeness: maximal use of off-record strategies.

S ——————————————→

(symmetrical)

←————————————— H

Brown and Levinson rightly note that low D and P relations facilitate the use of bald-on-record statements and lead to much use of positive politeness. However, to this it must be added that negative politeness may also be employed, so long as it is administered subtly and tactfully; that is, so long as it tends to be used in an off-record form, it may well be part of the intimacy which is generated by low D and P relations. In fact, off-record negative-politeness realizations often have a critical function to fulfil. They have to communicate two things at once, distance and intimacy. More precisely, they have to indicate distance within intimacy, saying something like 'Let us keep a distance while still not questioning our intimacy.' In real-life situations this is usually emphasized by a deliberate sequencing of switches between positive politeness and negative politeness (in both directions). Thus distances are constantly widened and narrowed as the verbal exchanges associated with a particular FTA develop.

We find, then, in Dyad III a variety of linguistic realizations (it is the widest of the dyads!) which range from bald-on-record through various shades of subtle on-record and off-record expressions of positive and negative politeness. That such richness should exist becomes clear when one stops for a moment and reflects about the nature of P. Only in certain formally organized groups with strictly defined role patterns and role hierarchies can social power between persons of similar status ever really be equal. In most, less formally organized, face-to-face groups, that is in 'natural' societies (in the sense in which languages may be distinguished as 'natural' and 'formal' ones), social power between 'equals' can never be predicted to remain equal for any length of time. On the contrary, P is always considered to be open to manipulation and this manipulation is anticipated by the speakers. Although two equals may have similar power today, tomorrow things may change. In fact, their verbal strategies may become the very factors which bring the change about. Brown and Levinson's formula for the computation of the weightiness of an FTA explains how this works. As I have outlined the argument already in detail (see 3.1) I need only repeat the most central points.

The formula $W_x = D (S,H) + P (H,S) + R_x$ compounds the three variables D, P and R into a single index of risk and any particular enactment encodes this risk. More correctly, it encodes the speaker's interpretation of the situation, the degree to which he considers a specific FTA to be dangerous or not. At the same time S's evaluation of P, D and R remains an open question because these are compounded in W_x. This leaves the information encoded in any specific W_x open to interpretation. Here lies the reason for the efficiency of FTA strategies in the manipulation of social power. A speaker can use the indeterminacy of the compounded factor W_x to exploit an FTA in such a way as to define and re-define the social relationship between himself and the addressee to his own advantage. Most importantly, he can increase his own P *vis-à-vis* the addressee. Brown and Levinson have given the example of a speaker who uses a bald-on-record FTA to claim (by implicature) that he is holding power over H. If he gets away with such a claim the speaker automatically asserts (or alters) the definition of his relationship to the addressee to his advantage. The same holds true for all realizations of positive and negative politeness, and nowhere do the struggles for a re-ranking of P thrive more vigorously than in the realm of off-record message construction.

By way of conclusion let me say that I have discussed here the dyads in the order in which they were presented by Brown and Levinson. Brown and Levinson's scheme moves from high D relations to low D relations. As far as I can see, this presentation does not attempt to be more than a preliminary listing of possible variations in the dyads. There remains therefore the question of how the different communicative strategies have arisen historically. Or, put differently, we still need a theory which shows how in the past specific social structures have determined the emergence of specific communicative strategies. For example, if we assume that kin-based 'face-to-face' societies have historically preceded state societies and societies based on distinctions of wealth, class, etc., it would make sense to begin the model of patterns of strategy distribution with low D relations and move from them on to relations of high D. A simplified historical scheme of patterns of strategy distribution would thus be based on the following sequence of dyads:

1) *Low D, High P*
   Prototype: parent–child relationship

2) *Low D, Low P*
   Prototype: age-mates

Predominant relationships in stateless societies

3) *High D, Low P*
   Prototype: market relationship
              between buyer and seller   Predominant
                                          relationships
                                          in state
4) *High D, High P*   societies
   Prototype: bureaucracy

Interesting as it may be, this possible extension of Brown and Levinson's theory is beyond the scope of this essay and has to be followed up elsewhere.

4 Symbolization and social domination

Symbolization constitutes a prevalent mode in which social competition and the struggle for social domination are conducted. This assertion does not, of course, come to us as something unexpected. In the preceding section we have already seen that off-record speech is not always used to evade and defend but is often used to do quite the contrary, that is, to persuade, impose and even attack. As the very notion of the face-threatening act (FTA) already implies, politeness is associated with something threatening and is not in every case as gracious as it appears. Beneath the surface of S's pleasing words may lie hidden intentions which are quite detrimental to H, and what is more, his pleasing words themselves may act as the very weapons with which S tries to harm another. What works well for ego to save the face of alter, also works well to destroy it. We could see this very clearly when looking at off-record positive and negative politeness and when examining the elements of positive politeness in what Brown and Levinson have called 'off-record strategies'. Also, general sociological theory tells us that symbolization and social domination may go together. Ever since Marx and Nietzsche launched their attacks on religion, sociologists have, in one way or another, tried to show how symbols play a role in social domination. The main thrust of the argument is that symbols help to create a false consciousness which in turn helps to perpetuate social inequalities and systems of exploitation.

Bourdieu has convincingly developed this position into a theory of symbolic violence. Symbols, says Bourdieu, censor, euphemize and distort the perceptions of the socially disadvantaged. The more powerful 'impose the principles of the construction of reality' on to the less powerful and both enter a complicity which disguises the unpleasant truth inherent in their relationships, that is, the truth of inequality and exploitation. The passage where, in my view, Bourdieu sums up this theory of symbolic violence most succinctly reads as follows:

The reason for the pre-capitalist economy's great need for symbolic violence is that the only way in which relations of domination can be set up, maintained, or restored, is through strategies which, being expressly oriented towards the establishment of relationships of personal dependence, must be disguised and transfigured lest they destroy themselves by revealing their true nature; in a word, they must be *euphemized*. Hence the *censorship* to which the overt manifestation of violence, especially in its naked economic form, is subjected by the logic characteristic of an economy in which interests can only be satisfied on condition that they be disguised in and by the strategies aiming to satisfy them. It would be a mistake to see a contradiction in the fact that violence is here both more present and more hidden. Because the pre-capitalist economy cannot count on the implacable, hidden violence of objective mechanisms, it resorts *simultaneously* to forms of domination which may strike the modern observer as more brutal, more primitive, more barbarous, or, at the same time, as gentler, more humane, more respectful of persons. This coexistence of overt physical and economic violence and the most refined symbolic violence is found in all institutions characteristic of this economy, and at the heart of every social relationship. (Bourdieu 1977: 191–2).

Bourdieu truly points here at the heart of the matter: in social life, physical violence is paralleled and works in conjunction with symbolic violence. Yet, while Bourdieu's analysis of symbolic and economic violence is extremely telling, it also is one-sided. Economic exploitation is not the only motive for symbolization. Rather it is one among several others, and consequently one has to study symbolization and social domination within a wider theoretical framework which embraces all the different motives which can lead to symbolization. This is what I have done in the present study. Having first examined the basic human faculty for symbolization (section 2), I have then gone on and asked to what purpose the faculty is put in human life.

Of the various possible intentions (aesthetic, cognitive, affective, etc.) I have isolated the social intentions, and after having dealt with politeness, I now turn to social domination, viewing both politeness and domination as subcategories of the overall class of social influence. I begin by showing how social domination operates in Hamar. First I present a set of six cases which I then discuss. In this way the cases will be more telling and the discussion will lead to one single connected argument. The cases all centre on the problem of language usage and social domination in the political domain of Hamar where P differentials and D values are generally low. The situation can be characterized by Dyad III above). In Hamar, Dyad III is associated with a multitude of everlasting struggles between members of the society who try to rerank, or reassert a positive ranking of their respective P values within the context of generally small P differentials.

4.1 Speaking and social domination in Hamar

SIX CASES

Case 1: speech as fighting

We drive through the dry river-bed of the Woito and on the savannah close to the mountains we meet the first Hamar-speaking herdsman, a Tsamai. Baldambe converses with him and I watch. The Tsamai not only speaks Hamar, he speaks like a Hamar. I am struck by the forcefulness of his speech, the decisiveness of his gestures, the distinct rhythm in the flow of his talk. This fresh impression supports my old finding that speaking and the ability to speak are here more highly valued than in other parts of the world that I have seen. There is even an excitement which goes with such speech encounters, an excitement which has to do not so much with the content of the speech but with the talking itself, or rather content and form merge and the excitement of the speaker consists in anticipating how he will say certain things. Watching the two men I have the feeling that I am watching two fighters, there are even movements and stances which remind me of fighting. Well, a kind of playful fighting. (Lydall and Strecker 1979a: 87–8)

Case 2: Baldambe dominates his conversational partners

Early in the morning, the men have coffee in Gemarro's house and then move over to Aike (Baldambe) where I join them. Aike is the one who talks the most. His older brother Surrambe sits quietly, looks depressed and moves his lips as if talking to himself. Nor does Gemarro say anything. He wears a dark expression and spits occasionally. Zinu, the old Kara man, speaks at times, but Aike, who addresses himself mostly to Zinu, dominates him completely. (1979a: 28)

Case 3: Gemarro excels at brideprice negotiations

Early in the morning Anti jingles into our house and, getting my coffee bowl, tells us that three young men have come demanding cattle and a gun from Baldambe as a marriage payment [for] ... the girl he stole into marriage. I get my tape recorder ready and record first the hushed talk in Aikenda's house where Baldambe and his brothers discuss how to meet the arguments of the in-laws. Then I record the arguments between the in-laws and the men of Dambaiti who speak on behalf of Baldambe. An 'informal' talk inside the cattle kraal follows, then an 'official' talk (again by the gateway of the cattle kraal) and, finally, a noisy and relaxed talk around the coffee pot after all the negotiations are over. Gemarro once again shows himself to be a magnificent speaker. He has an inexhaustible sense of drama. Is this why Baldambe hates him? Are they competing with each other? (1979a: 49)

Case 4: Competition between Baldambe and Gemarro

Early in the morning four young Kara men arrive. They bring a complaint and ask the Dambaitians for assistance: Gilo's son from Ande village has taken a gun by force from one of his Kara guests. Gilo's son took the gun because the Kara man owed him a leopard skin. The Kara have coffee with Baldambe first and later go over to Gemarro's house to talk to Kula the 'black', Banko, Balle and the others who have arrived there. Then they go back to talk with Baldambe again. It strikes me that Gemarro, Kula, Balle, etc., do not, however, talk with Baldambe! In the end the Kara are sent away with the remark that not all the men of Dambaiti are present today (which is not in fact true) and that they should return another day. Is this a trick to postpone negotiations and decisions? Maybe it is an important principle of Hamar arbitration, but it also seems to contain an element of competition for power and decision-making. Dambaiti is divided and it is not clear who is to be the decision-maker. Baldambe (as the Kara seem to think)? Obviously Gemarro, Kula and Balle think this should not be so. Gemarro has done his hair recently, has stuck a small white feather in his clay cap and has painted his face red. What a transformation! He has cleared his homestead and kraal of all weeds and dirt and has repaired the fences. (1979a: 75–6)

Case 5: Speech and self-glorification

Banko is here, looking neat and young with a splendid new clay cap. It strikes me that it is always after important events like hunting and trading expeditions that men tend to redo their hair. This fits in with the main purpose of such ventures: self-glorification. It is important to look good at the moment when one has something new to relate and talk about, for the listeners do not only lend you their ears, they also watch you. (1979a: 141)

Case 6: Wealth, verbal competence and leadership

Raised voices in Aikenda's house wake me before sunrise. The abbreviations, the pauses, the pace, the quick echoing responses, the varying levels of tone – all these tell me that great speakers have arrived. I can also tell where they come from – only the men of southern Hamar speak so powerfully. So I am not surprised to find Arbala Lomotor sitting next to the coffee pot. He, however, does not talk; he leaves the word to an old, grey-haired man. The old man, like many of those whom I meet from the south, has a strength and confidence and ruthlessness which I attribute to the environment of the wide open spaces on the south and their proximity to hostile neighbours. The south seems to select for strong and rich people. The south offers a regal way of life: large herds, especially herds of goats, periodically exchanged for grain in Banna, Kara, Tsamai. In the south, no poor man can survive. That is why the census shows more poor people the further one moves north.

In Hamar terms, 'poor' means lacking herds of cattle and goats. In some ways, wealth and oral competence go together, or, more exactly, oral competence and the ownership of herds! A remark of Choke's comes to my mind: he said that in the south everybody talks at the public meetings. He implies that this is bad, because it prohibits clear decision-making: 'Look at Assile, Wungabaino, Mirsha, the men of those places never stop fighting and raiding. Everybody does what he wants, nobody is listened to. Look at Angude and Kadja, those men only allow a small number of selected people to speak, and they stick to the decisions of those speakers'. (1979a: 236–7)

CASE DISCUSSIONS

Discussion of case 1

Case 1 sets out the perspective from which I have gained my knowledge. As an anthropologist entering another culture I was struck more by what was different than by what was familiar to me from my own society. It was speaking and the ability to speak that impressed me above all else in Hamar. In modern western culture writing and printing have taken over many functions of the spoken word, especially in the sphere of social control and decision-making. The emphasis on communicative competence has changed accordingly. It has shifted from the spoken word to print on paper. This does not mean that verbal skill and resourcefulness have become redundant, but it means that they are submerged and over-shadowed by other forms of communication. Therefore it is easy to overlook them. Not so, however, in Hamar. Here the spoken word reigns and has, until now, remained the supreme and undisputed tool of social competition. The spirit which goes with it is so strong and fierce that I have been led, as case 1 shows, to compare speaking to physical fighting.

Discussion of case 2

At the time I noted down case 2 (9 October 1970), I did not yet have much insight into what I was observing. Retrospectively this makes the case all the more interesting. Why does Baldambe's older brother Surrambe sit quietly, look depressed and move his lips as if talking to himself? And why does Gemarro keep silent, wearing a dark expression and spitting occasionally? The men are drinking their morning coffee and enjoying what should be an easy flow of conversation, yet the atmosphere is strained. Now, years after the event, as I have become more familiar with the dramatis personae, the reason for their uneasiness has become more clear to me: between Baldambe and Surrambe, and between Baldambe and Gemarro, a deep-seated rivalry existed, in each case belonging to a different social domain.

The Baldambe – Surrambe rivalry was one between brothers. Surrambe is the third child of Gino's (Berinas's) first wife whereas Baldambe is the first child of Gino's third wife (see Figure 14). The first son of Gino's first wife would have been the ideal head of the entire sibling group. He would have carried on the name of his grandfather (Biri), and his authority over his younger brothers and their families would have been unquestionable. However, Gino's first son died as a small child and was never able to perpetuate Biri's name. After Biri, a daughter (Maiza) was born and only then came Surrambe (Gapha). From the start, therefore, although he is the most senior of the brothers, Surrambe was stigmatized, and lacked the aura and authority of a truly first-born son (*djalepha*). Gino's second wife first produced two daughters (Goiti and Yayu) and then two sons (Tsasi and Lukusse). In terms of authority within the sibling group these brothers occupy even weaker positions than Surrambe. The third wife (Goiti) was lucky enough to produce a first-born son who was to live (i.e. Baldambe). Not only was her first child a boy but all her subsequent children were boys too. In Hamar terms this meant that the marriage of Gino and Goiti was truly blessed; it carried *barjo* (good fortune, well-being, etc.; see below). Gino married Goiti after his first two wives had died, and she undertook to bring up the children of these women as well as her own sons. Gino felt that only with his third wife did his real family life begin. Furthermore, both he and Goiti favoured Baldambe over and above his older brothers and in time he came to be regarded as a kind of *djalepha*. This position, however, is in conflict with the cultural prescriptions which make Surrambe the legitimate head with regard to ritual and control of the herds. His natural gifts, the support of his father, his strong-minded mother, his younger full brothers and Goiti's patrilineal kin, etc., have turned Baldambe into the *de facto* leader of the wider sibling group. Surrambe has withdrawn from the struggle for dominance. The strain has in fact been so much that he has become a stutterer and occasionally he has even retreated into a kind of madness (which interestingly has always been cured

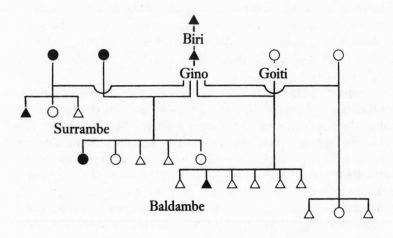

Figure14   Genealogy: conflict between Baldambe and Surrambe

ritually!). When it comes to ritual and the control of the herd which has been inherited by the sibling group from Gino, he still exercises authority which is much resented by Baldambe. So the two men are both handicapped and each is in some respect stronger and in another respect weaker than the other. What I was witnessing on that October morning in 1970 was one instance of their ongoing antagonism.

However, the main source of rivalry between Baldambe and Gemarro lies not in their kinship ties but in their position as co-residents who compete for political leadership. Both aspire to be the spokesman (*ayo*) of Dambaiti. Spokesmanship is not inherited but achieved through the good and effective use of speech. An *ayo* advises and commands and if his advice and his command lead to success this proves that he is a real *ayo*. But, as Baldambe has told us,

> if those [whom one *ayo* has directed] . . . don't kill the giraffe, the buffalo, the lion, the ostrich, the leopard, but if they meet the enemy and one of them dies, it will be said: 'His word is bad, his command is bad. Stop him.' And he will be stopped from taking command. Someone else will be selected to take his place. (Lydall & Strecker 1979b: 109)

The question of who should be, or rather who is naturally so well endowed that he should be, the *ayo* of any residential area in Hamar is always open to question, and as a result much of Hamar everyday politics revolves around this question. Baldambe and Gemarro are neighbours in Dambaiti and while Baldambe has a larger sibling group which supports him, Gemarro, who is slightly older, has many local allies who join forces with him whenever they feel threatened by the younger, yet ambitious, Baldambe. As leadership is equated with spokesmanship one can easily understand why Baldambe and Gemarro do not feel at ease when they find themselves sharing a drink from the same coffee pot. Or, rather, it is not the problem of sharing coffee from the same pot, but of sharing it with no one else to mediate.

This brings me to the fourth participant at the coffee session. He is Zinu, an old man from a neighbouring tribe, the Kara who live at the lower Omo river. His father was a bond-friend (*bel*; see page 75) of Baldambe's father, and Zinu and Baldambe have continued the relationship. Every year by October, the waters of the Omo begin to recede, and the Kara begin planting their fields along the banks of the river. From the time of planting until the harvest is ripe there is an acute food shortage. In order to overcome this shortage the Kara go up into the mountains and try to get grain from the Hamar who usually harvest a second crop at this time. Zinu is not, therefore, simply a guest. He is first and foremost a hungry man with a family back in Kara who are even hungrier than himself. Zinu has come to persuade Baldambe to let him have a share of what is already a meagre supply of grain. This makes him utterly dependent on Baldambe, and, naturally enough, he agrees to anything Baldambe may say and is also ready to act as a partner for Baldambe in that 'tight dialogue between two persons to exclude a third party' which I have described above (page 148).

As case 2 shows, Baldambe uses Zinu as a pawn in his verbal game against his two opponents. Surrambe and Gemarro have both been caught in an awkward situation and this is what makes them uneasy. As Zinu is Baldambe's man and not theirs, they can only sit, listen to Baldambe's disgusting speech competence, drink their coffee and leave as soon as they have quenched their thirst. Of course, the situation could quickly change. Zinu might leave the house and a close friend of Gemarro's might enter. This would in its turn leave

Baldambe with a gloomy face and cheer Gemarro up enormously. Or, a neutral person might enter, modifying the overall pattern of relationships in such a way that the situation does not allow any single participant to dominate the others thus making the situation more bearable for everyone concerned.

Discussion of case 3

When observing case 3, the competition between Baldambe and Gemarro had already become apparent to me, yet, at the time, the logic of the situation still evaded me. Why did Gemarro excel so much on that day? Why did he 'show himself to be such a magnificent speaker'? Today I explain the event as follows. Unlike case 2, on this occasion it is Baldambe who is caught and has to suffer Gemarro excelling in front of his very eyes (and ears!) without himself being able to do anything to counteract him. How does this come about? Baldambe had stolen a young girl into marriage some time earlier. The practice of marriage by theft, though customarily allowed, is rather risky and can only have a pleasant outcome if the 'thief' makes good his initial assault on the family of the girl by ostentatiously showing his eagerness quickly to fulfil all payments for the bride which they may demand and, above all, by demonstrating an attitude of great humility towards the girl's kin. When his bride's kinsmen arrived at his gateway, the great speaker, Baldambe, was, therefore, condemned to remain subdued and silent in public. Custom forbade him to speak for himself directly. Word was given, instead, to the local elders, among whom Gemarro was most prominent. Ironically, this meant that all that Gemarro said (and how he said it) was beneficial for Baldambe in one domain while being detrimental to him in another. As Baldambe's go-between Gemarro was able to ensure good relations between Baldambe and his new in-laws – but at the same time his excellent performance enhanced his own reputation as a spokesman to the disadvantage of Baldambe within the political sphere of Dambaiti. Not only did Gemarro show that he was a natural *ayo*, he also showed that he was greater than Baldambe, for from now on did not Baldambe owe part of his personal welfare to Gemarro's protection? This, I think, is the logic which explains why Gemarro performed so strikingly well when he defended Baldambe against his in-laws.

Discussion of case 4

Case 4 brings out the competition between Baldambe and Gemarro more clearly. The most interesting part of the case lies in the fact that it shows the divergent strength and weakness of the two antagonists. Baldambe's strength lies in that his and his father's names are known far beyond the confines of Dambaiti. So it is that when the Kara want to settle a dispute, they come first to Baldambe. They see in him the *ayo* of the area. But to be known and respected abroad does not necessarily mean one has similar support at home, and indeed Baldambe's position in Dambaiti is far from undisputed. As case 4 shows, the elders of Dambaiti back Gemarro rather than Baldambe. More correctly, they side with Gemarro to such an extent that Baldambe's power is successfully counteracted. It would, no doubt, have been proof and an expression of Baldambe's position as *ayo* if the Kara had received what they wanted at his homestead. For this reason, Gemarro is in no way motivated to help the Kara. To help them would mean to help Baldambe. This is the reason why the Kara were unsuccessful in their attempt to enlist Baldambe as their arbitrator. Had either only Baldambe or only Gemarro been present, the Kara would probably have found more support in Dambaiti. However, the competition between Baldambe and Gemarro produced a stalemate, where Baldambe's external esteem was counteracted by Gemarro's internal support. As a consequence, Baldambe did not get an opportunity to speak for the Kara (and outshine Gemarro) and the Kara had to go elsewhere to achieve their ends (they finally found support in another settlement area).

There is a further important element in the case. The event reminds us that the competition for spokesmanship is situational and that it is intimately bound up with the mental and physical energy of the contestants. A person's life never progresses on a straight line. Rather there occur numerous fluctuations in physical and mental well-being and in Hamar these fluctuations are forever affecting the actual social power of a man, especially his claim to be considered an *ayo*. Or, to put it differently, life is not such that men can aspire to be *ayo* in a regular and steady way. On the contrary, they are only able to aspire to it in bouts when they feel well and strong. This is a reflection of the overall pattern of Hamar life where few things are predictable: the rain may fall in Dambaiti this year and produce an abundant harvest and fail to be sufficient in neighbouring settlements, or vice versa; here the herds may thrive while there they may get decimated by tsetse fly; people who use this water-hole may get sick while the ones who use another may stay well; this part of the country may be raided while that part remains safe, etc. The fact that Gemarro has done his hair, has painted his face, has cleared his homestead and kraals and has repaired the fences are all part and parcel of a phase in his life when he has energy enough to muster his strength, ingenuity and his courage to compete with Baldambe for social power. One does, after all, compete not only with words as a speaker, but also with one's whole personality, which not only speaks to the ear of the listener but also to his eye. This observation brings us to consider case 5.

Discussion of case 5

Banko returned from a journey which had involved much travelling, hunting, meeting neighbouring tribes, visiting the cattle camps, etc. All this furnished him with a wealth of new information. To make the best of it he did not disseminate the information indiscriminately. Rather, he told the news on special occasions (the *pen gia* between age-mates; see page 85–87). Each time he did so he gained in esteem and status. The reason for this was not just that he entertained and satisfied curiosity, but also was closely related to some basic social needs, as the following observation shows:

> Choke has come for a visit and while he relates to us the 'talk of the country' I observe what I have often realized before: Baldambe and Gemerro listen to Choke's (well-told) accounts and are extremely interested in every detail. If a man is not fully informed of what is happening around him, who it was who died, who it was who consulted the intestines of an animal, who had a quarrel ... then he is not counted a full citizen. Nothing depresses Baldambe or Gemarro more than hearing of an important event long after it happened. The idea is to hear of an event while it is still going on or shortly afterwards and then to subject it to one's own evaluation, criticism, which, I think, may well feed back into the situation. As Hamar is a society without centralized institutions of social control, this eagerness of the men to be informed makes sense (1979a:80)

In case 5, Banko told the news just as Choke did, that is as well as he could. He used it as an opportunity to show that he was an indispensable member of the society, that people needed him in order to know what was happening ... All this inevitably took on a form of self-glorification. As I have already said, in Hamar you do not flatter others but yourself. You attend to your own 'face' and this is not only figuratively but also literally true. Hence, as soon as he had returned, Banko asked someone to prepare him a 'splendid new clay cap' (a hair-style where the hair gets intertwined and covered with clay; small cylinders are inserted and once the clay has hardened ostrich feathers can be stuck in the cylinders). Clad in this impressive hair-do and an extra string of beads, Banko related the news. In this way he glorified himself and at the same time fulfilled a task which was essential for the welfare of his community.

Discussion of case 6

This final case relates speech and social competition to their economic basis. When the men of the south visited Dambaiti I was reminded of what, in less exaggerated form, applies to all of Hamar. I observed that the southerners speak even more powerfully than the northerners. Reflecting on the source of their strength I concluded that it must have to do with two facts. First, in the south, the transitory zone towards the semi-desert east of Lake Turkana, hardly any poor families can survive. Secondly, the south is closest to neighbouring groups which can be raided for stock (Borana, Gabare, Samburu, Galeba). Naturally the southerners have been most involved in these raids.

In southern Hamar, then, most men are rich, otherwise they would not be there. By rich I mean, in Hamar terms that is, anyone who owns a considerable number of cattle, sheep, goats and donkeys. What is more, in the south each man thinks that he will become even richer overnight. That is, by raiding, which is part of the southerner's way of life and promises any day to suddenly increase his wealth and potential social power (each raided animal can be used in social transactions to gain influence over others). This is why, as Choke pointed out to me, the southerners all aspire to be an *ayo*. Each of them feels he is as good as (or better than) the others and that any day the fortunes of raiding may favour him so that he will outshine all his competitors. So, as he speaks, his confidence (in his tone of voice and in the way he tells a good story) reflects not only the achievements of his earlier life, but also his anticipation of future success (which may become a self-fulfilling prophecy). As one moves north in Hamar the amount of annual rainfall increases and people can survive even if they have little or no livestock; so the northern poor become the natural followers of richer and more influential *ayo* such as we have already met in the persons of Baldambe and Gemarro. In this sense Choke is right when he points to the fact that in the north fewer men aspire to the position of *ayo* than in the south. Yet even in the north economic inequality is very slight and in no way is any individual man able to estabish a lasting economic domination over a number of other men. In other words, the political rivalry and competition for power and influence is based on the very absense of any economic means to perpetuate inequality.

With this I end my presentation of the cases and move on to consider the linguistic means and realizations by which the struggle for social domination is fought.

4.2 Domination within the strategies of politeness

In section 3, I examined the strategies of politeness one by one. The task was arduous and led through a large amount of detail both because of the complexity of Brown and Levinson's framework and because of the detail of my data from Hamar. However, I think the effort has been worthwhile as it is the fineness of detail which, in the end, has shown us how and why people make use of symbolization. Furthermore, I think there can now be no doubt of the pervasiveness of symbolization in everyday life. As we have seen, this pervasiveness is not without reason, and over and over again people make use of the advantages and sometimes even the necessity of employing symbolic statements in interactional processes.

In the present section I want to bring out this point even more clearly by showing that the strategies of politeness may equally well be used for an opposite purpose. Rather than to save the face of alter and ensure his freedom from imposition, they may be turned aggressively against alter in order to damage his face and become a tool to put him down and dominate him. In other words, the strategies outlined by Brown and Levinson serve both the intention of redress (politeness) and the motive of aggression (domination) equally well.

4.2.1 BALD ON RECORD WITHOUT REDRESS

Imagine two complete strangers meeting in the street. If S were to address H with a direct imperative (with the exception of one carrying the desperate urgency and high noise level of a cry like 'Help!'), then such use of a direct imperative would be felt by H to be an unacceptable FTA. He would ask himself why S does not make the effort to soften the FTA by choosing a more elaborate linguistic realization. As the answer can only be an unpleasant one, he probably turns his back on the stranger. On the other hand, if the speaker and the addressee are familiar with each other, if they share common ground, often co-operate with one another, etc., then the use of the direct imperative is possible and becomes a tool with which S and H can communicate both directly and indirectly, and they can employ it to express special respect as well as disregard. We have already seen how the direct imperative many serve to show respect. Brown and Levinson have given the example of a pre-emptive invitation which I have interpreted as a 'flouting of an expected flouting' (3.2.1). In the same way as the strategy alleviates the weight of an FTA it may also aggravate it. If S is more powerful than H and has the option either to do an FTA bald on record or to choose a realization which involves some kind of redress, then the choice of the harder line automatically encodes an assault on H's face.

An example from Hamar illustrates this point. One day I noted down in my diary the following entry:

> Jean has 'discovered' that the power of the word which is so important in blessing and chanting is closely related to the actual command of men over women. Men always accompany the activities of the women with a command. A command which is seemingly unnecessary, yet part of the system of thought and action. (1979a:65)

Why do the men always accompany the activities of the women with a command? Certainly not because their commands are immediately necessary. Indeed, if they do anything they interfere rather than help, and when her man is away a woman runs her household just as, if not more, efficiently than when he is present. So the man is doing something else when he commands his wife, he is indicating something which he must not express directly and openly lest it lose its effectiveness. This is what Jean Lydall pointed out: the men use their commands at home as a living and constant proof of the power of their words. The responsive behaviour of the women (be they wives, sisters or daughters) serves to reassert an aspiration for power that goes far beyond the domestic domain. As, in the repetitive course of everyday life, the men find their commands successful in the social realm, they feel that the model may also be transferred into the realms of nature. But just as women do their work whether the men utter instructions or not, so nature in fact takes its own course whether the men chant blessings or not.

4.2.2 POSITIVE POLITENESS

When examining positive politeness we saw that to notice someone expressly is one of the ways in which S can 'anoint' H's face and make him feel that the imposition contained in an FTA is not really as threatening as it might seem. Thus to notice H is a strategy of politeness. Yet the same strategy quickly turns into one of social domination when the criteria by which S chooses to notice H are *de facto* more to S's advantage than to H's. The social categories in which a person may be classed are always manifold and they are not, in every case, the ones in which a person wants to be classed. To be classed as A or B may involve getting cornered and pinned down to particular dependencies, responsibilities, stigmata, etc., while to be classed as C or D may mean freedom from distraction and imposition. In short, the outwardly polite gesture of accepting someone as 'what he is' may hide a manipulation which is advantageous for S and, relatively speaking, detrimental to H. We have met examples of this kind in the Hamar use of terms of address (page 74).

When examining flattery (page 77–79) we could see that exaggerated interest, approval, sympathy, etc., becomes an imposition as soon as

S uses it beyond reasonable limits. As such limits are never really clear, exaggeration can easily go too far, and interlocutors may find it hard to stop. This inflationary process is well known in flattery and its inverse form, boasting. Both are typically competitive: the more A flatters, the more B flatters; the more A boasts, the more B boasts. In boasting the attempt to dominate is outright. By saying, 'I am great', S implies that H is not as great as he himself or at least that his power is greater than H might have thought. Note, however, that while the process of domination by boasting may be drastin, it never occurs between actors whose social power is very unequal. Rather it is characteristic of situations in which the P values of the interactants are roughly similar and not fixed, thus allowing for a perpetual wrangling for more power. Hamar, which in many ways resembles such a situation, is a society where boasting is prevalent and flattery is not. In flattery the element of domination is slightly more hidden than in boasting. S unduly compliments and overpraises H and by so doing S seems to humble himself. But does he really? Is not the essence of flattery that it is false and that, if accepted by H, it dislodges him from his real and secure position within the cultural and social context to which he belongs? What H gains by the flattery is problematic. His public image may seem to increase but the increase may well remain purely illusionary. S's gains, on the other hand are something real, that is, he has achieved progress in his attempt to manipulate H if H accepts the flattery. This is the reason why H usually feels awkward when he gets flattered and tries to return the flattery as quickly as possible, thereby trying to get rid of it. This in turn leads to further responses, and to the inflationary process mentioned above.

Brown and Levinson here observed that by telling a good story S can communicate his intrinsic interest and benevolent intention towards H. He can 'pull H in', as the authors put it. By the same token one might add that telling a good story may be used to push H out; that is, to intimidate him, make him feel without support and small and incompetent compared with S who excels and speaks ostentatiously well. All the different styles of Hamar speaking and the ways of telling a good story which have been described above (i.e. the invitation to echo, dramatization by means of directly quoted speech, onomatopoeic words and the imitation of voices and natural sounds, the use of summary words, etc.) can be used against H in order to dominate him and outdo him in the struggle of social competition. When describing the Hamar *pen gia* (telling the news) I indicated this double-edged aspect of narration. On the one hand a good story may benefit H but on the other hand it may implicitly put him at a disadvantage. This is what I meant when I wrote of the cruelty contained in poetics which leads H to enjoy the artistic elements in S's speech with a divided heart, knowing 'that the speaker's verbal art is closely related to aggression and social domination' (page 87).

When Brown and Levinson discussed the strategy of presuppose/raise/assert common ground they were thinking of a situation where S and H hold roughly the same social power (the P differential being minimal). Under such circumstances it is indeed polite to presuppose/raise/assert common ground, because by doing so S identifies himself closely with H by emphasizing the area where their separate social spheres intersect. But as the P differential increases, the situation changes: if S's power over H grows, the presupposition of common ground becomes more and more condescending and begins to ring untrue and if H's power over S grows, the 'raising of common ground' turns into presumptuousness. In both cases the use of the strategy begins to aggravate the FTA rather than to reduce its impact. In short, the strategy which once served to save face now begins to threaten it. In the case of condescension it threatens the face of the socially less powerful and in the case of presumption it threatens the face of the powerful (and is, in this latter case, a very risky strategy).

The positive-politeness technique of joking serves to put H at ease, as Brown and Levinson have shown, but once again it is not difficult to see that the opposite is also true. Just as joking may put H at ease so it may alternatively make him feel ill at ease. What is more, it may be used as a fine tool to chisel lightly, but effectively, little by little, at H's public image until in the end his face is damaged. Mockery, teasing, irony and all the countless forms of joking which force H to laugh with others at his own expense, where in reality he feels like crying, all belong to the daily drama of interaction where interlocutors jostle with each other and try to gain or keep the upper hand. Typically, however, the social distance between the interactants must not be too wide nor the P differential too great, for otherwise the joke will be out of place and may backfire on the one who has cracked it.

Distance also plays a central role in the strategy which conveys that S and H are co-operators. It may show true homage to H's face if S conveys that he and H are co-operating in the same activity and therefore share the same goals. In such a case the objective tasks associated with the activity justify and legitimate the behaviour of the interactants. As Brown and Levinson have pointed out, politeness can be altogether abandoned when the focus of interaction becomes completely task-oriented (see 3.2.1). But then, co-operation is a delicate matter and the way in which labour should be divided is often far from clear. In fact, often enough H may not want to work at all or at least not with S, etc. Thus the strategies which appeal to joint co-operation tend to put pressure on H (see Brown and Levinson 1978:130) and here politeness quickly turns into domination where S overruns and bullies H. The underlying mechanism is the 'point-of-view flip' already described above (page 90,106) in which S presumptuously implies that the addressee wants the speaker's wants to be satisfied.

Here are a few of Brown and Levinson's examples (1978:130–3) which, though given as instances of politeness, clearly show the aggressive and dominating way in which the strategies may be applied:

1. 'I know you can't bear parties, but this one will really be good – do come.'
2. 'Look, I am sure you won't mind if I borrow your typewriter.'
3. 'Let's have a cookie, then.'
4. 'Why not lend me your cottage for the weekend?'

The giving of non-material gifts has already been dealt with in the discussion of politeness. The giving of material gifts cannot be called a linguistic realization, and so this strategy needs (though very interesting in itself) no further discussion here. Yet let us note in passing that the gift is a well-known tool for social domination. In fact sometimes 'domination' may be too soft a word for it. Marcel Mauss preferred stronger terms when he described the competitive gift-giving among the Kwakiutl, Tlingit and Haida. He spoke of 'violence', 'antagonism' and the 'war of property' (Mauss 1954: 31–5).

4.2.3 NEGATIVE POLITENESS

Generally speaking, negative politeness is less likely to turn into an offensive strategy in which S dominates and unduly coerces H. The element of respect, avoidance and distancing is too strong to allow S to turn the tables easily and to attack. Yet there are a number of exceptions which show that even in the overtly defensive strategies of negative politeness, aggression may be hidden.

To begin with, hedges – which I have also called weasel words and chameleon words (page 99) – constitute a very general form of symbolization and they may be used equally well in defensive and offensive strategies. Whenever they are used, they shield S from being taken to task for what he has said. If H challenges him and S finds the challenge too strong and wants to retreat, he will always find a way out. Thus slander, insult, insinuations, etc., tend to work by way of hedges.

Similarly it may be an effective strategy of domination to minimize the imposition, Rx. There is no limit in the extent to which S can use this strategy to his own, rather than to H's, advantage. At first sight, however, this does not seem to affect H's face negatively. As long as H finds the minimization acceptable, the strategy leads to S humbling himself and there is no attack on H. (For the complicated feedback of material concession and social power, see page 101,125). The situation changes radically when H finds the minimization of R_x unacceptable. Now the imposition becomes a threat to his own face and in turn may be used by S to expose H and involve him in an interaction in which H can only lose. The reason for this is that any aggressive disagreement by H over the value of R_x leaves H with the problem of asserting, possibly even explaining, that R_x has in fact a higher value than S has implied. This is an extremely humbling thing to do and H tends to let S have his way and accepts the imposition, because any further insistence on a high evaluation of R_x is detrimental to his publicly recognized social power. All this is explained by our familiar formula which compounds the factors D, P and R into one index (W_x) which encodes the perceived danger of an FTA. As any politeness realization leaves open the question of how far D, P or R determines its particular value, S, by minimizing R_x, implies that H's P value is high. Now, if H then increases the value of R, he automaticaly lowers his own P. This is the logic by which the strategy of minimization may be deliberately used to attack H and either weaken him materially or reduce his standing in the social sphere. The strategy is thus a risky one because it is too effective and may lead to many latent bad feelings between the interatants. These bad feelings may in turn find their outlet in accusations which are familiar to anthropologists in the cultural idioms of witchcraft and evil eye.

Another strategy of negative politeness is to impersonalize S and H. As we have seen, this strategy embodies both an evasion and a threat. First, it provides S and H with an 'out'. This is brought about by a process which I have characterized as S switching the diectic anchorage of his utterance away from himself and letting the anchorage come adrift (page 106). Impersonalization then is a technique by which S disappears as the originator of the statement and one does not strictly know who is doing FTA to whom. In this way then the strategy is defensive and evasive. However, the vacuum tends to get filled quickly by an implicature which replaces the individual weakness of S by the collective strength of society. S now musters the support of intangible public opinion and morality behind him and in this way he begins to intimidate and coerce H.

The same happens in the strategy of stating the FTA as a general rule. Here the logic of the preceding strategy becomes explicit. S musters the support of the whole society against H. True, (as Brown and Levinson have pointed out) by stating an FTA as a general rule, S helps save H's face. But the element of coercion is, I think, also unmistakable. S backs up his FTA with the traditions of the society. If H refused to comply he would offend not only S, but society as a whole. We have seen above that 'stating the FTA as a general rule' plays a key role in Hamar social organization. In the form of a precedent it legitimizes the exercise of present power by invoking a historical authority. This historical authority, however, also acts as a brake on S's ambitions and forces him to check his exercise of power and to use it within the existing mould of his society's traditions (see page 108–111).

In a similar way, when using the strategy of nominalization, the speaker switches the attention away from himself. He does this by means of a metonymy in which the actor becomes an attribute of the action (page 113). The effect is the same as in the preceding two strategies in that S bullies H into doing something by threatening him with the powerful support of the anonymous.

4.2.4 OFF-RECORD STRATEGIES

At the beginning of this section I pointed out that it is misleading to speak of off-record strategies *per se*. Both positive and negative politeness may involve going off record. This strategy may be used as a device to increase the distance between S and H or to diminish it. By the same token it may also be used both as a tool to actually save H from the potential threat involved in an interaction or to make the threat even more effective.

Take for example the strategies 'give hints; give association clues; presuppose'. The polite aspect of hints, clues and the like may be expressed by the formula 'help yourself by helping the other'. This is how S reaches his aim without exposing himself and/or H to any threat of face loss. Furthermore, as hints and clues only work on the basis of tacit knowledge shared between S and H, the use of the strategy encodes an inclusiveness which can easily be turned into the exclusiveness of S and H if a third party is present. All the various forms of hints are ideal devices to create a complicity between S and H to be used by them against those who do not belong to their immediate in-group. I have already described the process when discussing metaphor and have given the example of Baldambe and Wadu, who joined forces together in order to intimidate a trader who had come to collect a debt (page 148). Hints and clues, while apparently softening an FTA, may none the less give it greater impact.

To visualize this let us remember once again the duke and the butler. The duke said, 'It's cold in here.' To put his command in this indirect way is polite as he substitutes a more engaging linguistic realization for a direct imperative ('Shut the window!'). The indirect statement attends to the butler's face, it even hides a compliment, for it implies that he is both intelligent and considerate. Yet it is here that, on a deeper level, the hint turns into something which certainly cannot be called a compliment – it becomes, as we have seen at the beginning of this chapter, a reminder and a criticism. Here lies the real power of the hint. Because something is not said openly, but is left for H to work out, it deeply involves and entangles him. The precondition for this to operate is that H is willing, at least to some extent, to work out the implicature contained in a hint. If S knows that H has such a disposition, then in order to give his commands an immanent and lasting force, he is well advised to administer them in an oblique form which forces H to think. In this way he extends his authority beyond his actual exchanges with H, becoming invisibly present in H's mind as a constant problem and worry. Obviously S dominates H much more effectively in this way than if he were using clear-cut direct imperatives.

To visualize the effectiveness of the mechanism at work, think of what would happen if, for a change, the butler operated with a hint towards the duke. Under normal circumstances the duke would not be bothered to think hard if he did not catch the butler's hint at once. Rather he would shrug his shoulders thinking, 'Let the butler make his meaning clearer if he wants to tell me something.' The butler, on the other hand would not dream of shrugging his shoulders. If he could not decipher a hint he would be worried until he had found out what the duke had meant. This, after all, is the way he earns his bread. Or, again, visualize the situation of two equals sitting in a room and one of them telling the other, 'It's cold in here.' Would not the addressee (H) feel piqued? He would understand that the other (S) was implying that he (H) was (and should be) concerned with his (S's) wants. But this is presupposing too much. Why should H be concerned? So H's answer might well be, 'If you feel cold, go and shut the window yourself, I am not your nanny.'

What about domination within such strategies as 'understate; overstate; use tautologies'? I think that some of Brown and Levinson's examples indicate how suitable understatement is as a means of damaging someone's face. The two examples I have quoted above (page 128) are of this kind. In the first instance, S says that nothing is wrong with Harry when he means that Harry is not very good, and in the second, S says that a dress is quite nice while he means that it is awful. Such seemingly harmless understatements can have a more devastating effect than appears on first sight. The reason for this lies in the fact that they are based on jointly shared background knowledge. This background knowledge is necessarily diffuse and allows a host of further implications to be associated with the low-key aggression encoded in the use of understatements. It is here that the resourcefulness of the understatement lies: it asserts the dominant and powerful position of the user, while at the same time putting down the person against whom it is directed. The extreme of such assertive understatement is total silence, where S deliberately abstains from speaking and leaves the situation to speak for itself; that is, where S leaves H to work out what S's statement would have been if he had felt inclined to utter it. To illustrate what I mean I give here an observation from Hamar:

> In the evening, as we drink coffee in front of Ginonda's house, Banko emerges from the dark. He leans on his spear and stands and waits. How much power can emanate from someone who just stands! Everyone knows that this stance constitutes a powerful command, so a cow hide is brought and coffee is served to him with speed and respect. (Lydall and Strecker 1979a: 229)

To read Banko's silence here as a sign of modesty and non-imposition would have been utterly wrong because it would have missed the point that his silence, given the social context in which it occurred, expressed his command more cogently than any words could have done. (Note that Banko is not a visitor 'guest' from far away but such a close friend, age-mate and neighbour that he almost belongs to the homestead of Berinas's sons; for a more detailed portrait of the man, see Lydall and Strecker 1979a.)

Overstatement differs markedly from understatement. While in the former S withdraws, in the latter he exposes himself. His exposure is, however, quickly compensated for, by the wide use to which he can put the strategy. As we have seen above (page 129–132), overstatement is a basic tool of persuasion. By telling a good story which communicates that he shares H's wants, S persuades H to do what he wants him to do. He acts positively and reduces the distance between himself and H. As long as he does this tactfully and does not impinge on H, he is polite. But often S goes on when H would like him to stop, and then the strategy becomes one of domination. S now indoctrinates H.

A Hamar elder comes to my mind as he sits opposite a number of younger men drinking coffee in one of the houses of Dambaiti. A coffee bowl stands on the ground in front of him and he leans across the steaming bowl towards the other men; stretching one arm out in a gesture that seems to take hold of each one of them, he emphatically calls out, '*Kansé, kate, kansé*!' ('Listen, listen well!') Then he speaks and the audience listens. The elder may speak for half an hour, for an hour, or even longer, and as he speaks and tells his good story he frequently comes back to the same points, uses similar images and generally covers the same ground, going over it again and again from many different angles as his speech unfolds. In this way he not only informs his listeners but actually influences and moulds their views. Or, to put it differently, the repetitiveness and other redundancies act as a tool of persuasion and instil in the listeners not only details and singular occurrences but also, and more importantly, underlying cultural generalities and structures. Furthermore, the repetitiveness leads, so to speak, to addiction, in that the listeners begin to feel that they have still heard too little, that the speaker has in fact missed certain implications of what he has said, implications which are also true and follow immediately from the premises that made him speak so long in the first place. When the coffee is finished, the youths go down to the dry river-bed and as they wait for the cattle to come to the water-holes, they sit in the shade of a tree and begin to talk again about what was said at the coffee pot.

One of the rhetorical devices which the elder might have employed during his speech is tautology (Strategy IV. 6). According to Brown and Levinson, tautologies embody a defensive and evasive strategy where S leaves it to H to 'look for an informative interpretation of the non-informative utterance' (Brown and Levinson 1978: 225) and thus does not threaten H's face. While this may be so, the opposite is also possible. The strategy may be employed to reduce H's face and encode S's dominating position over H. I pointed this out earlier when I said that tautology is particularly well suited for the assertion of authority and the affirmation of the *status quo* (page 133).

The strategies 'use contradictions; be ironic; use rhetorical questions' are similar. In the preceding section we have already clearly seen how these three strategies may be used by S to dominate H. Like tautology, they serve as a tool of the already powerful and they may not be openly employed against H if S's power is obviously smaller than that of H, for then S would harm himself instead of the other. In Hamar the use of contradiction (in the form of saying the opposite of what one means) is the privilege of the elders, who use it to make their commands more emphatic and involving, while at the same time drawing attention to the prevailing asymmetry of power (page 135). Similarly, rhetorical questions are typicaly used by speakers who already wield a certain amount of power. As the term implies, rhetorical questions are part of an orator's (a public speaker's) repertoire. He uses them as a device of positive politeness to assure his audience that he and they share common ground and once this first step is achieved, the rhetorical questions help him to persuade the listeners to think as he does (see page 138–140 above).

Irony is more complex and covers a wider range of social relationships where S's power might be higher than, lower than or equal to that of H. Whenever it is used, it manifests an attempt to assert a measure of control over a situation. This control is at once evasive and offensive. It is evasive in that what is said is different from what is meant and S can therefore retrieve his steps if this should be necessary, and it is offensive in that it expresses a disapprobation. Furthermore, as irony operates on the basis of tacitly shared background knowledge it is ideally suited for indirectly expressing hostility, while at the same time it encodes and actually generates the opposite, that is, a complicity. These inclusive and exclusive aspects lie at the heart of irony. Irony is never socially neutral but always works to the detriment of one and/or the advantage of another. This is why the figure is not only interesting to us as a tool for social domination but also as a test case to prove that symbolism is not only a cognitive but also a social mechanism (see 2.4).

Finally, let me turn to metaphor. When examining metaphor in the preceding chapter, I found that a socially important point is the question of how far a metaphor is on record and how far it is not. This, I said, is a empirical question. Thus the statistical variation in the interpretation of a metaphor becomes a factor in group formation and, seen from the oppostite angle, an index of the social identity of an actor. People who share the same interpretation of a metaphor share some kind of common ground, command similar tacit knowledge, etc. and recognize each other as being the same, the metaphor acting as a kind of secret password by which they can identify each other.

Now, it is perhaps quite easy to see that by its very nature metaphor is prone to act as a 'horizontal' factor which differentiates people on the ground, so to speak, into those who amicably adhere to one interpretation and those who adhere to another. The resulting antagonism between the different groups and their subsequent inclusion and exclusion practices is not difficult to visualize. But what about the 'vertical' factor? How can metaphor become a factor in the struggle for social domination?

The answer to this is difficult. I find it partly in the fact that the creation and use of metaphors is closely related to a usurpation of knowledge which in turn aims at a usurpation of social power. In order to show what I mean by this, let me utilize once again some observations I made in Hamar. Here are four cases which I quote straight from my notebooks.

Gemarro's fist of knowledge

I sit with Gemarro in front of his house and we are talking. I think I hear far away a truck making its way through the bush and ask Gemarro whether he too hears it. He does not answer but blows the warm air from his mouth into his hand, then turns the palm into a closed fist and moves it to his right ear where he then slightly opens it again. Through the cylindrical hole he listens intensely and after a while turns around to me with his typical fox-like smile: 'Brother-in-law, my ear is bad, it hears only the truth, it hears whether someone is going to live or to die.' No further explanation and also no further comment on what he is hearing just now follows. As so often before, I feel let down. Knowledge is so personal and hazardous, so political and antithetical that no systematic line opens itself for inquiry.

There are some basic axioms concerning the prophetical properties of the planets, the clouds, etc., but the evaluation of the cosmos is a matter of individual psychology and is motivated, as I have said above, by political antithesis: if a political opponent uses the stars to support his point you yourself use them to support your point. When Gemarro shows me his fist, which increases the power of his ear, this acts like a test by which he finds out how far he has influence over me, how far I would accept his bid for greater power. Baldambe, rather like Gemarro, is also constantly operating with such individually usurped super-knowledge. Whenever it seems possible in an argument, he forces his specific points on what he thinks is significant in the sky on to his listeners. He does this, of course, not modestly but by means of outright assertions. And yet there is no end to plausible interpretations of the sky, not only because the combinations of the known stars and other phenomena are innumerable but also because all objective phenomena are thought to have a subjective motivation. So Baldambe can say: 'There will be rain in this month because the sun will only go to rest in her "hole" [which she reaches on 21st December] if rain has cooled and softened it. The sun will only reach her "hole" when rain has fallen.' So the sun is not an objective measure of climate and seasons if the personal knowledge of a Hamar wants it not to be so. At another moment, however, it is, and Baldambe will say that no one should plant before the sun has reached its 'hole'. You can be sure that when he says this he has some political reason for it, that is the motive to establish a social hierarchy in which he ranks at the top and is accepted as a decision-maker. All this works, because everybody agrees that there is knowledge to be gained in the sky (and elsewhere) for him who is capable of catching it. The general discussions of the seasons, the weather, disease, hunger, war, etc., in terms of what the sky says, which I have witnessed so often, are like psycho-social experiments in the assessment and also in the exercise of personal power within the group, and it is interesting to note that some of those who keep quiet (offer no affirmation or rival interpretations) in one composition of the group are leading interpreters in other situations when the group is composed differently. Part of it all is the constant abuse of the knowledge of others. Either it is useful to you and you steal it from the others, pretending the interpretation derives from you yourself, or you dismiss it as false. Leaders especially like to slander one another in this way. Thus Gemarro, shortly after he has told me about the power of his fist, says that Wuancho, who like himself is a traditional spokesman of our area, is a goat and does not know anything. (Unpublished notebook 22: 22–4)

The rain-bringing moon

We look at the new moon. Its sickle is thin and lies almost horizontally. Above the thin bright 'bowl' of the new moon the grey heap of the moon is slightly visible. This picture means to the Hamar that this month will bring rain, for the grey moon looks like a cloud and the bright bowl beneath it will catch its rain. Who was it who first impressed his fellow countrymen with this cogent equation?

Whoever it was, he must have
laughed with delight inside when
he turned this metaphorical likeness into a causal prediction. (Unpublished notebook 19: 105)

Figure 15   *The rain-bringing moon*

The twitching eyebrow

Lukusse sits next to me and rubs his left eyebrow. It has been
twitching since yesterday and he asks Choke what it might be that his
eye will see. 'Meat, of course,' says Choke, 'from *galabu.*' If it had
been the right eye the meat would be from a family of the *binnas*
moiety. Often I have heard people refer to the twitching of a part of
their body and always the interpretation has had to do with a
premonition of food, that is, of meat. When your legs twitch you will
soon participate in a public assembly where an ox will be slaughtered
and you may rub your legs with the chime of the stomach. If your
buttocks twitch you will sit at a public meeting and eat ... etc. The
mentioning and the discussion of the twitching of a bodily part has
the same element of usurpation of knowledge as the interpretation of
the sky, or of the sounds of birds and the herds, but it seems to me to
be more stereotyped and simple. It's a matter of amusement.
(Unpublished notebook 24: 1–2)

A goat's sneeze, or how to keep your face

I have come to realize how important the various forms of divination
are as means of keeping one's face while modifying one's publicly
known decisions. Very prominent here is the mundane and all-
pervading sneeze of the goat. When Loborochir's son was to leap
over the cattle recently, some people (especially the initiate's family
and the neophytes) wanted the boy to perform the rite in the morning
following the day of the dancing after Oita Banko's son had leapt
over the cattle. Others, especially the more distant relatives and the
local people who wanted to eat and drink as much and as long as
possible, urged that the second initiate should only leap in the
evening [for a description of the ritual, see Lydall and Strecker
1979b: 77ff]. The matter was left open for some time. Some guests
then began to comment on the indecision of the families concerned.

Shortly afterwards Loborochir told me that the leap had been postponed 'because a goat has sneezed'. The sneeze was accepted by everyone and allowed both parties to keep their face in this difficult situation. (Unpublished notebook 24: 115–16)

I think the cases speak largely for themselves but I summarize here some of the central points. In the field I used the term 'usurpation' intuitively in order to stress that certain kinds of knowledge are simply assumed by a power of will. They are unfounded and cannot be validated and yet they serve the 'master' of that knowledge well and help him, as when Gemarro uses his 'fist of knowledge' in his struggle for social power over others or as in the case of 'a goat sneezes' when they help a person (or group) to save his (its) face.

As the example of the 'rain-bringing moon' shows, metaphorical likeness is easily turned into causal prediction. If I can say 'rain-cloud moon' then it is only a small step to say also 'rain-bringing moon' and predict that the moon indicates coming rain, just as the clouds indicate the coming of the rainy season and just as a cloud of rain empties itself over a dry country, which is empty like a bowl.

To understand more fully what is at issue it may be helpful to have a close look again at some of the technical properties of metaphor. According to Grice, a metaphor is created by flouting the first part of the maxim of quality, 'Do not say what you believe to be false' (see 2.3 above). As long as a conversation is a co-operative enterprise, S may make statements which are literally false (but note the social constraints on this which have been described above). Knowing that the literal falsity has been constructed deliberately, H then works out what the message may be and discovers the contextually defined meaning. The second part of the quality maxim is quite different. Grice has forumlated it as, 'Do not say that for which you lack adequate evidence.' A statement which violates this part of the maxim would thus be presumptuous. S would say something which he cannot validate! Nor can H for that matter and he is therefore forced to put the statement in quotes; that is, he is forced to treat it symbolically in the same way as he has to treat anything which violates the first part of the maxim.

However, the problems which arise from this point onwards are quite different for each of the violations. If S violates part one, then this is always more or less evident because it involves a plainly visible falsity. If, on the otherhand, he violates part two, then the violation is often not easily recognizable for H, because to validate or invalidate a statement may amount to an arduous task, and indeed H may often lack the opportunity and the tools for it altogether. Thus, the question whether a statement should be taken literally or figuratively may remain an open question. Furthermore, as Black and others have pointed out (see page 142–143 above), metaphors often combine different semantic elements in such a way that new entities result. These entities encode a deeper truth which no amount of literal use of language can convey. Such metaphors leave H utterly alone with no means of validating or invalidating them. The only thing he can do is to try to fathom what the deeper truth might be. If he takes this step, then he has been caught, as it were, in the net of the creator (or simply the user) of the metaphor and as he tries to imagine what, after all, the truth might be, he gets more and more in tune with the creator ('Aha, that's what he meant!'), who has thus subtly but effectively involved him and can now begin to exercise an influence over him.

Interestingly, all this brings us back to the beginning of our study, to Sperber. Remember, faced with the apparent paradox of symbolism, Sperber asked himself: 'Under what conditions is it logically possible to hold a synthetic statement to be true without comparing it with other synthetic statements which are susceptible of validating or invalidating it?' (1975: 99). The answer he has given is that we put these statements in quotes in the form of '"p" is true'. Sperber then provides among his examples the following statement by a Lacanian. 'The unconscious is structured like a language.' Here is Sperber's comment on this:

> A critical reader tries to see which statement is expressed by utterance (25) [see the sentence quoted above] so as to evaluate its truth. The structure of language being a part of the structure of the unconscious, he asks himself if the part is here a model of the whole, if the general properties of language extend to all the unconscious, if the unconscious is a code, or is made up of codes, etc. For my part, I am incapable of conceiving a true statement that would conform to the sense of (25). I doubt, however, that a Lacanian would yield to my arguments. If we ask him the precise import of (25), even though incapable of defining it, he will not

doubt its truth. The problem, for him, is not to validate or invalidate a statement. He knows that (25) expresses a valid statement, but he does not know which one. Thus he searches. Doing so, his mind opens itself to a whole series of problems, certain possibilities appear, certain relationships impose themselves. (Sperber 1975: 100–1)

The process which Sperber describes here is equivalent to what I have called the usurpation of knowledge. A Lacanian has the presence of mind which allows him to create (at least in a certain time in a certain place) statements which cause lasting focalization and rich evocation while eluding any efforts to validate or invalidate them. In this way does he not act like Baldambe who turns the 'rain-cloud moon' into a 'rain-bringing moon'? And does he not act like Gemarro who daringly reaches forward to grasp (where others dare not grasp) the unknown and by showing his fist of knowledge leads us to try to work out what truth he might be holding? Magritte, himself being one of them, once characterized the disposition of such 'masters' when he wrote: 'There is this need . . . in which an interest in the most difficult things and the passion for research are *replaced by an interest or desire for the result*' (Torczyner 1979: 51; my emphasis).

5 Symbolization and ritual

Back to the problem of symbolism in ritual

How do my findings affect the understanding of ritual? I began this study by asking how we interpret symbolism in ritual. Why do the Hamar, the Dorze and others retain a curious silence when asked about the meaning of their symbols? No anthropological theory has so far answered this question satisfactorily. True, there have been implicit treatments of the problem. Turner's notion of the structural perspective (see my introduction) implies, for example, the recognition of a partial silence on the part of the actor. Also Sperber gave, as we have seen (section 2.1), an answer when he said that meaning is by definition absent from symbolism. Another way to explain the silence is to relegate meaning to 'deep structures' or to say that it resides only in the system within which signs are related (Chomsky 1957; Lévi-Strauss 1962; Leach 1976). Also, the Freudian view that meaning is both expressed and repressed in symbolism (Freud 1963; Jones 1967) provides an answer, and so does Bourdieu's theory of 'habitus' and 'doxa' which implies an actor's unawareness of meaning (Bourdieu 1977). And finally even historical theories may shed light on the problem of silence by showing that meaning may be absent in symbolism because it has vanished in the course of history (Jensen 1960).

Yet, whatever truths these theories may contain, our understanding of symbolism will remain incomplete as long as we do not fully acknowledge people's competence for complex thinking, as long as we do not concede to them the competence for sustained intentional indirectness and multivocality. Only if we take into account the complete range of people's innate faculties can we hope to understand the different forms of culture which they have created. One part of these faculties is the ability to think in anticipation and to construct implicatures. Implicatures lie at the heart of symbolization. They are means by which indirect and multivocal communication is achieved. Furthermore, communication by way of implicature pervades everyday life. It is a tool which we apply constantly in social interaction. Life trains us, as it were, to become masters of the tool.

Now, if symbolization constitutes an immanent social practice then everything which applies to the grass roots of symbolization must also apply to the symbolism we meet in ritual. There is no dividing line between the sacred and the profane as so many anthropologists have been ready to assume. Such a dichotomy camouflages the fact that in reality the sacred is quite profane and the profane quite sacred. Both are generated by one single and all-pervading social practice.

Thus the symbolism which we meet in ritual cannot be different in its nature from the forms of symbolization which we find in the social practice of everyday life and consequently we must approach ritual in a similar way. That is, we must treat rituals as implicatures, as 'ways of not saying what is meant'. More specifically, we can now view rituals as realizations of strategies which have to do with the performance of face-threatening acts (FTAs). As strategies of politeness, rituals constitute means of maintaining face in situations of high risk. Ritual is thus a device which helps people not to hurt each other at socially critical moments.

When seeing ritual in this light, it becomes possible to understand something of the tact involved in ritual and something of its grace. This element of intention we claim as essential for the rituals and symbols in our own society, but when it comes to studying other people we tend to lose the understanding of the social thinking and consideration of the other which the author of a symbolic statement puts into its construction. We forget that he or she may have cared for the other and thought of him or her and therefore chosen a form of cultural suppleness which would shield and protect the other.

The suppleness of symbolism would, of course, not only shield the other, it also would protect the interest of the author of the statement. Indeed at times it may even do more than that. It may be used, as we have seen (section 4), offensively and against the interest of the other. Here, again, it becomes indispensible to take into account the actor's power to think in anticipation and his ability to put things indirectly, that is, by way of implication. Only in this way can we fully appreciate the exploitation which may be pursued in ritual. As we have seen, a successful implicature always involves an exploitation of the addressee by the speaker (see 2.3). Usually the exploitation is small, but it increases considerably when we enter the realm of metaphor and ritual symbolism. Then, as in the case of Gemarro's 'fist of knowledge' (see page 197), the speaker may become the master and the listener his slave.

5.2 A Hamar rite of passage explained by the theory of symbolization

I now want to show how the theory developed above applies to a Hamar rite of passage. I will keep my analysis short and will provide only the gist of my argument. A full investigation of the immensely complex rite I intend to offer in a separate publication.

There exists an indigenous description of the rite (Lydall and Strecker 1979b: 74–99) and also a film which depicts the various episodes which make up the rite (Strecker 1979b). Jean Lydall has written a short introduction to the film which may serve here as a summary of what happens:

The film, which is set in southern Ethopia, follows a single Hamar youth through a series of initiation rites at the climax of which he leaps across a row of cattle. Rituals are always full of mystery, even, or perhaps especially, for those who enact them. The commentary of the film, which consists of a description of the rituals by Baldambe, an older brother of the initiate Berhane, retains this essential mystery while providing information about such details as the passage of time and the nature of relations between actors.

Almost immediately we are introduced to Berhane as he drives cattle into a kraal. He is dressed in a white cloth which hangs from his shoulders like a toga. He is called over by Baldambe who tells him it is time to take the stick so that he might leap over the cattle and thus qualify for marriage. But first of all we see Berhane give away his personal attire; all his beads, his white cloth, his stool are taken by his age-mates and he is left with only a small ragged loincloth and his sandals. From an elderly clansman he receives a small club-shaped stick which he will carry from now on as a special symbol. Next, the hair on the front of his head is shaved off, and hereafter we follow a progressively unkempt-looking

Berhane as he hastens from one event to another: he goes to get an iron ring which he wears upon his arm; he collects white gourds and gives them to people to fill with milk; he shows his stick to others who give him iron rings for each of which he bores a hole in the club end of the stick; he receives a skin cape and a necklace of beads from a young girl; and then he chooses himself a youth to be his aide.

Baldambe's commentary informs us: 'Then it is time for him to sew on the phallus.' We see how he goes to a man who makes a small object with antelope skin and cow dung, and fastens it on Berhane's little finger as Berhane stands naked before him. Berhane and his aide are then bombarded with cow dung as they flee from the scene. They come to a sandy creek where the aide pours handfuls of sand over Berhane's naked crouching form: 'He washes away all that was bad in his childhood.' The aide binds two strips of bark around Berhane's chest before they set off again. We see them dash into the homestead at immense speed so that no woman may touch Berhane who finally puts his phallus object safely away in an empty beehive.

Our attention is now turned away from Berhane towards the guests who are arriving for the occasion of the leap. On the path to the homestead come groups of women and girls, shining red with butter and ochre, singing songs about the initiate and brandishing wooden staffs. Men and youths arrive with less exuberance but are dressed and painted with more originality and colour. Down at the dry river-bed we find the *maz* who, we are told, are those who have already been initiated and are about to make Berhane one of their number. As they paint each other's faces we hear them singing and strumming the lyre in the background. Now everyone gathers in an open space where women and girls dance around the cattle which men have brought together.

Berhane makes his appearance on the scene again. He is made to sit down on a cow hide opposite a *maz* who wears a cowrie-shell belt and Berhane's skin cape. Other *maz* surround the two, and between their legs and arms we get glimpses of a set of curious ritual acts: whips are jerked up and down; iron rings are thrown off Berhane's stick; a *maz* tries to make Berhane laugh; and a gourd of milk is passed up his outstretched legs.

Next we witness an extraordinary scene where women and girls taunt the *maz* into whipping them: 'Our boy will come and stand naked like a dead man in the middle of the cattle. The inventors of this ordeal are the *maz*. Let us kick them, let us punch them, so that they may whip us.' Older men separate the girls from the *maz* so that the rituals may continue. As the girls predicted, Berhane enters among the cattle and stands there naked except for the two bark strips which he still wears around his chest. Meanwhile several *maz* encircle the cattle rapidly while other *maz* line up in a squatting line and chant.

Next, with great commotion the *maz* grab hold of a number of cattle; one holding the head, another the tail of each animal, they bring them into a row. At last we will see the initiate leap. And now he runs towards the row of cattle, and springing high into the air he steps on to the back of the first cow, then on to another and another until he reaches the last and jumps down to the ground. He returns the way he came and repeats the leap several times. While he leaps, his mother's brothers and sisters hold their wooden staffs horizontally above their heads in order, we are told, to prevent him from falling and hurting himself. And then the leap is over and the initiate gets blessed, first by the *maz* and then by his mother's brothers and sisters.

With the next scene we are taken away from ritual and on to the festivities which follow. Now the people come to dance, and feast and drink.

In a fleeting moment of darkness we see a foot extinguish fire, and that is all we are to witness of the ritual ordeals through which Berhane must pass during the night after his leap. By morning light we see him again as he is blessed for a final time by his relatives who are preparing to return to their own homesteads.

Next Berhane's head is shaved: 'Now the boy has become a *maz*. His head is shaved, he is bald. When the children get up they see it: he is a *maz*. When the men get up they see it: he is a *maz*.' And then he is blackened from head to foot with charcoal mixed with butter. In this state he throws green *gali* leaves at the side of cattle and encircles the same cattle in the midst of whom stands another youth who is about to leap.

Again the scene changes to one where three *maz* slaughter a goat and feed Berhane with blood and fat. It is with relief that we see Berhane, by now thoroughly exhausted, led to rest on a bed of green leaves in the shade of a bush. Here he is fed like a child with milk and honey. Later, in a revived state, he washes off the black with which he has been covered for four days. The *maz* who now acts as his ritual helper gets a dikdik skin and cuts in into a long thin strip which is twisted and then wound around Berhane's waist. Now, we learn, Berhane can go and get married, but he is best advised to wait for his father to find him a wife. Meanwhile he decks himself out in all his finery – a clean white cloth, splendid necklaces of beads, metal arm bands – and a special marking to show he is a *maz* is shaved upon his head. At last we have before us Berhane transformed into a proud and handsomely dressed initiate who is ready to marry and assume full adult status in Hamar society.

We have here then, in rapid succession, most of the episodes which constitute the drama of the ritual. Certain episodes are missing such as, for example, some ordeals which the initiate has to suffer during the night when his head is shaved. Also the final episodes which lead to the initiate's marriage are missing. But this incompleteness does not matter for the moment. The general scene has been set and it is sufficient to know that the initiate does in fact pass through something, that he gets transformed and completes, as it were, a journey from one social status to another. The passage is not simple and straightforward though, but complicated with many twists and turns which all seem to mean something and carry specific intentions.

Now, how does one explain the rite of transition in terms of the theory of symbolization developed in this study? The theory predicts that when we find elaborate forms of symbolic action there will exist some underlying motive of persuasion. Some people must be trying to use subtle means to influence others and realize their interests in such a way that they shield themselves and others from the social dangers associated with the pursuit of their interests. Our central question is therefore: 'Who is trying to influence whom through the Hamar rite of transition?'

I have often discussed this question with Jean Lydall and at the moment our answer is as follows: it is the parents and a number of close relatives, especially the siblings of the father and the mother, who are trying to influence the young man. Through the ritual they assert their control over the young man's labour. Controlling others and forcing them to work is a very problematic and face-threatening act. We hypothesize that this is the reason why such elaborate symbolization has ocurred and the ritual procedures have been invented. It would need many pages of background knowledge about Hamar society and culture to uphold and substantiate this thesis. But there is no space for this here. As I have said above already, a full description and explanation of the rite I will present elsewhere. Here it must be sufficient to show the general direction of my argument.

The explanation starts, of course, with the facts of Hamar economic life.

Hamar economy is based on a number of food-producing activities in widely dispersed areas: sorghum cultivation, herding of goats, sheep and cattle, keeping bees, gathering wild produce, trapping and hunting wild animals. Generally, there is no need for large corporate groups. A livelihood is better gained by living in a multitude of small, largely independent groups who in times of crisis lend each other support. The typical economic unit consists of a *donza*, a married man, with his wife or wives and his children. He, the *donza*, is most interested in controlling the age at which his sons are allowed to gain economic independence. He is interested in keeping them dependent so that they can provide the labour necessary to herd the family's sheep, goats and cattle in the distant grazing areas and protect these herds from theft by enemies, as well as maybe augmenting them by raiding animals from enemy country. Close relatives and neighbours who do not have adult sons of their own are also interested in controlling the age at which a man gains independence. In fact the sheep, goats and cattle of many domestic units are grouped together in order to be herded by available young men in the distant grazing areas. In different ways, the transition rite requires the participation of all the people who are interested in a young man's labour, i.e. the parents, close relatives and neighbours. Any one of these can impede the performance of the rite by refusing to participate. A man cannot perform his rite without the consent of the interested parties, which is implied by their participation in the rite.

Although a young man's parents, kinsmen and neighbours have crucial roles to play in the rite, the rite is so designed that it seems that the real control lies elsewhere. A man's father, the most interested party of all, only figures in the rite at the very beginning when he ritually grants his son the right to take the *boko* stick and proceed with the rite. A man's mother only figures in the rite when she cooks him some sorghum food, a piece of which he throws away at the foot of a *gali* plant before going off with the *maz*. The roles played by the father and mother are deliberate understatements so as to hide the real locus of power. Instead of the parents, relatives and neighbours, the rite makes it seem that it is the *maz*, other initiates, who grant adult status to a man.

This emerges from the following facts: immediately prior to leaping across the cattle the initiate is involved in a set of rituals in which a *maz* ritually gives birth to him. He becomes the child of this *maz* who is referred to as both his mother and his father. The 'mother/father' who ritually gives birth to the initiate wears the cowrie-shell belt of the initiate's mother and sits on a cow hide with his legs spread apart. The cowrie-shell belt is acquired by a woman only after she has given birth to her first child. Accordingly, the belt is strongly associated with her child-bearing capacity. It is not until his hair is shaved off that the initiate is finally declared a full *maz*:

> Next morning they get up with the sunrise. Now the *ukuli* has become a *maz*, his head is shaved, it is blunt ... Then his head and body are rubbed all over with charcoal and butter ... In his first days the young *maz* is like a child ... His *mansange* feeds him with milk and honey. (Lydall and Strecker 1979b: 94–6)

The new *maz* is blackened with charcoal and butter for a period of four days, and then he is smeared with butter alone for another four days. All these acts imitate the newborn child which typically has little or no hair and whose head is bald, or blunt as the Hamar say. Also, the infant is at first very pale, almost white, for it takes some time for the pigment in the skin to darken. The newborn child is covered with waxy fat and is breastfed with sweet mother's milk. The bald head, the blackening of the body, the rubbing on of butter and the feeding with milk and honey all imply an analogical relationship between the new *maz* and a newborn child. It is therefore *maz* who give birth to *maz* in the rite. This makes the ritual seem self-generating and the true locus of control remains hidden.

Yet the real control is exercised not by the *maz*, but by the *donza*, the 'fathers' of the initiate and it is the *donza* who have created a set of beliefs and practices which help them exercise their control. Most important here is the institution of *barjo äla*. At a *barjo äla* married men join together in a chant. The oldest person present leads the chant and the others answer in a chorus, repeating the last word or words of each phrase. There is an example of a *barjo äla* on my Hamar record (Strecker 1979c) which goes as follows:

Leader	*Chorus*
The rain shall fall,	fall (*hanshe*)
the children shall play,	play (*yege*)
the plants shall smell good,	smell good (*game*)
the rains shall stand in puddles,	stand in puddles (*kate*)
the rain shall turn into plants,	turn into (*mate*)
the herds shall enter the homes,	enter (*arde*)
the flood water shall flow upwards,	flow (*mirse*)
(it shall be like) butter,	butter (*bodi*)
rain,	rain (*doni*)
well-being,	well-being (*nagaia*)
sickness shall go away,	go (*yi'e*)
it shall fall like a dried-up leaf,	fall (*pille*)
away.	away (*wollall*).

The verb *äla* means 'to call' or 'to call forth'. The noun *barjo* is very difficult to translate and there are many aspects to the concept. Plants, things, substances, places, body parts, animals and people may, for example, all be *barjo* or have *barjo*. Also certain actions may contain or cause *barjo*. Most often Jean Lydall and I have translated *barjo* as 'luck', 'good fortune' or 'well-being' (Lydall and Strecker 1979a and 1979b).

Only *donza* may call forth *barjo*. This privilege is associated with their social and economic position. The *donza* are the heads of the basic economic units of Hamar. In political matters they act collectively with other *donza* of the same settlement area. Whenever economic or other reasons make it necessary, a *donza* may leave one settlement and join the *donza* of another. And wherever he goes he carries his *barjo* with him and may join other *donza* to call forth *barjo*. For a number of purposes the *donza* delegate the *barjo äla* to specific persons; for example, to the guardian of the fields (*gudili*) or to one of

the two guardians of all of Hamar country (the *bitta*). Yet in spite of a
certain amount of delegation of their privileges the *donza* remain the
basic agents in Hamar politics.

Although Hamar social structure is not centralized, none the less
there exist important differences in the amount of freedom of action
which different members of the society have. Especially, there are
the hierarchies between old and young and male and female. It is
within these hierarchies that the concept of *barjo* functions. Who
controls whom can be seen by who is allowed to call *barjo* for whom.
As I have said, only the *donza* may call *barjo* for the women,
unmarried men and children and not vice versa.

Young men lack *barjo* in some way and are said to be immature,
deficient, generally no good and, above all, sexually unclean. The
Hamar term with which they are characterized is *mingi*, which
conjures up pollution, source of ill luck, unnatural. If they want to
become clean and acceptable members of society they have to purify
themselves by performing the rite of passage. Thus the rite acts like a
gateway which both excludes and includes the youths. First it bars
them from becoming socially mature although physically they may
long have reached maturity. Secondly, after having excluded them, it
allows the youths to enter the stage of proper manhood and gives
them the right to marry and the contingent rights to claim children
and livestock on their own. Having performed the rite they now may
aim at independence, found their own families and join the *donza*
whose right it is to perform the *barjo äla*.

All in all I think one can say that the Hamar rite of transition is a
brilliant strategy with which the *donza* exercise control over others
while at the same time inhibiting the control of others over
themselves. The concept of *barjo* plays an intrinsic role in the
strategy. It sanctions and justifies the rite of passage which in turn
justifies and sanctions the prolonged control of the *donza* over the
young men's labour.

5.3 Limits to the explanation of symbolism: the problem of displacements

As we have seen, the Hamar rite of transition can be explained as a
strategy to reduce social danger in a situation where people exercise

control over one another. The intention of control generates as it were the symbolic output. But this symbolic output cannot be univocally defined in its meaning. It is off record, as Brown and Levinson would say, off record not only for the actors but for the anthropologist too. All our explanations are therefore faced with the limits inherent in symbolic forms. In order to clarify this point let me return to the problem of displacement which, as we have seen (section 2.2) lies at the very heart of symbolism. To recognize and make sense of displacements is the central problem of interpretation.

Here are some examples of displacements in the Hamar rite of passage:

(1) Plants from the bush are displaced by putting them across the gateway of the goat enclosure.

(2) An iron ring is displaced by taking it from the leg of a woman and putting it on the wrist of the initiate.

(3) Cow dung is displaced by taking it from the ground of the cattle kraal and rubbing it on to the chest of the initiate.

(4) Sand is displaced by taking it from the dry river-bed and pouring it over the initiate's body.

(5) Cattle are displaced by driving them together on to a ridge in the bush.

(6) The initiate is displaced by being made to leap over the cattle.

In terms of Grice's theory of implicature such displacements would be called 'violations' or 'floutings'. But what are being flouted here are not conversational maxims but the practical maxims of placement. All cultural life is based on a practice (or *habitus* as Bourdieu would call it) where objects, substances, living beings, etc., and their names have a practical place. People know of these practical (often in fact natural) placements, and they know that other people know of them. Just as people co-operate daily together in their work, they share similar expectations about where things should be at particular times. That is, they have created a practical order of which they have a shared knowledge. In *The Said and the Unsaid* Stephen Tyler has examined this shared conceptual order as the 'collocation of commonplace knowledge' (Tyler 1978). Anthropological studies of classification and categorization have also amply demonstrated the internal coherence and order of folk taxonomies (see, for example,

Brown, C.H. 1984, Ellen and Reason 1979, Rosch and Lloyd 1978, Spradley 1972, Tyler 1969).

Now, given such shared background knowledge about the order of things, people may then at times deliberately flout the maxims of putting things in their proper places, or letting them stay in their proper places, and use the displacements in order to imply something, thereby doing on an action level something they also do on a verbal level (see our findings on the practice of symbolization).

According to Sperber, any displacement may be treated symbolically. It may be put in quotes, the mind may focus on the 'defectiveness of the conceptual representation', and then evocations may be set into motion which become the essential gain of the 'symbolic mechanism' (see section 2.1).

I have objected to this view because if one looks closely one finds that not every displacement is treated symbolically. Only those which are not simply displacements, but are in fact artful placements get the status of the symbolic and do not end up in the waste bin.

Now, if one holds such a theory of symbolism, how does one as an ethnographer demonstrate or at least illuminate the artfulness of a displacement? Indeed, how does one recognize the displacement itself, or even that any displacement has occurred at all? Obviously a host of problems arise here and the questions bring us straight to the heart of ethnographic practice. Also, we are right back to the problems of observation and description with which I began this study (see pages 11–15).

The ethnographer is a stranger, a foreigner in an alien culture where, at first, he has no inkling of the order of things. Only through a long and complex process of learning does he come to know the order and in turn reaches the ability to recognize and understand the displacement of things. For example, in one episode of the Hamar rite of passage a youth pours sand over the naked body of the initiate (see above). If one witnesses this event as a complete outsider, one realizes that evidently something has been displaced. The sand does not belong on the body of the boy because it does not fulfil a recognizable practical function there. Thus the outsider will be inclined to think that the act has a symbolic meaning. But here his thought process ends and he shrugs his shoulders. In Sperber's terminology, his thought process ends because his memory provides no material for evocation. In my terminology, his thought process ends because he lacks the competence for analogical thinking. He is not able to recognize the analogical potential of the displacement.

Perhaps I should concede a bit more to our total stranger. He comes, after all, from somewhere! He has lived his own life and this may well provide him with evocations when he watches the boy pouring sand over the initiate. Yet these evocations are specifically his own. He has imported them into the situation. This is the reason why they can't serve him as a key to an understanding. The ethnographic question is not (or at least primarily not) what he, the ethnographer, thinks or may think, but what the Hamar think or may think in a situation where a displacement has occurred. In other words, the question is how a displacement may act on the minds of the Hamar. What is its potential? The possible answers cannot come from outside but can only be found in the culturally specific experiences and memories of the Hamar; that is, in their shared knowledge about their practical everyday life. Only the ethnographer who knows this practical life well is competent to fathom the analogical potential of a displacement. To take the displacement of the sand as an example: the specific displacement of the sand (from the river-bed on to the naked body of the initiate) at the particular moment when it occurrs asserts something in Hamar because of the following reasons (which are not exhaustive).

First, Hamar country is dry. Rain falls only sporadically and after the rains the rivers dry out quickly. People then have to dig holes in the sand in order to reach water. Hence the water is usually in the sand. When a Hamar wants to cleanse either himself or some object of dirt which is difficult to remove, he uses sand and water. Sand is the soap of the Hamar.

Secondly, the geological formations of Hamar contain much quartz. The sand in the dry river-beds is therefore often very light in colour, sometimes even snow-white. Each time a flood passes through a river-bed, the sand is washed anew and gets a fresh appearance, which strikes the Hamar in rather the same way as we are impressed by the 'virginity' of newly fallen snow.

Now, given the cultural context of Hamar, one can (but may or may not) use these facts of Hamar everyday life to recognize the following analogies, which all reveal a similar intention of cleansing.

1. The sand in a dry river-bed is an impressive example of something clean and something recently cleaned. As I have said

already, floods periodically pass along the river-beds, taking with them all the dirt which has accumulated. The flood removes filth, it erases all traces of human and animal use of the river-bed, and it moves the sand itself around so that, after each flood, the sand in the river-bed has a new appearance. Because of these striking characteristics, the sand of an untouched river-bed epitomizes any physically clean state and any kind of erasure of past states of pollution which one has observed in the world. And this metaphorical extension also reaches into the social and moral realm so that one can say that in the ritual the initiate is brought into contact with sand in order to become socially as unpolluted as the untouched sand in a dry river-bed.

2. The sand which is poured over the naked body of the youth can be seen to represent a cleaning substance. One arrives at this conclusion via three different paths of thought:

2.1. Watching the sand being *poured* over the body of the initiate, one may say that the sand is poured *like* water. Sand, resembling water in that it is pourable, would thus stand metaphorically for water. And water being a cleaning agent would indicate an act of cleaning. But as the act of cleaning in itself is not what matters, one would have to conclude that the act of cleaning metonymically stands for a state of cleanliness. This state of physical cleanliness can then in turn be extended to the domain of social life and metaphorically express social and moral purification.

2.2. One may make sense of the enigmatic picture of displacement by arguing that sand is being substituted for water just as in so many other metonymic ritual tropes where the container is substituted for the contained. In Hamar, water is mainly collected from holes which are dug in the sandy river-beds. Sand is perceived of as the container of water and can be used metonymically to represent the latter by replacing it.

2.3. By a synecdochical mode of thought the sand may be seen as a part standing for a whole. In Hamar the mixture of sand and water is a widely used cleaning agent, the abrasive part of which is the sand. Knowing of no other technical term, I suggest we call the replacement of a mixture (sand and water) by one of its components (sand) an 'ingrediental' synecdoche. The replacement of a mixture by a component has what Sapir calls a *particularizing* character, like the replacement of a whole by a part in the anatomical mode and the replacement of genus by species in the taxonomical mode of synecdoche (see Sapir 1977: 13).

Note that the use of water instead of sand at that particular point in the ritual would not make one think strongly of sand. The reason for this is that water without sand makes sense in that context on its own, while sand without water does not. Also, water would have been a much weaker displacement because it would not have evoked the emphatic (abrasive) removal of dirt. In fact it is the very *absence* of water which counts. The absence of water makes the displacement 'speak' and provokes one to enter the metaphorical realm where physical acts and agents make one think of non-physical referents – for example, social and moral purification.

3. The sand is poured over the initiate, not sprinkled, rubbed or otherwise placed on him. The action, taken by itself, looks the same as when a Hamar man scoops up water from a water-hole and pours it with his hands over another man's body to clean him. The *pouring* of the sand over the initiate may thus metonymically represent a state of cleanliness (means for end) which may in turn be metaphorically extended to refer to the desired newly purified state of the initiate.

The different semantic aspects of the displacement of sand which I have outlined here are charted in Figure 16.

It has become clear by now that the displacement of sand in the Hamar rite of transition is not 'rubbish', because the young man over whom the dry sand is poured is not just a physical body but a social person, an *ukuli* who is told that he is morally defiled. Therefore the displaced activity of pouring dry sand over him makes sense. It is meant to wash away some invisible dirt. In short, pouring the sand over him is an act of moral and social purification. Within Hamar life the displacement of the sand thus has a specific potential for saying things. Anyone who is motivated to work out this potential, or some of the potential, may do so.

Furthermore, he will find that, as in the instance of the sand, the analogies which are possible, which make sense in the context of the situation, are not only multiple but also condense into one general intended meaning. It is this condensation which makes the displacement such a powerful tool of intention and here lies both the artfulness and the effectiveness of symbolism. The Germans call poetics the art of condensation (*Dichtung*). In this sense then all rituals must be viewed as poems, as *Dichtungen*, and because the

218

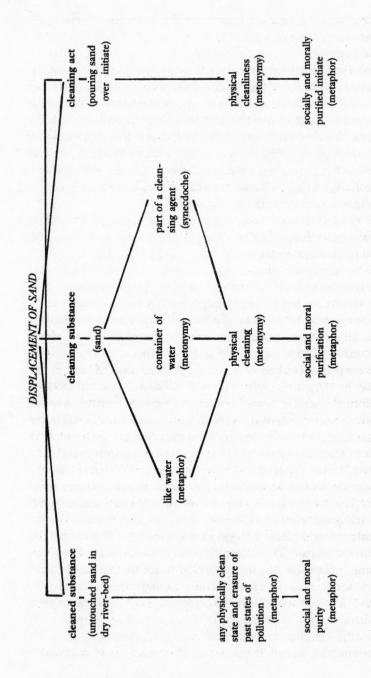

Figure 16 Semantic aspects of the displacement of sand

displacement of sand in the Hamar ritual of transition contains such *Verdichtungen*, the act of pouring it over the initiate's body entails a skilful placement.

This skilful placement speaks within the context of the totality or *Gestalt* of the ritual. Having been removed from its usual location, an element (object, quality or action) has been given a place in the newly constructed order of the rite, and this order in turn explains the choice of the element. Somewhere else the displaced element might indeed be truly out of place, but as part of the particular *Gestalt* of the rite it has been artfully placed. Using the terminology of structural anthropology one could say that the syntagmatic chains and the paradigmatic associations furnishing the *Gestalt* of the rite link and relate displacements. Each displacement relates both to the other displacements within the rite and to the initial order of things from which it has been displaced.

Thus, the Hamar rite of passage is composed of more than fifty different episodes which occur over a period of several months. In their totality these episodes have a common goal which all the participants in the ritual know: the young man who stands at the focal point of interest is to gain the right to marry, have legitimate children and become a grown-up man with full adult status in the society.

The syntagmatic chain of events aims at a dramatic development. Gustav Freytag in his early study of classical drama (Freytag 1887) has likened the structure of a drama to that of a pyramid. After an introduction and a number of exciting events the action within the drama rises continually until it reaches its climax. Then, after the climax, the action begins to fall and ends either in a happy end or in a disaster. I have found that the development of the Hamar rite of passage closely follows this pattern and that everyone acting in the rite or just watching it is first and foremost carried along by this dramatic development of the ritual acts. But then there is also the mental process of paradigmatically associating the different episodes within the ritual. The dramatic structure involving time now becomes a timeless structure of logical relationships. As the mind reviews the events it has experienced, or (in the case of someone who knows the ritual already) may be about to experience, it relates them paradigmatically (Lévi-Strauss 1958). The relating is done hier-archically. That is, the formulation and development of structural oppositions begins with the most important ones which stand at the apex of the *opus operatum*. In the Hamar rite of passage the crucial opposition which generates, so to speak, the power for all the events within the ritual, is found at the climax of the rite. Here in one episode the initiate first stands *within* a herd of cattle and then, in the next episode, he leaps on to and runs *over* the backs of the cattle. Anyone who notices these displacements may ponder and ask himself what the relationship between the young man and the cattle is. He may ask himself in the form of a riddle, 'What is it that relates to the young man as cattle do?' If he (or, of course, she) is a Hamar or if he (or she) has some background knowledge of Hamar life, then he may well find that the answer is *women*. As women the cattle constitute an artful placement for the following reasons:

(1) In Hamar, women are often metaphorically referred to as cattle. When Hamar men speak of women and girls, they like to use the expression *oto* (calf) and *wungo* (cow). 'Has so-and-so still got a calf in his enclosure?' I have heard, for example, one Hamar ask another. What he meant was, 'Has so-and-so still got a marriageable daughter?'

(2) The equation of cattle and women occurs not only in the metaphorical usage described above. In practical everyday life there exist many correspondences between cattle and women. The most obvious of these is, of course, the fact that cows give milk and serve as 'wet nurses' which feed infants. In this sense cows are equated with women because cows may be a substitute for women. Children often drink from the teats of the cows directly, just as they drink from the breasts of their mothers directly. They drink from the animals when they are out in the bush and get hungry during the long hours of the day. Once they are no longer children, that is, when they have married, they are forbidden to use this direct access to milk. In a certain episode in the ritual the initiate drinks, in fact, expressly for the last time from the teats of a cow and says, 'From now on I will never do this again!'

(3) Cows are not only 'wet nurses' (substitute mothers) whose milk one drinks, but are also 'sisters' and 'daughters'. This equation comes about by metamorphosis: any man who has sisters and daughters loses them after they have been married. But as compensation for this loss he receives cattle in return. The sisters and daughters burst their cocoons, so to speak, at

marriage (more precisely when they have been brought to their husband's homestead) and reveal themselves to be cattle.

(4) The wives, in a sense, are cattle too. Here the reasoning is metonymic and runs as follows: a man can only found a new herd together with his wife. Only through having a wife does he receive livestock from his relatives. These livestock will become the nucleus for his future herd. The possession of a wife therefore leads to the possession of cattle. As the wife has an active role to play in this, the relationship between wife and cattle is one of cause and effect, the wife causing the cattle to materialize. This relationship of cause and effect may be used as the basis for the mental and linguistic figure of metonymy in which an effect (the cattle) is replaced by the cause (the wife).

Thus the initial puzzle may be solved by equating cattle with women. Yet this solution leads immediately to a further puzzle. One asks oneself, if the cattle are women, why is the initiate first between them and then above them? What has he to do with these cattle-women? And who precisely are these cattle-women, for there are many different categories of women? If one thinks of the central intention of the rite and then focuses on the relationship between the artful placements in the two episodes, the puzzling questions may receive the following answers: although in both episodes the cattle are women, they represent in each episode a different category of women. The physical relationship between the initiate and the cattle which changes drastically from one episode to the other symbolizes the *change* in social relationships which the young man is undergoing *vis-à-vis* two categories of women.

At first, the initiate stands in the midst of the cattle. They surround him and, if one looks closely, one can see how the initiate leans on them, hangs on to them and while he does so, tries to step not on the ground but rather on to fresh cow dung which is lying on the ground. If these cattle who surround him so closely are women, who else could they be but the women of his close family, that is, his mothers and sisters. Later the initiate has left the herd. The cattle are now fewer in number and have been brought into line, about a dozen or so cattle standing side by side. The initiate now runs towards the cattle, and, clearly visible to all the guests who are present, he leaps on to the cattle and runs across their backs four times.

If one assumes that these cattle on whose backs the initiate steps are wives, then the events furnish a logical pattern. The opposition of 'in the midst of the cattle' and 'above the cattle' now becomes a model for the social relationships between the initiate and the women. The formula would be, 'initiate among the cattle: initiate above the cattle:: boy to mothers and sisters: husband to wives and children'.

When he was a child, the initiate was only the son of mothers and the brother of sisters who nursed him, fed him, looked after him. In short, he was *dependent* on women. But this situation is now to be changed.From now on the young man will establish a completely new relationship with a certain category of women. Together with them he will beget children and will exercise *authority* over them (wives and children) as he has never done before in his life. Just as he is raised above the 'cattle-wives' in the ritual, he will be raised over his wives and children in everyday life.

This, one could say, is the central meaning of the ritual as it reveals itself at the climax of the dramatic events. But note, I am saying 'one *could* say' because the meaning of which I am speaking is hidden, must not be arrested and can never be exhausted. If I have found order and meaning in what at first looked like chaos, then this still does not prove anything. Nothing says that I have reached the end of the analysis. Nothing assures me that things *must* be the way I have seen them and I can force no one to accept my argument as being correct. I have simply discovered relationships which are *possible*. That they are necessary I cannot say. Yet, as the reader of this study will know by now, all this has to be expected because the people who have created the ritual have aimed at indirect communication by choosing to speak through symbolism. They want the intended meaning to be there but also to be not there, so that each participant in the rite may be safe from criticism by others. There should be no room for argument, only for mystery. At the same time, the symbolic statements are aimed at generating a mental movement which provokes all the participants to think of everything which may have to do with the central intention of the rite. The task of the ethnographer consists of following this open process. For him the events of the rite can be only a starting point and a point of return. His actual journey leads him into the political and practical life of the people enacting the rite. This involves working out the significant context of the symbolic statements within a rite in the way which Turner has advised (Turner 1967). However, now we can say that the context is only significant because it is significant to the people who are enacting the rite. To be aware of the significant context of symbolic statements is not and cannot be the sole privilege of the anthropologist who, almost in an attitude of superiority, works out with pencil and paper the positional meaning of symbols. If there is such a positional meaning to be worked out, then this is so because the people have, in the first place, positioned the symbols so meaningfully. This question of positioning is totally absent in Turner's approach to symbolism and also in most other recent contributions to the subject. Yet positioning or, as I prefer to call it, artful placement, is not the result of mysterious social and psychological forces which lie beyond individual consciousness and intentionality, nor is it the result of chance (though it occasionally may be). It is the result of a creative act. Or is it not an art to displace a single element within a cultural order in such a way that the displacement influences others?

Only those who master the culture as a whole can master the art of displacement and create positional meaning. Therefore the positional meaning lies first and foremost with the people who have created the symbols, and the task of the ethnographer can only be to rediscover it.

This rediscovery necessitates its own kind of ethnography which may well depart from some of the established ways of describing other cultures. For by its very nature the meaning of a symbolic statement may not, as we have seen, be arrested. If one arrests the oscillation of thought which has been produced by the symbol, one destroys the meaning. Thus one needs an ethnography which is also able to speak at times indirectly and by implication. At the end of my fieldwork I was thinking of such an ethnography when I noted down the following lines in my work journal:

I pick up *The Brothers Karamazov* and drift into the Russian world. The story and the setting are distant, but there is something peculiarly familiar about it. It takes me a while to realize: it is Dostoyevsky's capacity to embrace contrarities. This is splendidly demonstrated when he describes old Karamazov, or rather lets him act. Dostoyevsky never gets stuck with one static characterization, he always creates the contrasts that make up the dynamics of any real individual personality. On a psychological level he does what a great anthropologist would do on a cultural level. Read the chapter 'The old buffoon' and you will know what I mean. A capacity like Dostoyevsky's is most important for ethnographic writing. You need detachment and the ability to see the actual as just one manifestation of the potential. Furthermore, you have to show the lines along which the actual can develop. Not only this: you also have to show what it is in terms of *what it is not*, not now, not yet, possibly never will be, yet potentially always can be. This negative aspect of the actual is always hidden. Will anyone ever produce such an ethnography? (Lydall and Strecker 1979a: 271)

I think the intuitions I had in the field do in fact apply to the ethnography of symbolism very well. How do I communicate the artful placements of symbolism and the competence for analogical thinking which go with it? Will I not destroy what I want to say by using an inadequate, that is, arresting, way of saying it? Remember what I have said above about tactfulness and ritual. Now, how do you communicate tactfulness? Is it not already tactless to try to reduce tact to words about tact? Would silence not be a much more appropriate answer? The problems are manifold but I think we can now appreciate much better the Hamar, the Dorze and others who meet the inquisitive ethnographer with silence when he asks them about the meanings of their rituals.

To speak about the unsaid requires speaking about it indirectly. Yet to speak about something indirectly presupposes a shared common ground, which does not and cannot at first exist between the ethnographer and the people he has come to study. Only as the ethnographer joins in the life of the people, takes part in their practical activities, shares sorrow and joy and health and sickness with them, and as gradually a history of joint experience develops, can he hope that people will begin to communicate with him as they communicate with each other; that is, indirectly by way of implicature. And only from this point onwards will he make headway in the understanding of what is meant but not said in everyday life. Knowing that he knows the order of things, the people can now confidently introduce a certain measure of disorder. They can violate conversational maxims or create displacements which they know the ethnographer will interpret correctly.

When this level of discourse has been reached, adequate communication about ritual symbolism becomes possible because now the ethnographer and the people can converse without being afraid of ever breaking what I might perhaps call the 'law of symbolism': that no one may reduce a symbolic statement to any single meaning. Being in agreement on this law (an agreement which is not theoretical or contractual but has proven itself in the practice of symbolization during the history of joint experience) discussions may now develop about the various intentions that lie behind ritual acts. Such discussions will not be directly about meaning but will simply be aimed at enriching the ethnographer's already existing background knowledge. The initial silence has now given way to a sympathetic smile and to hints which the people know the ethnographer will be able to use to work out for himself the implicit relationships which establish the potential meaning of a displacement.

Epilogue

Some critics of this essay will perhaps say that symbolic production does not procede as artfully as I have argued. True, people may simply enact their rituals out of habit. But this does not explain how the ritual forms were invented in the first place. As an example for the conscious invention of meaningful displacements I like to mention here Melissa Llewelyn-Davies's beautiful and very telling film *The Women's Olamal*. I saw the film some time after I had completed the present study. It shows a dispute about the scheduling of a Maasai fertility rite which the men had refused to perform for the women. After the conflict was resolved and the ceremony had been completed, one Maasai woman said to Melissa:

> Some *olamals* stand out as especially good compared with others. We may say of one: 'It was very good.' We may say of another *olamal*: 'It was good, but it had some small defects.' Of this one we say that the *Nyankusi* blessed us very well indeed. They had some items which aren't usually seen in *olamals*. They started things of their own. This blessing was wonderful. The thing Ole Kopio had ... to do like this with [she imitates waving something] ... we'd never seen it before. We'd never seen it before, the thing he did this with [imitates waving something].

Melissa asked: 'When the women came under the heifer?' The Maasai woman continued:

> They also brought fronds of the *oltukai* tree. You know that word? ... They put them on both sides of the gateway. They also had honeycombs ... which we knelt on as we drank. Those were three things which have not been done at other blessings. So Ole Kopio had elements ... which went beyong previous blessings ... three elements altogether.
> So we say his blessing was a great one.

Bibliography

ALMAGOR, U., 1978. *Pastoral Partners: Affinity and Bond Partnership among the Dasanetch of South-west Ethiopia*, Manchester: Manchester University Press.

ARISTOTLE, 1942. *Poetics*, in *The Student's Aristotle*, vol. VI, ed. W.D. Ross, Oxford: Oxford University Press.

ARISTOTLE, 1954. *Rhetoric*, with intr. and notes by Friedrich Solmsen, New York: Modern Library.

ARISTOTLE, 1969. *Nicomachean Ethics*, Harmondsworth: Penguin.

AUSTIN, J. L., 1962. *How to Do Things with Words*, the William James Lectures delivered at Harvard University, Cambridge, Mass.: Harvard University Press.

BACHOFEN, J. J., 1859. *Versuch über die Gräbersymbolik der Alten*, Basel: Bahnmaier.

BANTON, M. (ed.), 1965. *The Relevance of Models for Social Anthropology*, London: Tavistock.

BARTHES, R., 1964. *Eléments de Semiologie*, Paris: Editions du Seuil.

BATESON, G., 1958. *Naven*, 2nd edn, Standford, N.J.: Stanford University Press.

BEATTIE, J., 1964. *Other Cultures*, 3rd impr., London: Cohen & West.

BEATTIE, J., 1966. 'Ritual and social change', *Man* (N.S.) 1, 60–74.

BECHERT, J. *et al.*, 1970. *Einführung in die generative Transformationsgrammatik*, München: Hueber.

BENEDICT, R., 1934. *Patterns of Culture*, Boston Mass.: Houghton Mifflin.

BERGER, P.L. and T. LUCKMANN, 1966. *The Social Construction of Reality. A Treatise in the Sociology of Knowledge*, Garden City, N.Y.: Doubleday.

BERLIN, B., D. E. BREEDLOVE and P. H. RAVEN, 1974.*Principles of Tzeltal Plant Classification: An Introduction to the Botanical Ethnography of a Mayan-Speaking Community in Highland Chiapas*, New York: Academic Press.

BLACK, M., 1962. *Models and Metaphors*, Ithaca, N.Y.: Cornell University Press.

BLACK, M., 1979. 'More about metaphor', *in Metaphor and Thought*, ed. A. Ortony, 19–43, Cambridge: Cambridge University Press.

BLOCH, M.,1976. Review of D. Sperber, *Rethinking Symbolism*, *Man* (N.S.) 11, 128–9.

BOURDIEU, P., 1977. *Outline of a Theory of Practice*, Cambridge: Cambridge University Press.

BROWN, C. H., 1984. *Language and Living Things: Uniformities in Folk Classification and Naming*, New Brunswick, N.J.: Rutgers University Press.

BROWN, P. and S. LEVINSON, 1978. 'Universals in language usage: politeness phenomena', in *Questions and Politeness. Strategies in Social Interaction*, ed. E. Goody, 56–324, Cambridge: Cambridge University Press.

BROWN, P. and S. LEVINSON, 1987. *Politeness: Some Universals in Language Use*, Cambridge: Cambridge University Press.

BURKE, K., 1945. *A Grammar of Motives*, New York: Prentice-Hall.

CASSIRER, E., 1923. *Philosophie der symbolischen Formen. Erster Teil: Die Sprache*, Berlin: Bruno Cassirer Verlag.

CHOMSKY, N., 1957. *Syntactic Structures*, Janua linguarum, Nr. 4, 's-Gravenhage: Mouton.

COHEN, M. and E. NAGEL,, 1934. *Introduction to Logic and Scientific Method*, London: Routledge & Kegan Paul.

COLE, P., 1975. 'The synchronic and diachronic status of conversational implicature', in *Syntax and Semantics*, vol. 3: *Speech Acts*, ed. P. Cole and J. L. Morgan, 257–88, London: Academic Press.

COLE, P. and J. L. MORGAN (eds), 1975. *Syntax and Semantics*, vol. 3; *Speech Acts*, London: Academic Press.

CREUZER, G.F., 1819–28. *Symbolik und mythologie der alten Völker, besonders der Griechen*, 2, völlig umgearb, ausg. Leipzig und Darmstadt: Heyer & Leske.

CROCKER, J. C. and J. D. SAPIR (eds), 1977. *The Social Use of Metaphor. Essays on the Anthropology of Rhetoric*, Philadelphia: University of Pennsylvania Press.

CUTLER, A., 1974. 'On saying what you mean without meaning what you say', in *Papers from the Tenth Regional Meeting of the Chicago Linguistic Society*, 117–27, Chicago: Department of Linguistics, University of Chicago.

DIDEROT, D., 1956. *Jacques le fataliste et son Maître*, Geneva: Les amis du Livre.

DIEZ, M., 1933. 'Metapher und Märchengestalt III. Novalis und das allegorische Märchen', *Publications of the Modern Language Association of America*, 48, 488–507.

DUBOIS, J., F. EDELINE, J. M. KLINKENBERG, P. MINGUET, F. PIRE and H. TRINON, 1970. *Rhétorique générale*, Paris: Larousse.

DURKHEIM, E., 1912. *Les Formes élémentaires de la vie religieuse*, Paris: Alcan.

ECO, U., 1972. *Einführung in die Semiotik*, München: Fink.

ECO, U., 1973. *Il Segno*, Milano: Istituto Editoriale Internazionale.

ELLEN, R.F. and D. REASON (eds), 1979. *Classifications in their Social Context*, London: Academic Press.

EMPSON, W., 1930. *Seven Types of Ambiguity*, London: Chatto & Windus.

EVANS-PRITCHARD, E. E., 1937. *Witchcraft, Oracles and Magic among the Azande*, Oxford: Clarendon Press.

EVANS-PRITCHARD, E.E., 1940. *The Nuer*, Oxford: Clarendon Press.

EVANS-PRITCHARD, E. E., 1951. *Social Anthropology*, London: Cohen & West.

EVANS-PRITCHARD, E. E.,, 1956. *Nuer Religion*, Oxford: Clarendon Press.

FEUCHTWANG, S.,1974. *An Anthropological Analysis of Chinese Geomancy*, Vientiane: Editions Vithagna.

FILLMORE, C.J., 1971. 'Towards a theory of deixis', in *Working Papers in Linguistics*, 3, Honolulu.

FIRTH, R. W., 1936. *We, the Tikopia*, London: George Allen & Unwin.

FIRTH, R. W., 1951. *Elements of Social Organization*, London: Watts.

FIRTH, R. W., 1973. *Symbols Public and Private*, London: George Allen & Unwin.

FLEW, A., 1979. *A Dictionary of Philosophy*, London: Pan Books.

FORTES, M., 1945. *The Dynamics of Clanship among the Tallensi*, Oxford: Oxford University Press.

FORTES, M., 1949. *The Web of Kinship among the Tallensi*, London: Oxford University Press.

FORTES, M., 1969. *Kinship and the Social Order*, London: Routledge & Kegan Paul.

FREUD, S., 1958–63. The standard edition of the complete psychological works of Sigmund Freud, vols 4–5: *The Interpretation of Dreams*, vols 15–16: *Introductory Lectures on Psychoanalysis*, London: Hogarth Press and the Institute of Psychoanalysis

FREYTAG, G., 1887. Die Technik des Dramas, *Gesammelte Werke*, vol. 14, Leipzig: Verlag von S. Hirzel.

FRYE, N., 1957. *Anatomy of Criticism*, Princeton, N.J.: Princeton University Press.

GEERTZ, C. (ed.), 1974. *Myth, Symbol and Culture*, New York: Norton.

GLUCKMAN, M., 1955. *Custom and Conflict in Africa*, Oxford: Blackwell.

GLUCKMAN, M., 1963. *Order and Rebellion in Tribal Africa*, London: Cohen & West.

GLUCKMAN, M. (ed.), 1962. *Essays on the Ritual of Social Relations*, Manchester: Manchester University Press.

GLUCKMAN, M. and F. EGGAN, 1965. Introduction in *The Relevance of Models for Social Anthropology*, ed. M. Banton, ix–xi, London: Tavistock.

GOFFMAN, E., 1959. *The Presentation of Self in Everyday Life*, Garden City, N.Y.: Doubleday.

GOFFMAN, E., 1967, *Interaction Ritual: Essays on Face-to-Face Behaviour*, Garden City, N.Y.: Doubleday.

GOMBRICH, E.H., 1960. *Art and Illusion*, London: Phaidon.

GOODY, E. (ed.), 1978. *Questions and Politeness: Strategies in Social Interaction*, Cambridge: Cambridge University Press.

GREEN, G., 1975 'How to get people to do things with words: the whimperative question', in *Syntax and Semantics*, vol. 3: *Speech Acts*, ed. P. Cole and J. L. Morgan, 107–41, London: Academic Press.

GRICE, H. P., 1971. 'Meaning', in *Semantics: An Interdisciplinary Reader in Philosophy, Linguistics, and Psychology*, ed. D. Steiberg and L. Jakobovits, Cambridge: Cambridge University Press.

GRICE, H. P., 1975. 'Logic and conversation', in *Syntax and Semantics*, vol. 3: *Speech Acts*, ed. P. Cohen and J. L. Morgan, 41–58, London: Academic Press.

HAYWOOD, B., 1959. *Novalis, the Veil of Imagery. A Study of the Poetic Works of Friedrich von Hardenberg*, 's-Gravenshage: Mouton

HUMBOLDT, W. von, 1876. *Ueber die Verschiedenheit des menschlichen Sprachbaues und ihren Einfluss auf die geistige Entwicklung des Menschengeschlechts*. Berlin: Königliche Akademie der Wissenschaften.

JENSEN, A. E., 1960. *Mythos und Kult bei Naturvölkern*, 2. bearb. Aufl., Studien zur Kulturkunde 10. Wiesbaden: Franz Steiner Verlag.

JONES, E., 1967. *Papers on Psycho-Analysis*. Boston, Mass.: Beacon Press.

JUNG, C.G., 1948. *Symbolik des Geistes*, Zurich: Rascher.

JUNG, C. G., 1949. *Psychological Types*, London: Routledge and Kegan Paul.

KAMLAH, W. and P. LORENZEN, 1967. *Logische Propädeutik. Vorschule des vernünftigen Redens*, Mannheim: Bibliographisches Institut.

LAKOFF, R., 1972. 'Language in context', *Language*, 48, 902–27.

LAKOFF, R., 1974. 'What you can do with words: politeness, pragmatics and performatives', in *Berkeley Studies in Syntax and Semantics 1*, XVI, 1–55.

LEACH, E, R., 1958. 'Concerning Trobriand clans and the kinship category tabu', in *The Developmental Cycle in Domestic Groups*, ed. J. Goody, 120–45, Cambridge: Cambridge University Press

LEACH, E. R., 1976. *Culture and Communication*, Cambridge: Cambridge University Press.

LÉVI-STRAUSS, C., 1958. *Anthropologie structurale*, Paris: Plon.

LÉVI-STRAUSS, C., 1962. *La Pensée Sauvage*, Paris: Plon.

LEVI-STRAUSS, C., 1964. *Mythologiques I. Le cru et le cuit*, Paris: Plon.

LÉVI-STRAUSS, C., 1966. *Mythologiques II. Du miel aux cendres*, Paris: Plon.

LÉVI-STRAUSS, C., 1968. *Mythologiques III. L'origine des manières du table*, Paris: Plon.

LÉVI-STRAUSS, C., 1971. *Mythologiques IV. L'homme nu* Paris: Plon.

LÉVI-STRAUSS, C., 1963. *Structural Anthropology*, New York & London: Basic Books Inc.

LEVIN, S.R., 1977. *The Semantics of Metaphor*, Baltimore, MD: Johns Hopkins University Press.

LEWIS, D., 1969. *Convention. A Philosophical Study*, Cambridge, Mass.: Harvard University Press.

LEWIS, I. M. (ed.), 1977. *Symbols and Sentiments: Cross-Cultural Studies in Symbolism*, London: Academic Press.

LIDDELL, H. G. and R. SCOTT, 1968. *A Greek-English Lexicon*, new edition revised by H. S. Jones and R. McKenzie, Oxford: Clarendon Press.

LOEWENBERG, I., 1973. 'Truth and consequences of metaphors', in *Philosophy and Rhetoric*, 6, 30–46.

LOEWENBERG, I., 1975. 'Identifying metaphors', in *Foundations of Language*, 12, 315–38.

LYDALL, J., 1976. 'Hamar', in *The Non-Semitic Languages of Ethiopia*, ed. M. L. Bender, 393–438, East Lansing: African Studies Center.

LYDALL, J., 1978. 'Le symbolisme des couleurs dans le rituel Hamar', in *Voir et nommer les couleurs*, ed. S. Tournay, 553–75, Nanterre: Laboratoire d'ethnologie et de sociologie comparative.

LYDALL, J. and I. STRECKER, 1979a. *The Hamar of Southern Ethiopia*, vol. I: *Work Journal*, Arbeiten aus dem Institut für Völkerkunde Göttingen, Bd. 12, Hohenschäftlarn: Renner.

LYDALL, J. and I. STRECKER, 1979b. *The Hamar of Southern Ethiopia*, vol. II: *Baldambe Explains*, Arbeiten aus dem Institut für Völkerkunde Göttingen, Bd. 13, Hohenschäftlarn: Renner.

MAHOOD, M.M., 1957. *Shakespeare's Wordplay*, London: Methuen.

MALINOWSKI, B., 1922. *Argonauts of the Western Pacific*, London: Routledge & Kegan Paul.

MALINOWSKI, B., 1944. *A Scientific Theory of Culture and Other Essays*, The University of North Carolina Press, Chapel Hill.

MAUSS, M., 1954. *The Gift*, London: Cohen & West.

MAYBURY-LEWIS, D., 1967. *Akwè-Shavante Society*, Oxford: Clarendon Press.

MEGGITT, M. J., 1965. *The Lineage System of the Mae-Enga of New Guinea*, London: Oliver & Boyd.

MERLEAU-PONTY, M., 1960. *Signes*, Paris: Gallimard.

MOOIJ, J. J. A., 1976. *A Study of Metaphor*, Amsterdam: North-Holland.

MORRIS, C., 1938. *Foundations of the Theory of Signs*, Chigago: Chicago University Press.

NADEL, S.F., 1942. *A Black Byzantium*, Oxford: Oxford University Press.

NADEL, S. F., 1951. *The Foundations of Social Anthropology*, London: Cohen & West.

NADEL, S. F., 1954. *Nupe Religion*, London: Routledge & Kegan Paul.

NAGEL, E., 1961. *The Structure of Science. Problems in the Logic of Scientific Explanation*, New York: Harcourt, Brace and World

NIETZSCHE, F., 1887. *Zur Genealogie der Moral*, Leipzig: Naumann.

NIVELLE, A., 1950. 'Der symbolische Gehalt des "Heinrich von Ofterdingen"', *Tijdschrift voor Levende Talen*, 16, 404–27.

NOVALIS, 1802. *Heinrich von Ofterdingern*, Berlin: Buchhandlung der Realschule.

ORTONY, A. (ed.), 1979. *Metaphor and Thought*, Cambridge: Cambridge University Press.

PARK, G., 1963. 'Divination and its social context', *Journal of the Royal Anthropoligical Institute*, 93, 195–209.

PARTRIDGE, E. H., 1968. *Shakespeare's Bawdy*, London: Routledge & Kegan Paul.

PEIRCE, C. S., 1931–58. *Collected Papers*, 8 vols, Cambridge, Mass.: Harvard University Press.

PERRET, D., 1976. *On Irony*, Pragmatics microfiche, 1.7.:D3. Dept of Linguistics, University of Cambridge.

POLANYI, M., 1966. *The Tacit Dimension*, Garden City, N.Y.: Doubleday.

POPPER, K., 1935. *Logik der Forschung*, Wien: Springer.

POPPER, K., 1960. The Logic of Scientific Discovery, London: Hutchinson

RADCLIFFE-BROWN, A.R., 1922. *The Andaman Islanders*, Cambridge: Cambridge University Press.

RADCLIFFE-BROWN, A. R., 1952. *Structure and Function in Primitive Society*, London: Cohen & West.

RICHARDS, I.A., 1925. *Principles of Literary Critisicm*, New York: Harcourt, Brace.

RICHARDS, I. A., 1936. *The Philosophy of Rhetoric*, Oxford: Oxford University Press.

RICOEUR, P., 1970. *Freud and Philosophy: An Essay on Interpretation*, New Haven and London: Yale University Press.

RICOEUR, P., 1978. *The Rule of Metaphor*, London: Routledge & Kegan Paul.

ROSCH, E. and B. B. LLOYD (eds), 1978. *Cognition and Categorization*, Hillsdale, N. J.: Lawrence Erlbaum Associates.

SAPIR, E., 1921. *Language*, New York: Harcourt, Brace.

SAPIR, E., 1977. 'An anatomy of metaphor', in *The Social Use of Metaphor*, ed. J. C. Crocker and J. D. Sapir, 3–32, Philadelphia: University of Pennsylvania Press.

SAUSSURE, F. DE, 1968. *Cours de linguistique général*. Ed. critique par Rudolf Engles. Harassowitz, Wiesbaden.

SEARLE, J. R., 1969. *Speech Acts: An Essay in the Philosophy of Language*, London: Cambridge University Press.

SEARLE, J. R., 1975. 'Indirect speech acts', in *Syntax and Semantics*, vol. 3: *Speech Acts*, ed. P. Cole and J. L. Morgan, 59–82, London: Academic Press.

SEBEOK, T. A. (ed.), 1964. *Approaches to Semiotics*, The Hague: Mouton.

SHIBLES, W. A., 1971. *Metaphor: An Annotated Bibliography and History*, Whitewater: Language Press.

232 *The social practice of symbolization*

SMITH, N. and D. WILSON, 1979. *Modern Linguistics*, Harmondsworth: Penguin.

SØRENSEN, B. A., 1963. *Symbol und Sumbolismus in den ästhetischen Theorien des 18. Jahrhunderts und der deutschen Romantik*, Kopenhagen: Munksgaard.

SPENCER, R.F. (ed.), 1969. *Forms of Symbolic Action*, American Ethnological Society, Proceedings of the 1969 Annual Spring Meeting, Seattle: University of Washington Press.

SPERBER, D., 1975. *Rethinking Symbolism*, Cambridge: Cambridge University Press.

SPERBER, D. and D. WILSON, 1986. *Relevance, Communication and Cognition*, Oxford: Basil Blackwell.

SPRADLEY, J. P. (ed.), 1972. *Culture and Cognition: Rules, Maps, and Plans*, London: Chandler.

STEINBERG, D. and L. JAKOBOVITS (eds), 1971. *Semantics: An Interdisciplinary Reader in Philosophy, Linguistics and Psychology*, Cambridge: Cambridge University Press.

STRECKER, I., 1969. *Methodische Probleme der ethno-soziologischen Beobachtung und Beschreibung*, Arbeiten aus dem Institut für Völkerkunde Göttingen, Bd. 3, Hohenschäftlarn: Renner.

STRECKER, I., 1975. *Baldambe Spricht. Versuch zu einer zeitgemäßen Ethnographie*, Berlin: SFB 23.

STRECKER, I., 1976. 'Hamar speech situations', in *The Non-Semitic Languages of Ethiopia*, ed. M. L. Bender, East Lansing: African Studies Center.

STRECKER, I., 1979a. *The Hamar of Southern Ethiopia*, vol. III: *Conversations in Dambaiti*, Arbeiten aus dem Institut für Völkerkunde Göttingen, Bd. 14, Hohenschäftlarn: Renner.

STRECKER, I., 1979b. *The Leap across the Cattle* (film). Göttingen: Institut für den wissenschaftlichen Film.

STRECKER, I., 1979c. *The Music of the Hamar*, Berlin: Museum für Völkerkunde.

TORCZYNER, H., 1979. *Magritte*. London: Thames & Hudson.

TURBAYNE, C. M. (ed.), 1970. *The Myth of Metaphor*, Columbia: University of South Carolina Press.

TURNER, V. W., 1957. *Schism and Continuity in an African Society*, Manchester: Manchester University Press.

TURNER, V. W., 1961. *Ndembu Divination: Its Symbolism and Techiques*, Manchester: Manchester University Press.

TURNER, V. W., 1967. *The Forest of Symbols*, Ithaca and London: Cornell University Press.

TURNER, V. W., 1968. *The Drums of Affliction*, Oxford: Clarendon Press.

TURNER, V. W., 1969, *The Ritual Process*, London: Routledge & Kegan Paul.

TURNER, V. W., 1974. *Dramas, Fields, and Metaphors. Symbolic Action in Human Society*, Ithaca and London: Cornell University Press.

TYLER, S. (ed.), 1969. *Cognitive Anthropology*, New York: Holt, Rinehart & Winston.

TYLER, S., 1978. *The Said and the Unsaid*, London: Academic Press.

VAN GENNEP, A., 1977. *The Rites of Passage*, London: Routledge & Kegan Paul.

WEBER, M., 1960. *Soziologische Grundbegriffe*, Tübingen: Mohr.

WERTHEIMER, M., 1959. *Productive Thinking*, New York: Harper & Row.

WORSLEY, P., 1956. 'The kinship system of the Tallensi: a revaluation', *Journal of the Royal Anthropological Institute*, 86, 37–75.

Index